Reading Madeleine

Books by Roger Greaves

NADAR, OU LE PARADOXE VITAL

ALLAN RAMSAY'S FABLES AND TALES

ANTOINE HOUDAR DE LA MOTTE: FABLES NOUVELLES 1719

ROBERT SAMBER: ONE HUNDRED NEW COURT FABLES 1721

NADAR QUAND MÊME!

HISTOIRES D'ENTREVAUX

MONSIEUR PROSPER

LOTTE H. EISNER: THE HAUNTED SCREEN

PIERRE LEPROHON: THE ITALIAN CINEMA

JEAN JULES-VERNE: JULES VERNE

FRÉDÉRIC GRENDEL: BEAUMARCHAIS, THE MAN WHO WAS FIGARO

MAX KALTENMARK: LAO TZU

READING MADELEINE

Mrs Robert Henrey, authoress

Roger Greaves

All writers are vain, selfish, and lazy, and at the very bottom of their
motives there lies a mystery. Writing a book is a horrible, exhausting
struggle, like a long bout of some painful illness. One would never
undertake such a thing if one were not driven on by some demon
whom one can neither resist nor understand.

—George Orwell, 'Why I write'

*La vraie vie, la vie enfin découverte et éclaircie, la seule vie,
par conséquent, réellement vécue, c'est la littérature.*

—Marcel Proust, *Le Temps retrouvé*

CONTENTS

AUTHOR'S NOTE

BY PURE CHANCE in April 2021, I tuned in to a rare cable TV screening of Carol Reed's classic movie *The Fallen Idol* (1948), which I hadn't seen till then. To my amazement I found myself watching the spitting image of a small English boy I had been in the year the film came out. No doubt about it: I put the video on pause and checked the old albums. There I was with my mother and siblings snapped in 1948 by a roving photographer on the seafront at Cleethorpes, looking just like the little boy in the movie: dark short trousers, white shirt and longish hair (his fair, mine dark) falling in a fringe above penetrating eyes. It was almost like coming face to face with myself in a mirror. Or so I thought.

When I returned to the movie, I realised that my *alter ego* was speaking to me from a different world. His posh accent sounded vaguely foreign, whereas my vowels in 1948 were still native Derbyshire. I looked him up and discovered that he was French, the son of two well-known London writers, and that he himself had become famous as a child because of the film he starred in. This seemed so unusual that I dug deeper and hit upon *Through Grown-up Eyes* by Robert Henrey, a book of memoirs describing how the boy in the movie, my non-identical twin, struggled all the rest of his life to survive his childhood fame, quite unlike me.

The book was so brilliant and the struggle so moving that I felt I had to get in touch. He answered my email almost immediately from his home in Connecticut. One thing led to another. I learned that his bicultural parents created a feminine projection of themselves in print—a certain 'Madeleine'— and published many titles under a joint mixed-gender signature purporting to tell the absolute truth about this character's life and times. That approach seemed so modern, despite the books' vintage, that I began collecting them from libraries and second-hand sources. By the summer I had gathered a hefty bookshelf of forty-five titles, all out of print, and had more or less decided to write something about them.

The problem was, Robert told me, that his parents destroyed virtually all their private papers, as if they wished to go down to posterity in their published works alone. This didn't daunt me, as the books themselves provided so much detail about people and places that I felt they could be sorted, paraphrased, checked and contextualised to give a fairly accurate account. The real challenge, it seemed to me, lay in reconstructing a coherent story from the sheer number of books they produced in just anyhow order.

In early September 2021, Robert and his wife Lisette put me up at the Normandy farm where he was born. I slept in his father's room, surrounded by his parents' bookshelves and pictures. On a small table under a portrait of his mother Robert laid out whatever literary stuff was left: archive copies, photographs, contracts, royalty statements, illustrations, business correspondence. Then Lisette and he cleared out, leaving me alone in his parents' house to find out what I could.

When I left the farm, I said: 'Now all I have to do is write my book.' On the train back to Paris, I realised that I had entered a new universe and that this book would be more than a book: a voyage, a spiritual adventure.

A FAMILY CHRONOLOGY

1839

HANNAH, second daughter of Europe's greatest banker, **NATHAN MAYER ROTHSCHILD** of New Court in the City of London, disobeys her Ashkenazi father and marries **HENRY FITZROY**, an English politician of royal descent, second son of **2nd Baron Southampton**, at St George's Church, Hanover Square.

1864

BLANCHE ('PELI'), the Fitzroys' only child after the tragic death of her younger brother **ARTHUR**, marries (and funds) artist baronet Sir **COUTTS LINDSAY** of Balcarres in Fife. They eventually separate and she lives very comfortably in Hans Place, Knightsbridge, until her death in 1912. Her first cousin **LIONEL, 2nd Baron Rothschild** of Gunnersbury Park, born in 1868, likes children but dies unmarried in 1937.

1897

EUPHEMIA ('EFFIE'), the Lindsays' elder daughter (whose sister **HELEN**, a missionary, goes to China), marries Rev. **SELBY HENREY ('BURR')**, vicar of St George's Church, Brentford. They retire from their vicarage to a fine house and garden in Godalming paid for by Effie.

1921

ROBERT ('BOB'), their son born in 1901, drops out of Oxford, partly to spoil his father's plans for his career but mainly to try his luck in America. His sisters **Kitty** and **Blanche** have no wish to marry, and never do.

1905

In France, the three daughters of grocer-hatmaker **JEAN BERNHARD** run away from their village near Blois. **MARGUERITE** and **MARIE-THÉRÈSE** emigrate to England as chambermaids, while pretty **MATHILDE** aged eighteen sets up as a seamstress in Clignancourt on the north flank of the Butte Montmartre, catering mainly for prostitutes and demi-mondaines.

1906

MATHILDE BERNHARD, unmarried, gives birth in Paris to a female child, father unnamed. The child registered as **MATHILDE BERNHARD** *faute de mieux* is taken in charge by the Assistance Publique. A few months later, **MARIE-THÉRÈSE BERNHARD**, back from the Colman's mustard family in England, unmarried, gives birth in Paris to a female child, father unnamed. Registered as **ROLANDE BERNHARD,** the child gets the same Assistance Publique treatment as her cousin.

1908

MATHILDE BERNHARD marries **ÉMILE GAL**, a boozy coal-miner from the Midi hanging out as a labourer in Clignancourt and Clichy. Her child **MATHILDE**, known unofficially as **MADELEINE**, is officially adopted as **MATHILDE GAL**. A similar adoption-by-marriage operation takes place in 1911 when **MARIE-THÉRÈSE BERNHARD** marries **LOUIS SOILLY**, a Paris gentleman's gentleman almost certainly not **ROLANDE**'s father.

1929

MARGUERITE BERNHARD brings **MATHILDE** and **MADELEINE** to London, where a chance encounter at the Savoy Hotel in 1927 leads to the girl's marriage to **ROBERT HENREY**, back in London as a newspaper columnist. He calls her **MÉ**, she calls him **BOB**. They have a lot of fun.

1940-

BOB and **MÉ** become famous as the middlebrow authoress **MRS ROBERT HENREY**. Their only child **ROBERT HENREY** born in Normandy in 1939, now resident in Connecticut with his wife **LISETTE**, is also a writer.

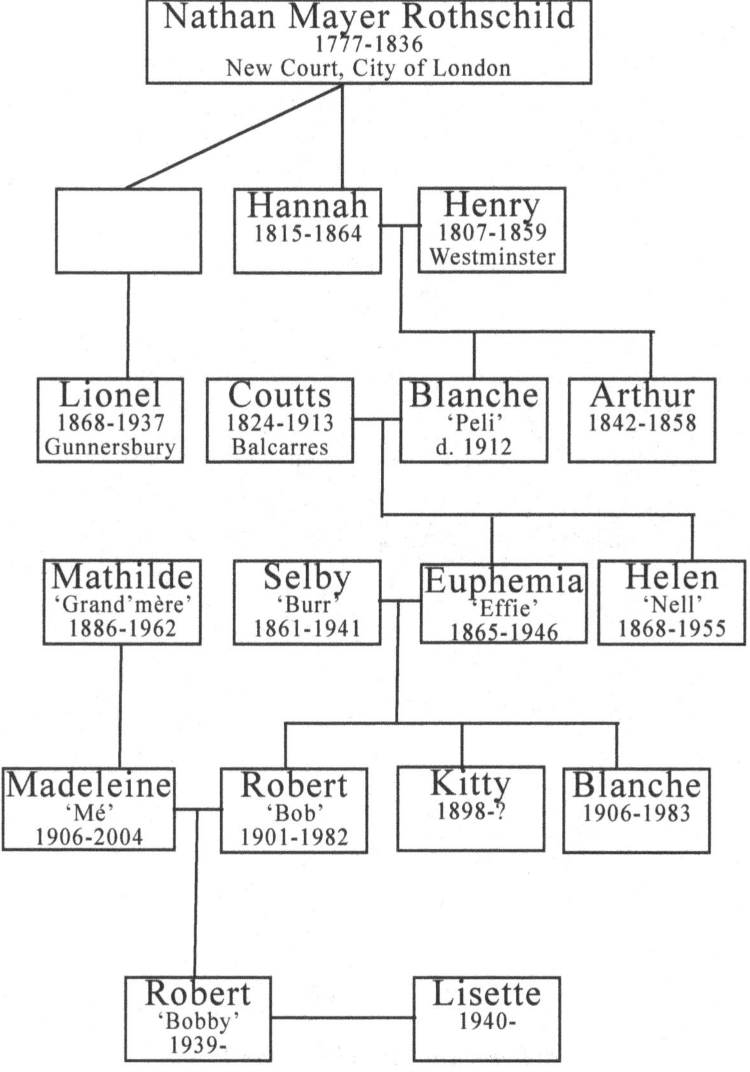

Nathan Mayer Rothschild
1777-1836
New Court, City of London
Hannah
1815-1864
Henry
1807-1859
Westminster
Lionel
1868-1937
Gunnersbury
Coutts
1824-1913
Balcarres
Blanche
'Peli'
d. 1912
Arthur
1842-1858
Mathilde
'Grand'mère'
1886-1962
Selby
'Burr'
1861-1941
Euphemia
'Effie'
1865-1946
Helen
'Nell'
1868-1955
Madeleine
'Mé'
1906-2004
Robert
'Bob'
1901-1982
Kitty
1898-?
Blanche
1906-1983
Robert
'Bobby'
1939-
Lisette
1940-

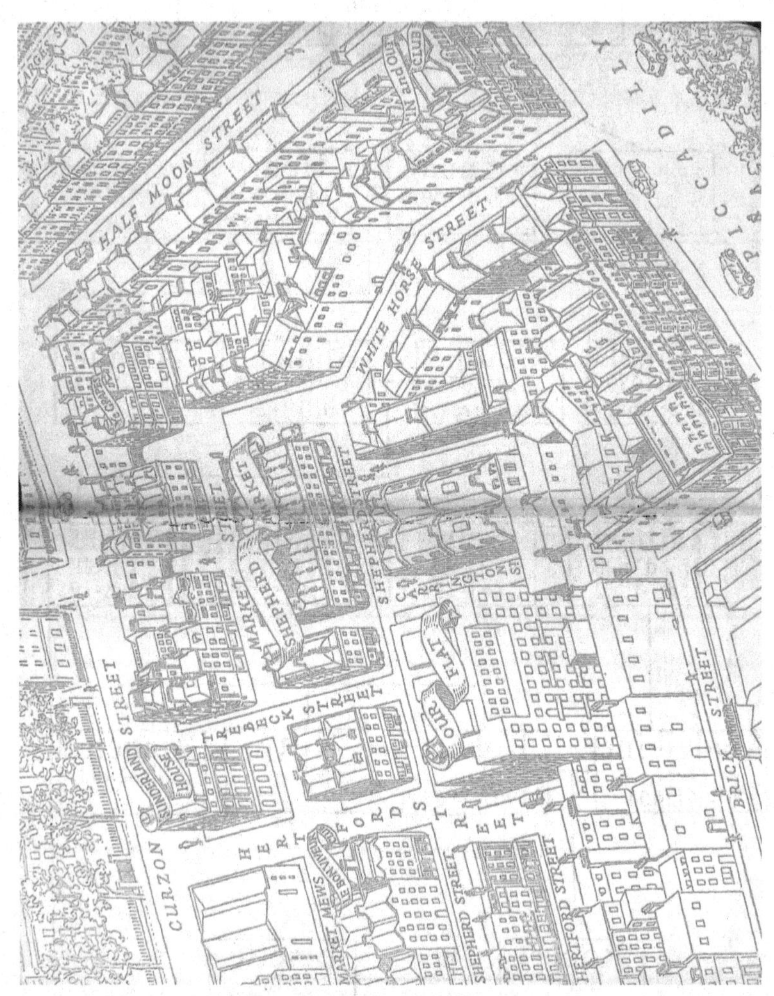

Shepherd Market with 'Our Flat''

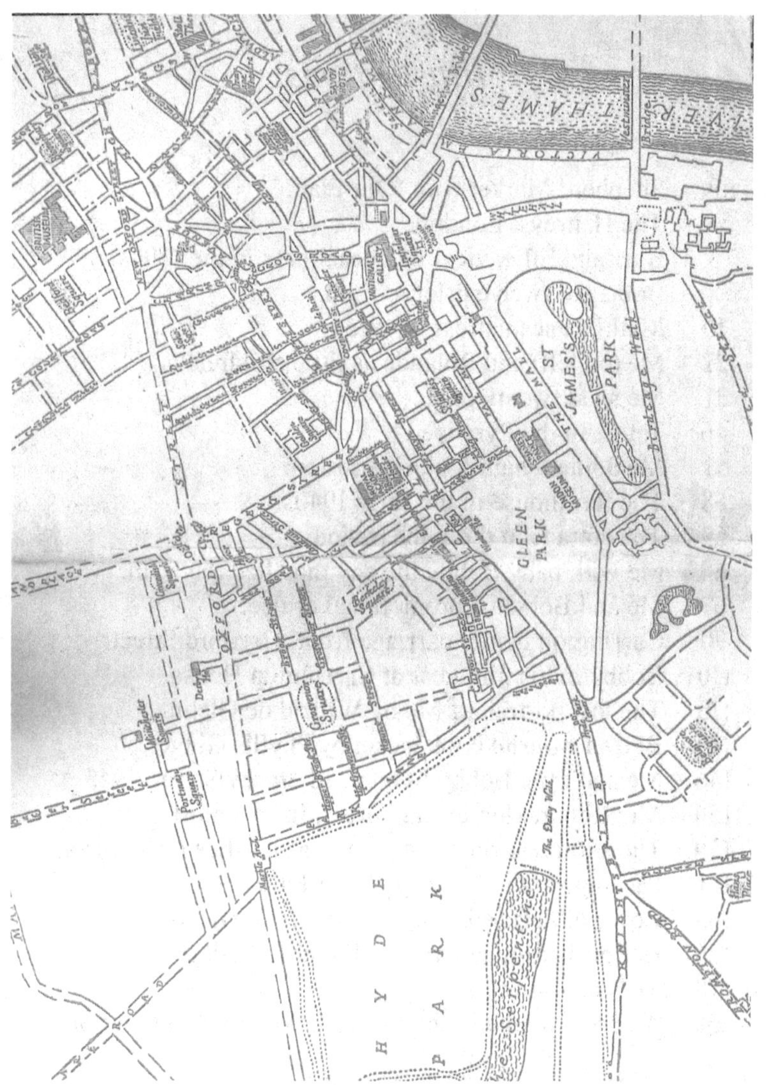

The Henreys' London

Illustrations

All illustrations courtesy The Henrey Estate
digitised by the author
see also https://qr.net/eV6DqB

PART ONE

Premisses of Madeleine

His Lucky Start

IN THE EARLY 1900s Brentford was a grimy bottleneck in West London on the road to Richmond. The Anglican church of St George, on the High Street opposite the gasworks, had recently acquired a peal of bells. But it was a squat Victorian building, uninspired and uninspiring. (When Google drove that way in 2021, it stood derelict.)

The vicarage, two hundred yards farther down the road, was an old house, so old that nobody could tell for certain its age. Without a doubt it had been a farmhouse in the days when stage coaches from the West of England changed horses in the High Street. It had only one storey and an attic, but the rooms were spacious. It was hidden from the street by an iron gate against which grew a clump of acacia trees. A slope bordered by evergreens curved down to the entrance, which was framed by pillars like those of a Grecian temple.

The main part faced the garden on the other side with nothing in front but water and trees: the Thames and the long view across the river to Kew, with an eyot where swans nested among the osiers and willows. A screen of lilac trees and a high wall divided the garden on one side from the wharf of the Brentford brewery. On the other side the garden stretched away unopposed until it died against an inland creek where barges were mended. Beyond were the gasworks. Leaning on a stout oak fork in the centre of the lawn stood a giant mulberry, probably as old as the house itself. In spite of the stench when the wind blew from the gasworks or the brewery, a lovelier haven would have been hard to find.

The bachelor vicar, a Yorkshireman called Thomas Selby Henrey, son and grandson of Yorkshire vicars, tended his garden amid his mixed flock of merchants and working folk, but before long felt the need of a deaconess to help him with the ladies. He

went to Mildmay, an Anglican mission in the north of London, and recruited a newly qualified deaconess who duly came to Brentford. She liked it and him, he was satisfied with her, and a year later they were married. She called him Burr, like those seed heads that prickle and stick. He called her Effie.

Euphemia Lindsay was the grand-daughter of Henry FitzRoy, deputy speaker of the House of Commons, and Hannah Mayer Rothschild, daughter of the founder of the London House. Her brilliant mother Blanche FitzRoy married the Scottish baronet Sir Coutts Lindsay of Balcarres and they founded, mainly with her money, the Grosvenor Gallery which fostered the Pre-Raphael-ites. Little Effie their daughter grew up in opulence among famous poets, musicians and painters until her father's faithlessness led to a stormy separation. Her mother rescued what was left of her money, which was quite a lot, and Effie and her younger sister Helen kept their ends up decently on the family crumbs.

Burr felt safe with Effie—as he could, for she had a sound head for money while practising her Christian beliefs with love and understanding. She built a new wing at the vicarage to provide him with a study giving straight into the garden and ruled their servants with strict economy and truly fond generosity. Burr was, however, the undisputed head of the house as he was of the parish. A conservative in both senses of the word, he didn't like change. If his 'parliament', as he called his parish council, had a socialist among its members, it was on condition the man kept his trap shut.

Burr took a cold bath every morning. Since he was haunted by the fear of fire, electricity wasn't allowed in the vicarage. The gas was turned off at the main when they all went up for the night holding their candle. As Burr also feared burglars, there was a ceremony before lights out at ten while he checked that the big safe in his study was properly secured, tugging at the handle and asking others to do the same. The doors and windows were naturally locked, chained and barred.

Effie's life revolved around her 'little room', where she studied science and the scriptures, received visits, ran her charities. She held her Bible Class in the church's Green Room and wrote a regular newsletter for the lighthouse men on the British coasts which she printed off on a little machine on the dining room table before putting it in the post with the latest magazines. She slept sparingly, spending much of the night looking after things, opening drawers and cupboards, roaming from room to room with her candlestick.

Bob was born on 14 August 1901, and called after Effie's late Uncle Bob, Robert Loyd-Lindsay V.C., Lord Wantage, who liked to say with some truth that he was the largest farmer in England.

* * *

BOB'S SISTER KITTY was three years his elder and struck him as 'wiser in everything'. She wore printed cotton frocks and her hair fell in magnificent curls. One of Bob's earliest recollections was taking turns with her at being the Boer spy hunted for by Mr

Stamp, one of their father's churchwardens, amid the undergrowth of the lilac bushes in the vicarage garden. Mr Stamp could tell stories of the South African war and was a good amateur conjurer when the necessity arose.

When their little sister Blanche came into the world in 1905, Kitty and Bob were left alone in their schoolroom and hit on the idea of producing a snowstorm by clambering on chairs and spitting furiously into space, wondering whether the new arrival would deprive them of some of their mother's affection.

The children saw their parents mainly in the evening, when they were admitted to their father's study while Effie sewed, knitted, or looked over Burr's letters, pencil in hand, before he sent them off. 'Have you put the tick?' he would ask as she handed them back one after the other. In the mornings, Bob and Kitty took their breakfast alone, though they occasionally looked into the dining room where their parents were breakfasting.

They had nurses of different nationalities, mainly German, who changed frequently, and a French governess who came every morning. The nurses were good-natured on the whole, but the governess wasn't to be trifled with. She came from Falaise in Normandy, like William the Conqueror, and taught remarkably well in French. She was to have been called Mademoiselle, but that was too much for Bob at the tender age when first he came under her spell. The best he could do was to call her 'Mallalal', and that was the name she was evermore known by. The fascination she inspired undoubtedly accounts for Bob's lifelong passion for all things feminine and/or French.

Mallalal arrived at nine o'clock. Her ring at the front-door bell was short and peremptory. She would walk up the stairs and arrive on the children's landing just as the cuckoo came out to sing the hour. Kitty and Bob would be seated on either side of the schoolroom table, with pencils and books all arranged on the green cloth, and as Mallalal opened the little gate that their mother had fixed across the top steps so that they should not fall down the stairs, their eyes would become grave and expectant. Then the schoolroom door would be pushed wide and Mallalal would say: *'Bonjour, mes enfants.'* Wasting no time, she would take her seat between them at the top of the table, and they would read, alternately, a few verses from the New Testament in French. That was the start of the lesson.

Blanche didn't come to these lessons because she was still small. At midday Bob and Kitty closed their school books and went out for a walk. Mallalal timed these walks to perfection, just as she timed her own arrival in the morning. They would be back at the top of the vicarage slope at five minutes to one exactly. They would troop up to the bathroom to wash their hands and brush their hair before the gong went.

They all lunched together. The vicar would ask if they had earned any good marks that morning. When the pudding came along, their mother asked them if they wanted a second helping, but they had an idea that their governess didn't approve of this manifestation of greed and generally they refused. Mallalal watched their manners closely, and they were never allowed to accept the last cutlet or the last pancake on the dish.

After lunch Mallalal went home and they were handed over into the care of their nurse. This was the time when they made a bee-line for Gunnersbury Park. It belonged to their cousin Leopold Rothschild and they had the run of the wonderful place. To reach it, they followed the High Street for half a mile between the brewery and the gasworks on one side and their father's church on the other, and a bit higher up here was Kew Bridge. Then a sharp turn to the left just beyond the railway and there was a lane with hawthorn bushes and dandelions. There were still market gardens and orchards around here resisting the factory invasion to the bitter end.

Once through the park gates they could change their walks every afternoon. As Blanche was not yet considered by them of any useful age in the park, they would leave her with the nurse, who sat on a tree stump reading a German novel while she gently rocked the pram. Sometimes they ran into their cousin Leopold himself. He had a magnificent head, with laughing eyes and white moustaches. He would take them back to the house and offer them chocolate cake, and four months ahead of time ask them what they would like for Christmas. His gifts were always princely: if they requested a book they would receive a library. Afterwards they went off to wheel their hoops in his park wearing their round hats of panama straw, fastened under the chin by elastic that they chewed to bits.

From time to time Bob was taken to see his grandmother Blanche Lindsay, known as Peli (like Pelican), in Hans Place, Knightsbridge. Lady Lindsay of Grosvenor Gallery fame had produced four novels and several collections of poems and songs. Bob was expected to show her how well he recited a French poem taught him specially by Mallalal and was then told to sit on the Persian carpet and keep still, unless Peli sent him to nearby Harrods with her secretary and instructions to buy him whatever he liked best. Once it was a trumpet and it didn't go down well back in Hans Place when he blew it.

In summer Bob's parents would sometimes give parties in their garden for 'dear good souls in black-beaded bonnets' (as he described them later) or members of the local Conservative club. These festivities generally took place when Bob had been dismissed for the night, but happily his window overlooked the garden and from his bed he enjoyed a privileged view. There would be masses of strawberries and cream and buns and a loud brass band, and Mr Stamp would arrive with his conjuring apparatus. Then as night fell the little coloured lamps that they had all helped to fix in the loganberry bushes were lit and the place was a real enchantment.

Every August Burr carted his family off to Rottingdean by train. It was just a village then, no trippers ever came to mar its peace. In the morning they sat on the sands and watched their father swim. He stayed in the water for nearly an hour each day. Then there was a cove to which the children walked to take dips, sure of never seeing a living soul.

One August for some reason they went to Folkestone, where Burr had taken a house overlooking the harbour. It was a tall, rambling place commanding a magnificent view. The children watched the cross-Channel ships that lay just below their window and regulated their bedtime each evening by the siren of the outgoing Ostend packet. They had with them Effie's Pekingese dog, a fierce and beautiful creature who adored her. He fought anybody who came near her, and during mealtimes rushed under the table to bite the maid's shins each time she made her round with the dishes.

Several times Kitty and Bob crossed the Channel with their father while Blanche stayed at home in her nursery. It wasn't that

Burr had affinities with the continent. He liked no foreigners but the Swiss. He loved crossing the Channel, however, for the bracing air, the waves, the lively movement on the steamer. As soon as they arrived, they took the next boat back.

One night there was a great commotion in the house at Folkestone. Bob's mother, looking white, came in to see him, for he was then ill with appendicitis. She looked worried and was off to the station to catch a train back to London. A few days later the children learned that their grandmother Peli had died.

* * *

THROUGH NO FAULT OF HIS OWN, Bob's first appearance in print came in the form of a classical inscription on the dedication page of his father's *Attic Salt: The Saving Grace of Humour*, a compendium of wit ('Attic salt') first published in October 1913 and several times reprinted:

TO
MY DEAR SON
ROBERT SELBY HENREY
THE SUNBEAM OF HIS HOME
I AFFECTIONATELY DEDICATE THIS VOLUME
MAY HE EVER BE A SUNNY CHRISTIAN
AND MAY HIS SPEECH ALWAYS BE SEASONED WITH
ATTIC SALT

Burr's plan for his beloved son, aged twelve, was that he should go to Eton and Oxford and become a bishop. The first step was highly successful. One evening in 1914, just after the outbreak of war, his parents took him in a train bound for Windsor. They sat in the ill-lit compartment and looked at one another with damp eyes. For the first time in his life, Bob was going away to school.

He loved Eton passionately. The gardens, the rules, his house tutor, his class masters, the nonchalant elegance of school and town suited him perfectly. He spent most of his first term learning how to swim properly at the bathing place more than a mile away across the fields. He was to row, but he was in no hurry to pass the swimming trials. He enjoyed the bathes, and afterwards would seek out the shade of a willow tree and read a book until dusk.

Though at times he was somewhat ashamed of living between a gasworks and a brewery, when his schoolmates took pride in talking about their theatrical first nights and their fox hunting, Eton left a deep mark on him. He would never wear a tie unless it was an Old Etonian tie, and whenever he lacked a belt he knotted an Old Etonian tie round his waist. He went back repeatedly on Fourths of June in the 1930s, and when he died his gravestone bore at his request 'The Lord is my shepherd' and *Floreat Etona*.

Eton gave him just enough idea of the outside world for him to chafe at the restrictions life at Brentford necessarily imposed. He really knew nothing about London and decided to spend his holidays exploring it. It took about forty minutes to get into the heart of the West End from Brentford. He spent each day walking round, arriving home much later than he should have done. Neither then nor later did his father agree to give him a latchkey. As he knocked at the front door, long after the household had gone to bed, he would be filled with remorse to see his mother, tired and reproachful, standing before him in a dressing-gown, holding a dripping candle in her hand.

He was just ready to leave Eton for Sandhurst when one day the news of the armistice broke. That evening his house-master climbed down into his cellar and brought up a dozen bottles of hock. He placed them on the long tables at supper and, lifting his glass, bade them drink to their victory. The war had passed over Bob's head without so much as a ripple.

* * *

AFTER ETON, Oxford was quite a different kettle of fish. Burr had been at St Edward's School in Oxford but to his eternal regret had not entered the university. However, his epilogue to *Attic Salt* had appealed for contributions from any reader knowing a good story that wasn't included in his collection. 'It shall be inserted, if suitable, to the next edition, the name of the sender being given.' It so happened that among his willing correspondents was Sir Herbert Warren, President of Magdalen College, Oxford, who sent in some Senior Common Room witticisms for the later editions of Burr's book.

Thanks to the Warren connection, Bob managed to circumvent whatever examinations were required for admission and was given rooms at Magdalen overlooking the Deer Park. He went up in Trinity term 1920, along with a great many young men just back from the trenches in France. The usual rules for undergraduates were relaxed to accommodate this unusual intake, and Bob was free to roam more or less as he pleased.

While poring over the visitors' book at the Mitre Hotel in quest of likely people to meet, he hit upon the wife of the illustrious French playwright, novelist and librettist Francis de Croisset. She was there to show Oxford to her daughter Marie-Laure de Bischoffsheim and a Russian girl, Princess Galitzine, who had fled the Bolsheviks. His tall slim figure, blue eyes and excellent French made a favourable impression on these ladies. He showed them round Magdalen, ciceroned them at other colleges and the usual university monuments, filled a punt with champagne and took them on the Cherwell to display his skill with the pole.

His prowess must have impressed them, as the Croisset connection became highly useful to him later on in Paris. Above all, Marie-Laure, after their happy hours gliding down the Cherwell under the red and white hawthorn, sent him *À l'ombre des jeunes filles en fleurs,* winner of the Prix Goncourt the previous year, and *Du côté de Guermantes* inscribed and hot off the presses, which set him thinking about his own relationship with literature.

During the long vacation his father gave him a third-class rail ticket to Switzerland, telling him: 'Don't look out of the window, there's nothing worth seeing as you cross France.' It seems he got

10

no further than Rouen, where he wanted to check up on the recently canonised (March 1920) Joan of Arc. On his return he spent most of his time in town, and his room at Brentford became a mere place to sleep.

The following winter at Magdalen he joined the team of the newly launched student paper *Cherwell* and, as their drama and music critic, became absorbed by the West End theatres and life in the wings. He is said to have produced an Oxford play, but nobody knows which. At the end of Hilary term in April 1921, he flunked the compulsory Divinity examination known as 'Divvers', perhaps deliberately, and either he or Magdalen or both decided that repeating university responsions just wasn't for him.

* * *

ONE MAY EVENING IN LONDON he decided at a Ludgate Hill news stand that one of the morning papers was going to give him his first job. His bookshelves were stuffed with French novels describing the effervescence of the postwar period, Europe was seething with great events, and he was anxious to take some active interest in what was going on, preferably by writing about it.

His Old Etonian tie and his offer to work immediately for no pay got him a week's trial on the copy desk at the *Daily Express*. He sub-edited little six-line paragraphs for all that first week, after which he was handed over to the news editor and sent out on his first assignments as a reporter on the night shift. He covered several big stories involving night clubs, restaurants and theatres which woke him up to the facts of life. His passion for ballet began with the Ballets Russes season at the Alhambra—he didn't miss a single performance.

Suddenly that winter the ticker announced that Sinn Fein raiders had kidnapped a hundred unionists, Orange leaders and magistrates as part of a border protest. The situation was approaching the state of civil war. In the office it was decided to send a couple of men to Ireland. At that moment Bob walked in from his fish and chips and because it was late and because the man who generally made these trips preferred not to run into any more shooting, the choice fell on Bob. He was sent over as the assistant to a good, hard-boiled reporter who never even troubled to go home for his toothbrush.

In Belfast, the civil war looked tame. They searched for something to cable home, but there was really nothing except a few pickings from the local papers that might be rehashed. There had been just one spot of bother, however. A party of Ulster special constables had been driving in an ambulance when they lost their way. They were guided by civilians to Monaghan, where the ambulance was commandeered and the constables taken off to an unknown destination. Bob offered to ride down in the day train and see what was happening.

The trip through the Irish countryside was delightful, but when the train reached Clones it was ambushed by a group of Republican soldiers. Two of its carriages contained armed Ulster special constables. Somebody opened fire and in the mêlée a Republican officer was killed. Seeing this, his men started to shoot indiscriminately. A hail of bullets swept through the carriages and four Ulster constables were shot dead in their seats. Bob had the wisdom to open the opposite door and dive out on the centre track. He was arrested and told he deserved to be shot.

He alerted his colleague in Belfast, and this man got him released via their paper, the Colonial Office and Michael Collins, the independence leader, who was himself shot in a civil war ambush a few months later. Back in Belfast, Bob was told to file a story about his adventure and then return by the night mail. The following morning, 13 February 1922, he found his 'Men Shot for Less' story plastered over the front page of the *Daily Express*.

After a while he was sent to Paris to work under a senior correspondent. He took the same pleasure in learning his way about Paris as he had taken in making himself acquainted with London during his school holidays. No language difficulties arose, for thanks to Mallalal's teaching he found himself thoroughly at home. He lived at the Louvre Hotel next to the Comédie-Française, where he went so often that he began to know their repertory by heart. He also made many friends in the law courts, where the great barristers of the day drew huge crowds to hear them speak. And the Croisset connection worked at full steam. He was moved to meet Mme de Croisset's mother, Mme de Chevigné, a descendant of Sade portrayed by Proust in his character Mme de Guermantes.

In the third week of November 1922, he got a cable from London instructing him to accompany Poincaré and Curzon to Lausanne for the Near East Conference. Expecting this to be a simple assignment covering the journey to Switzerland, he carried no luggage, only what was necessary for his return by sleeper the same night. But things dragged on in Lausanne, not at all unpleasantly as it happened. Quartered at the Lausanne Palace, the newspaper men were treated as royally as Poincaré's own staff. Bob eventually bought a collar and shirt and then another and a pair of socks, and finally a suitcase to put them in.

Then a cable arrived at Lausanne sending him to Athens, where the military revolution had just executed several ministers, including an old man who could barely walk and who was dragged from his sickbed to be shot. Traversing Europe in his *wagon-lit*, he looked out with eyes full of wonder—Venice, Zagreb, Belgrade, Sofia, Salonika in ruins, and then past Mount Olympus to Larissa—slowly, slowly, down on the way to Athens. Years later, he remembered: 'Oh, those Greek hills and olive trees so evocative of the past with hardly ever a living person to destroy the illusion of having stepped back into classical times.' Callous in so many ways, he wept.

In Athens he met several of the colonels, but had trouble getting his stories out because of the censorship. Learning of the numerous deaths occurring in Athens from an epidemic caused by refugee ships from the Black Sea, he struck a deal with Colonel Plastiras allowing him to get his cables through by not mentioning politics. An American doctor whom he rowed out to interview offshore told him his death-ship held only four hundred survivors out of an initial passenger list of two thousand. Owing to the danger of infection, the bodies of the victims were burnt in the ship's furnace. Chutes were arranged from the decks to the stoke-hole down which the bodies were thrown.

This story went down well at the *Daily Express*, but after his first few cables interest dwindled because France had occupied the Ruhr. After a while Bob felt an urge to get back and cabled London to ask whether there was any point in his remaining longer in Greece. Ten days later, he was ordered home.

* * *

Having exchanged the violet mountains of Greece for London fog, he was almost immediately sent off to Düsseldorf to cover a conference between the Allied chiefs of staff discussing fresh penalties for German resistance in the Ruhr valley. As usual, he began by buying a much needed shirt and collar, for he had left London once again at short notice. He was now accumulating quite a wardrobe of wearing apparel from different parts of Europe. The people in Düsseldorf appeared courteous and keen to help and he found no open antagonism. The scattered railway strikes harmed the local population more than the invaders, he reported, because they were unable to find means of transport.

That spring he was sent back to Paris, where he was well acquainted with the routine. The office had a fixed-time call every evening with London at nine, and his chief generally left it to him to call over their day's copy, at least a column of politics rehashed from *Le Temps*. Bob often felt inclined to abridge this when the wire was bad, for his chief's copy seldom made more than three lines in the paper the next morning. By nine-thirty Bob was usually free and would then make a dash for some rendezvous. He learned his way about Paris as he would never have done otherwise. As darkness fell, a thousand night clubs would hurl their lights across the pavements, and the noise of jazz bands would blare into the crowded streets. People from all over the world came to empty their pockets in Paris.

In early August he received a cable one morning to go immediately to Doorn, in Holland, to interview the ex-Kaiser. But the veteran war correspondent Sir Percival Phillips, with whom he dined, had beaten him to it. For a couple of days, Bob just stayed around. He hired a bicycle and for an hour or so each afternoon would get some exercise pedalling round the village. The Crown Prince, in golf stockings and field grey suit, would roar past him in his sports car. On the day of his departure, Bob came across him standing despondently in front of his machine and helped him change a tyre.

* * *

Back in London, he began planning to cross the Atlantic. One October evening by his mother's fireside in her little room at

Brentford, Effie asked him whether he had saved any money. He had saved just the fare, twenty pounds. His mother gave him a reproachful look and said quietly that she and Burr would be putting a hundred pounds to his name at the Bank of Montreal.

A few days later, she sat with him for a few moments in the ill-lit compartment of the Southampton train before his departure. At twenty-two he was leaving a comparatively well-ordered life to court adventure, curious to see how far he could travel round the world by the exercise of his craft, using newspapers as stepping-stones. His mother commended him into the care of God, and bade him goodbye.

His passage was booked on the *Andania,* a slow but comfortable cabin ship bound for Quebec and Montreal. It was his first trip across the Atlantic. On arrival in Montreal, he took a room at the new and luxurious Mount Royal Hotel in order to have the benefit of its address. Although he hadn't yet worked on an evening paper, it struck him that the best idea was to storm the office of the first publication he bought at the news-stand. This proved to be the *Star* and he sent up his card. The reception wasn't exactly warm but it proved to be successful. He was accepted on a linage basis and told to report the following morning. This was just what he wanted, for it gave him a chance of making good first and talking money later.

His first assignment was to inquire into the prospects for Christmas turkeys. This was an easy story to write, for there were only two possible outcomes: either turkeys would cost more that Christmas or they would cost less. His story hit the front page with double-decker headlines. For a week he wrote over a column a day for the *Star* but his pay packet wasn't encouraging, so he walked over to the *Gazette* where he was offered a salary of twenty dollars a week. This was considerably less than even a beginner could earn in London, but he was glad to get it. Much of the time he covered the law courts and learned the intricacies of the French-Canadian mind with its peculiar language, religion and folklore. In one case a farmer described how he had seen a birch-bark canoe piloted by the devil flying rapidly over the tops of his spruce trees under a full moon.

The following spring he was sent to a village near the United States border. It was still prohibition, and there were wild stories of bootlegging. He got a splendid story about two nuns on a sled loaded with logs who were driving across the border. They turned out to be men in disguise with a cargo of hollow logs full of booze.

Bob enjoyed Montreal and the *Gazette*, but when he looked at a map of Canada he wanted to move on. He needed the thrill of attacking another newspaper office. He decided to collect his savings and make Toronto his next stepping-stone. Travelling on the night train he reached Toronto first thing in the morning. He made another bid for an evening paper and tried the *Toronto Star*. He got his job and a salary of thirty dollars a week within four hours of his arrival.

His first assignment was unexpected. Although Ontario was a 'dry' province, publicans had the right to sell a weak and sickly beer. It was rumoured that this law was being totally disregarded, and the *Star* was apparently eager to prove that the beer sold in the majority of bars wasn't far off the real stuff. Bob went to Woolworth's and bought a small syringe and a number of small medicine bottles. He concealed these in his overcoat pocket and for the next two days pub-crawled, taking from each pint of beer a sample that was later analysed. His story covered most of the front page and created a sensation, though for some days he feared reprisals from angry publicans.

This beer adventure gave him a good start. For the next month he flew over forest fires, raced up to the gold-mining district of Timmins and even carried on a campaign against the city's dog-catchers. He was sent to Niagara to investigate a rumour that an organization had been formed for passing aliens into the United States. The 'passengers' were collected in Toronto or Hamilton, taken by car to the Canadian bank of the Niagara river a couple of miles below the Falls and a crossing was attempted by night. The immigrants were packed in a small boat and the other side would be signalled with a flash lamp. However, the tangle of branches and undergrowth proved a good hiding place for United States immigration officers, who were always on the watch. Bob saw a real battle at Lewiston with sub-machine guns and rifles, while in the distance came the muffled roar of the Falls.

He stayed in Toronto till the end of the summer and was able to radiate on a fairly wide scale. It became clear, however, that his original intention of working his way to the Pacific would take too long if he remained for six months on each newspaper. He knew that he mustn't stay away from London too long or he would run the risk of returning as a stranger. Quite suddenly, also, he felt a desire for no particular reason to visit South America. One morning when his city editor took him off news for a week, telling him to work in the library, he took the order as an insult and walked out of the building for good.

He bought a third-class passage from New York to Buenos Aires and that same night took the mail train to Grand Central Station. It was early September. He didn't know a soul in New York, but it took his breath away and for about half an hour he walked the streets trying to get his bearings, finally landing up at an hotel somewhere near Times Square. Technically, he had no business to look for a job, because he was an alien without a work permit, but he secretly thought his old luck might last. It did, but not quite as he thought.

It so happened that the chef of the King Edward Hotel in Toronto had given him a letter to a friend of his who ran the kitchens at the Bankers' Club in New York. Bob thought it would be an excellent idea to look this man up. He took a taxi and drove there. The lift was halfway up the building when two shots rang out as they passed one of the floors. Bob jumped out. Facing him was the half-open door of a diamond merchant. A couple of men rushed past as the elevator came level with this office. Bob walked across to the door and looked inside. A man was lying with his face to the floor with blood trickling from the back of his head. Bob picked up the phone on the reception desk and asked for an evening paper. Its city editor had laughed in his face earlier that morning, telling him he wouldn't get a story in a month. Bob dictated his story.

By the time the excited crowd that had gathered back down in the lobby was released by the police, he heard the newsboys in the street yelling out his story. He rushed to the newspaper office, hoping to get hired, but the editor wasn't available to see him. He was paid six dollars for information and left white with rage.

The next day he took his liner to South America. The steerage accommodation on the *Vauban* was fairly dreadful, but as he was the only passenger down there the purser moved him up into second class, and he got sunburnt by the swimming pool, spending part of the three-week voyage lying on a plank provided by the ship's doctor. On arrival in Buenos Aires, he felt intimidated: he knew nobody, didn't speak the language, and had very little money left. But as he observed the midday crowds thronging the pavements he suddenly thought that there must be greater fools than he among them. Could he be less able to live in this city than the humblest of these folk?

He repeated this sentiment to himself several times and felt better. He did have a letter of introduction to the owner of an *estancia* in Rosario, but life on a ranch wasn't really what he wanted. Within a short time he discovered that there were three newspapers in Buenos Aires that held out reasonable prospects. Two of them were printed in English and the third in French. He called on the owner of the *Herald* and was put on the salary list.

Alas, the damp heat in Buenos Aires kept him awake at night. One morning, just as he was carving out a place for himself on the *Herald*, he felt an urge to return home. Walking down the Calle Florida he suddenly realised that he was heading for a shipping office. The *Almanzora* was due to sail that afternoon. He booked a passage and hurried back to his lodgings, where he collected his cabin trunk, never daring to return to the *Herald* for fear of changing his mind but conscious of the fact that, as when he had quit Oxford on an impulse, he was doing something wrong by clearing out from purely selfish motives.

Her Rough Lot

THE TRUTH ABOUT HER CHILDHOOD was never told. The official version[1] was that she was born in Montmartre ('under the shining loftiness of the Sacré-Cœur') to a married couple called Émile and Mathilde Gal. In actual fact, she was born out of wedlock at the Lariboisière Hospital in the tenth arrondissement of Paris, father unnamed, and was immediately taken into care.

Her unmarried mother Mathilde Clotilde Bernhard was from Blois, the third daughter of an invalid zouave from Alsace and a local washerwoman. She was a tiny redhead of eighteen with no self-confidence and a hard-bitten eldest sister. This Marguerite set Mathilde up in Paris as a dressmaker on the Clignancourt side of the Butte, halfway down, where most of her customers were prostitutes or prostitutes' maids. A family innuendo suggests that she met a Russian student at this time who made her pregnant and scarpered, as too often happened in the Belle Époque when girls were poor.

Her child was born and named Mathilde like herself (no other name having been provided to the hospital) on 13 August 1906.[2] Three days later the baby was packed off to a foster home in Soissons under the Assistance Publique scheme known as *prévention de l'abandon*.[3]

There are conflicting stories about how baby Mathilde acquired the name Madeleine. The most likely godmother wasn't Marguerite, as that interfering aunt claimed, but the Soissons wet-nurse. Terrorized by the parish priest's saying she was giving her milk to a pagan, this lass chose the name at the font from peasant lore because her fosterling was forever weeping, like the proverbial Magdalene in the Bible. In any event Mathilde's daughter didn't become Madeleine officially until she was styled 'Mathilde Madeleine, daughter of Emile Gal, gentleman' on her marriage certificate in London. There's something pleasing about that.

One of Bob's fondest nicknames for her was Mé. Meaning 'mother' or 'wife' in Norman dialect, it's useful as a cognomen to distinguish her private self from the literary Madeleine with whom her identity partly overlapped.

When the Assistance Publique's two-year fostering subsidy ran out, Mé's mother married Émile, known as Milou, who recognised her daughter as his whether she was or wasn't.[4] It's fairly clear that Mathilde married him mainly to get her daughter back. He was from a mining village in the Midi and earned his living in Paris as a bricklayer or general labourer. His base was Mme Berthier's café on the corner of Rue Marcadet, downstairs from Mathilde's one-room flat via the courtyard back door. He was strong and handsome, a real meridional male with flashy charm, but he turned to drink whenever he was out of work, and could be violent. Serious-minded Mathilde, as clever a dressmaker as ever lived, worked herself to a frazzle to keep the wolf from the door and found him increasingly objectionable.

He bore a grudge against Mathilde's pretty elder sister Marie-Thérèse, possibly for reasons unspeakable, though he claimed it was because she forgot to wash his socks. She turned up at the café one evening with labour pains. Milou took her to the usual hospital for illegitimate births (Lariboisière), but they were so full they packed them off to an annexe. On the way, a little bundle dropped on the pavement—Rolande, who was promptly dispatched to Soissons, where little Mé born to Mathilde by her Russian absconder (or A.N. Other) was already in care. Thereupon Milou gave Mathilde a baby boy who was sent to Soissons too and died almost immediately from food poisoning, then a second son after their marriage whom she called Robert Émile. Her little Bébert was the apple of her eye, but he died in a Paris hospital of diphtheria at the age of two, leaving her disconsolate for the rest of her life.[5]

Marie-Thérèse eventually fulfilled every poor girl's dream by marrying a kind and well-to-do husband, Louis Soilly, who adopted Rolande.[6] With Marguerite established in Beckenham as the wife of an elderly Armenian merchant and Marie-Thérèse set up by her Louis as a successful milliner in the smart Rue de Longchamp, only Mathilde seemed to have missed the bus. All she had was Milou and Mé housed outside the Paris limits in the rough district of Clichy, quite some way from her former friends and customers in Clignancourt. This unfavoured fate increased her bitterness. When Milou was invalided out of the war with a blind eye and permanently injured a leg at work, he took more than ever to drink and started hurling things out of the window. Though it seems he never struck her, she left him and took little Mé off to her mother's home in Blois.

The girl was ten by then. She had been to school from time to time at a Protestant establishment on Rue Souchal in Clichy where much of the day was devoted to praying and hymn singing, but frequent illnesses and a general lack of family incentive due to her parents' pover-ty had kept her away more often than not. Most of her time was spent playing with her surrogate little sister Rolande, sew-ing with her mother or running errands. With two other little girls from the street she learned how to jump the ration queues by holding a soldier's hand to benefit from his priority status. Once she spent several  months in Milou's home village in the Midi, supposedly to re-pair her health with clean air and sunshine, and frequented a local nuns' school unenthusiastically for a week or two.

In Blois she discovered Juliette, her granny, a fey creature who claimed her great-grandfather was a marquis and that a treasure wrapped in leather trousers awaited her buried in the woods if only she could find it. She went off early every morning pushing a wheelbarrow to collect the linen she washed in the river and spread out to dry on the bushes before starting her treasure hunts, not returning home until dusk. Once while her three daughters were small, Juliette forgot Marie-Thérèse in the woods and the terrified child spent a whole dark night on her own until she was found crying at the foot of a tree the next morning.

Juliette's old zouave husband took up his hat and stick one day and walked away to die in an almshouse. Somehow she acquired a ramshackle old house in the Rue des Violettes under the castle walls in which she let rooms. Two of her tenants were prostitutes who catered mainly for farmers coming to town for the market. Mé and Mathilde became these girls' neighbours, and poor Mathilde was several times mistaken in the early days for a newcomer in the same business, though she soon made it plain that she was no such person.

Before long, Milou discovered where they were and begged them to come back to him in a new flat he had found across the street in Clichy. This they did, but he soon became violent again, forcing Mathilde to stop seeing Marie-Thérèse because he thought the two sisters were in league against him.

Little Mé secretly sought refuge in a top floor flat opposite inhabited by a prostitute working as Didine Garcia, whose invented name matched her dark Spanish beauty. She was the mistress of an Italian shoemaker, who worked exclusively for women like her. She arrived in the morning, slept till four, visited the baker and the dairyman and invited the little girls playing in the street to come up for an hour. She would serve them a flaming rum omelet, and they would sit with their plates on her unmade bed, staring with envy at her orange lingerie garnished with black velvet.

At six she would send them away. Then she would dress, and an hour later they would see her come out, painted up, wearing her lovely high boots, smelling good, hardly looking at them, thinking only of what the night would bring or rather bring in. On these evenings, Mé would sulk into her soup plate. Her father would scold, while her mother, thinking she was ill, would worry. Mé dared not say she had been with Didine.

Another neighbour opposite was the impoverished daughter of a once famous actor. Brought up in a fine house in the aristocratic Rue des Saints-Pères on the left bank of the Seine, she had personally known the Comtesse de Ségur, Théophile Gautier, Émile Zola and other famous authors. She had seen the czar, the czarina, the grand duchesses, kings and queens, and had been in Paris as a young girl during the Commune.

She was nineteen when her father died in his sleep and her mother downed a phial of laudanum from his bedside table to die by his side. When everything was sold, there was no question of a rich marriage. She had to do what any pretty young woman did in those days who wanted to get on: she became the mistress of a much older man, a diplomat, married, famous and selfish. But she lacked boldness, she asked him for nothing. She believed this failing ruined her life and told Mé that what a girl wanted in life she should ask for.

This Mme Maurer (the name of a municipal customs official who eventually married her) lived in a flat full of Second Empire furniture and fine objects.[7] Imperceptibly, she took Mé in hand and excited her imagination. She showed her miniatures hidden in drawers and lent her books which precipitated her into a world she knew nothing about. Mme Maurer loved the streets of Paris and walked interminably, taking Mé with her and explaining what they saw.

Under her tuition Mé began to see the unusual and picturesque in people, to become an onlooker. The reading she did under Mme Maurer's guidance began to form her intelligence. After running wild with her playmates in the street or under the fortifications, she would return dishevelled, dirty, unrecognisable, and discover in some novel by Gyp a whole world of châteaux and rich people that seemed to come from another planet. She wept over George Sand's *Indiana*, but sunshine filled her day when François le Champi married the girl he loved. Montmartre cemetery became a place of pilgrimage after she read *La Dame aux Camélias*.

She had nightmares. Waking, she would see her mother looking like an icon, a tiny, shaded, flickering lamp beside her golden hair, for she too had fallen under Mme Maurer's spell and had begun reading deep into the night.

Mme Maurer took her two protégées to matinees at the cinema in Avenue de Clichy, where the programme included a weekly serial with Pearl White and a Max Linder comedy. When the bell went announcing the start of the programme at two, Mé's excitement was immense. It began with a flickering Pathé newsreel. Weary soldiers trudged along in long lines. Lloyd George and Clemenceau walked jerkily across the screen. King George V and his handsome son, the Prince of Wales, shook hands with soldiers and climbed over trenches and barbed wire. It always seemed to be raining. Mathilde found her first moments of real pleasure in these visits to the cinema.

A few of the boys with whom Mé flew kites over the waste land under the fortifications were nice, but most of them spoke and acted like their fathers. It was obvious they would continue in the male tradition. As soon as they were married they would drink too much and pick quarrels with their wives in one-room flats with the children looking on, not understanding, afraid. Mé was gladder than ever to be a girl. It gave her a feeling of superiority.

After the armistice in 1918, Mme Maurer, who was an atheist, prevailed on Mathilde to send her twelve-year-old daughter to a state school where religious education was banned. Though neither Mathilde nor Milou went to church and never mentioned Jesus, the girl was far too pious in Mme Maurer's view, too influenced by the teaching at the Protestant school, where she was apparently confirmed despite her baptism in Soissons as a Roman Catholic.

At her new school, Mé was found to be very backward, fortieth out of forty girls. This drastic change upset her, but she was determined to do better than the other girls and began to climb higher in the class by sheer hard work. She was helped by having read enormously under Mme Maurer's guidance and having learned to observe closely what was happening around her. She was eighth by the beginning of the third term. She wrote French without a mistake, no mean feat even among educated Frenchwomen, and her reading made her so enthusiastic that she rose to be second in the class. She was up at five to go over her homework on the kitchen table. Three hours later she made her own breakfast before going off to school.

Her young, pretty, elegant French teacher praised her essays. This Mademoiselle's combination of beauty and intelligence seemed to Mé the most desirable thing on earth. Already Mé dreamed of becoming a famous woman writer like George Sand, but even as this idea took shape, she decided it must not interfere with her having a broad velvet hat like Didine nor being clever with her needle and iron like Mathilde.

Neither her mother nor her father showed any great desire to have their daughter distinguish herself academically. Mé worked to please herself. 'The force to succeed grew within me, beyond my control, and often my gaiety was tempered with envy and discontent so that, never satisfied, I was thrust further and further forward.'[8]

Only eight of her class passed the school certificate in July 1919. When Mé's name was called out, a surge of inward satisfaction made her blush. She didn't hurry to go home and announce the news to her parents, wishing first to savour it herself. To her surprise, her mother was peeping through the curtains of the flat waiting to see her come down the street. Seeing from her daughter's face that she had passed, Mathilde just kissed her and that was that. Milou wept.

As these were Mé's last holidays, her mother thought the girl should make herself useful. Mathilde had built up quite a busy dressmaking business in Clichy and needed materials, trimmings or buttons from the Magasin du Printemps or the Galeries Lafayette in the heart of Paris. Mé was sent to do these errands on her own for the first time. Followed from counter to counter by old gentlemen or pinched and groped on the Métro, she became used to this and developed her own defences. Clearly her days of playing hopscotch in the street were over. Now she would know the joys of growing up, the satisfaction of seeing men turn round in the street to take a second look at her.

For her first job, her Protestant minister sent her to see two Dutchmen who ran a factory in Clichy where they made imitation pearls. Mé learned how to classify correspondence and run errands through the ranks of women dipping the pearls in tiny cauldrons. The main office was full of young clerks who came in to work from Paris. All they could talk about was marriage. Mé, almost dangerously slim with her long blonde hair caught up in a bun as prescribed by the rules, was teased because a boy of seventeen from the gas company further along the boulevard courted her.

At the end of her first month, she brought a hundred francs home and handed it to Mathilde. Milou wept. When one of the girls in the office encouraged her to learn shorthand to become a secretary, she signed up for night classes at her own expense and practiced assiduously, but she wasn't good at it. The speed refused to come.

After five months at the factory, she was laid off on account of a slump in the economy. There was a heat wave, then it snowed. Milou fell ill in bed, cost a lot of money for care because Mathilde wouldn't send him to hospital, and died on 9 April 1920.

* * *

ONCE THE BILLS HAD BEEN PAID, Mé and Mathilde were penniless. As usual Mme Maurer made a suggestion. A small advertisement in a newspaper got Mathilde a job sewing and mending at the home of a staff officer near the École Militaire, followed by a similar job at a luxurious mansion with butler, chauffeur, cook and maid at the Étoile occupied by a demi-mondaine, and yet another at the Crillon hotel for two young American showgirls who walked around their suite stark naked much of the time. Mé went to see them one day but was disappointed because she found them fully dressed.

With her mother out all day from eight to eight, Mé went to her secretarial classes every morning and did the housework and cooking when not reading and writing. She wasn't well, however. Years of undernourishment had taken their toll on her frail constitution. She took her shorthand examination in mourning clothes and gave up halfway through the dictation.

Suddenly a telegram came from Beckenham. Marguerite's husband Vahan Garabedian had died. Mathilde in despair wrote to her widowed sister asking for help. Marguerite came to Paris, saw how wretched her sister and niece were, and to get Mé out of the mess enrolled her for a year at a convent school in Tooting, sharing the fees half and half with Mathilde.

Although the nuns confiscated her Protestant bible, life for Mé at the Convent of the Holy Family was entirely pleasing. Her schoolmates were French, Belgian, Polish, German, Russian, Greek girls. She prayed feverishly to learn English as soon as possible. The sisters taught with remarkable clarity and she made swift progress. Though she remained true to her Protestant faith acquired in Clichy, she appreciated the advantages of this regular, cloistered life with its superb teaching, and felt as her mind expanded that she was at last building up a personality of her own.

Towards the end of her time at Tooting, she began suggesting to

26

her seamstress mother that as life was so hard for her in Paris she should come to London. The French mother of one of her friends at the convent, a successful dressmaker in Soho, promised to look after Mathilde and give her enough work to keep her busy till she could build up a business of her own.

Mathilde came over to explore the idea and quickly went back to Paris to sell everything she could. A month later, she had found a single room on the second floor of a house in Stacey Street, a narrow dead end on the fringe of Soho, where Mé joined her at the end of her last term at the convent.[9] At thirty-five, Mathilde still looked amazingly young, with a fine head of golden hair, slim legs and a waist that a man's two hands could span easily. When she and Mé went out together, people took them for sisters. Everything was delightfully new and they were both convinced they had left their cares behind them.

* * *

IN STACEY STREET, things looked pretty good for Mé and Mathilde to begin with. Having left her convent, Mé happily helped her mother with her new dressmaking venture. But it turned out that Aunt Marguerite had been up to her scheming again and was pulling strings behind the scenes. She had a friend, a pastry cook from Lyons, who had led an adventurous life in kitchens all over the world till he ended up in London. This Étienne Thibert was a widower with two children, a girl and a boy, both born in London. After his wife's death from overwork and anæmia the girl was taken in charitably by the nuns in Tooting, while the boy ran wild before being apprenticed to a West End chef. The girl showed no inclination for the veil, quite the contrary in fact, but she was the indirect reason why Mé was sent from Paris to Tooting in the first place. The direct reason, it transpired, was Marguerite's plan to wed her widowed sister Mathilde to her widowed friend Étienne. And she pulled it off.

Just two years after Milou's death, Mathilde walked off alone with Étienne one Tuesday morning and married him round the corner at the registry office, having bought her own wedding ring.[10] To her tearful daughter she said she was doing it for her. He was ten years Mathilde's elder, a talented cook but too adven-

27

turous, constantly changing from one place to another. His latest
venture was his own invention, he claimed, though it sounds like
the Belgian *cigarette russe* by Delacre. He called it the cigarette
wafer, and he made it in his gas ovens at his flat in, of all places,
Stacey Street.

* * *

MARGUERITE'S NEXT MOVE was to cart Mé off to a tiny village near
Saumur, where she had taken over the management of a coopera-
tive store. The move was fairly disastrous. The newcomers were
ostracised for quite a while by the locals. Mé brought in some
petty cash by collecting eggs for a grocer in Saumur and selling
cans of cut-price petrol to passing motorists.

A rich cousin from Tours turned up as if by magic, supposedly
to hide from his parents because he had failed his *baccalauréat*,
more likely because Marguerite was trying to induce him to marry her niece. Mé showed him round the store. They were alone
in the attic when he suddenly pulled her towards him and kissed
her brutally, her head thrown back, her lips parted. 'I would have
smacked him if I had dared, but a penniless girl hesitates, whatever people say, before smacking a rich young man.'[11] That kiss in
the attic was her first, but she spat it out. Her cousin left in a huff.
Then a bashful young farmer started stopping regularly by the
shop and finally asked Mé to become the mistress of his farm. But
a letter from her mother ordering her back to London immediately
saved her from having to decide. She was only sixteen, after all.

* * *

MÉ AT ONCE REALISED that her mother's relations with Étienne had
become strained. He couldn't open his mouth without getting on
her nerves. When he spoke nostalgically of the lark and snipe *pâtés*
of his native Lyons, she snapped back in French: 'You'd do better
to earn enough to pay the rent. What do I care for your snipe and
your larks? A hunk of dry bread is more to the point.'[12] Étienne's
wafers it seemed were not selling as well as before. Competitors
were copying and undercutting him. Obviously, Mé's urgent recall
to London was intended to help pay the rent, which was seriously

28

in arrears and urgently in need of being paid up.

The home that Mathilde, Mé, Étienne, his daughter, son and ovens shared was a two-roomed flat on the third floor of 14 Stacey Street. Though the flat was pleasant enough, the promiscuity was unbearable. When the boy brought home a racing bicycle he had bought with money patiently put by from his small pay as an apprentice, Étienne exploded in French, which neither of his children understood, ranting that his son took him for a fool, his daughter treated him like a stick of furniture, his wife and her daughter spent the weekend gossiping in the basement with that Italian woman, supposedly doing the washing, but in fact showing off to that Italian signor with his tenor voice and gypsy hat, did they think he was blind? After this outburst, supper was morose.

Étienne moved his ovens to a basement in nearby Phoenix Street and, ever-optimistic, decided to expand his business by growing mushrooms in two adjacent cellars. The whole family collected cinders from the neighbours, horse dung in the streets and stole earth at night from St Giles's graveyard. His mushrooms grew magnificently, but they were nibbled as fast as they popped up by legions of mice that made a mockery of whatever traps they set. The whole project collapsed. Étienne was once again obliged to admit that a dream had ended in failure.

Mathilde found a job in a dress factory. Mé, at seventeen, after a number of distressing rebuttals trying for shop jobs, eventually spotted a vacancy at the Librairie Parisienne, a newspaper shop in Old Compton Street, and was taken on despite her lack of experience for a pittance with long hours.

One evening her mother told her Étienne had made her pregnant. How could they cope with another mouth to feed? The story doesn't tell how the miscarriage occurred but it did. When Mé came home from the paper shop that night, she sensed that there had been a violent quarrel. After this, her step-father was quite changed. He was angry with Mathilde for not wanting a child, and this increased his suspicions that she must be in love with the Italian in the basement, with the result that he was continually trying to surprise her, bursting into the room where Mé and Mathilde were quietly sewing. Even their mother-and-daughter connivance annoyed him, and he began to hate seeing them together.

After a more violent quarrel than usual, Mathilde reached an important decision. She told the rent collector what was happening, that her husband brought no money in, and asked whether he could give her a really nice room to work in as she was going to leave him. The rent collector, drawing the window curtain aside, pointed down to the second floor opposite at number seven and said he would bring her a new rent book the following week. She and Mé moved in without the least fuss at all, leaving Étienne and his daughter on their own at number fourteen, the boy having gone off to work in the kitchens of a transatlantic liner.

By this time Mé had begun a series of new jobs as a shop girl at Galeries Lafayette in Regent Street, then as a junior typist with a silk merchant in the City, followed by a similar position at Gaumont in Denman Street, Piccadilly, hoping to get a screen test and become a film star. Her own life was beginning to take shape in the shadow of her mother's misery. The harder she worked the more anxious she was to dance. Short dresses, cloche hats, and the rhythm of jazz filled her young mind during these critical months. She made and altered her own dresses now. The Kit-Kat club where she went dancing was neither rich nor elegant, but all its members were young—shorthand typists, milliners, sewing hands, shop girls, waiters, apprentice chefs, tailors, market youths from Covent Garden.

Mé sometimes felt guilty when she returned late from her club and found Mathilde alone, looking sad, even sometimes sulking. She kept a pair of binoculars beside her sewing machine with which she would look up across the street towards the third floor at number fourteen. On 12 December came a boxful of violets with a tin of wafers, a mocha cake and a note from Étienne wishing Mathilde a happy birthday. It was the only time in her life she ever received flowers for her birthday.

Mathilde gradually built up a reasonably successful dressmaking business in their new flat. Their one room was always too hot, too lived-in, but so cosy. They never lost time looking for anything, no object being further than a yard away. There was a gas stove, surmounted by enamel pots and a frying pan, and in the same corner a pail for washing vegetables, the only running water being from a tap down in the yard. Then there was the table, the immense table covered with an inch-thick plush rug. Mathilde kept her sewing machine and cut her dresses on the table, pushing back part of the rug at meal times to make a dining room. Mé slept under the window against the wall. Mathilde's divan was near the door.

One of her dressmaking customers, a manicurist who earned a great deal of money catering for the French prostitutes in Bond Street and Jermyn Street, spoke to Mé, who had reached twen-ty by now without really getting anywhere, suggesting she try manicuring like her. There was a school in Paris that trained girls in twelve days to be top-notch hairdressers and manicurists.

Mé went over with Mathilde, took the course and passed the final examination. But her handbag was stolen while she was working on a hairdo as part of the examination. She ran out into the street distraught, imagining mistakenly that her passport had gone with her bag. An elderly passer-by comforted her, gave her a sherry at the Café Régence, drove her around Paris in his open car, showed her the hotel he was building near the Étoile as a hedge against inflation, bought her a new handbag, and finally gave her a letter to a man he knew in London who could help her.

Back in Stacey Street, Mé worked for a while at a basement barber's shop halfway between Piccadilly Circus and Leicester Square, then used her Paris well-wisher's letter to see the Belgian hairdresser Monsieur Adolphe at the Savoy. Adolphe liked her looks and gave her a job starting in October 1926 or February 1927 depending on which story is correct.[13]

Their Fairytale Romance

On his return from South America, Bob joined the *Morning Post*, an ultraconservative daily that loaned its office during the nine-day General Strike in May 1926 to the government broadsheet edited by Winston Churchill known as the *British Gazette*. Bob found life there extremely dull and jumped at a chance that cropped up to bring some sparkle back in his life by falling in love. It happened one day when he dropped in for a haircut at the Savoy. He climbed the stairs from the basement barber's shop and presented his bill to the girl at the cashier's desk. She was new, very young and had obviously not learned yet how to give change quickly.

Mé looked up from her flustered arithmetic and saw his eyes fixed on her in an incredible way. They were blue eyes, light blue, and very cold, and she had the feeling of being transfixed as with daggers. She was scandalized and angry, but for several seconds she could not break away. She thought he was too young, too slim, too elegant in his black suit, and his stare was insolent. Few young men came to the Savoy. Young men didn't own newspapers, oil wells or shipping companies. Their hair wasn't turning grey and their faces were not creased with experience. They had no place in the Savoy's world of maharajahs, Hollywood moguls, famous barristers and Dominion prime ministers.

He stopped staring at her, picked up his change and walked out. Mé noticed that he had his hat on. Men of forty were more polite than that. No millionaire had ever spoken to her with his hat on. She went home for lunch and indignantly told her mother that a man had stared at her with his hat on. What was odd about that? asked Mathilde. Surely she had been looked at by a man before? Not like that.

She hurried lunch and dawdled back to the Savoy, where the regular cashier she stood in for at lunch hour told her she had an appointment for a manicure at four. No name, the appointment had been made by telephone. The other three manicurists were intrigued, none of them had appointments that afternoon.

At four Mé was downstairs, putting some powder on her nose, when the page boy came to call her for her customer. She suddenly found herself facing the insolent young man who had made her so angry before lunch. She was much too surprised to say anything. He appeared calm, as well he might, having arranged it all several hours ago. The page boy filled her silver finger bowl with warm water, lit her table lamp, and relieved her customer of his black felt hat. She invited him curtly to be seated, determined to turn herself, like Lot's wife, into a pillar of salt.

He made himself comfortable in the armchair, crossed his legs and put a French novel on the edge of the table. Instinctively she looked at the title. It was *Mademoiselle Dax jeune fille* by Claude Farrère, one of her favourite authors. She exclaimed that she hadn't read it yet. Having sworn to keep silent she could scarcely credit the sound of her voice. Yes, the book had just come out, he said.[14] But did she know that she had unusually pretty teeth? And then he laughed about something and she forgot all about her surroundings.

One of her colleagues, thinking she was trying to be nice to earn a good tip, frowned at her through the cubbyhole and whispered 'a bob', meaning the cheap shilling tip that was all she could hope to get out of him. But Mé was thoroughly enjoying herself. Her young man wasn't nearly as bad as she imagined. He was very polite, and asked neither how old she was nor where she was born. When at the end she gave him his bill he gave her a two shillings tip and the novel by Claude Farrère. Then he went upstairs and she was called to another customer.

At seven, having left her colleague Scotty at the bus stop by Woolworth's, she began walking home, when she felt somebody quite close to her. She gave way a little, but the presence came nearer, and something touched her shoulder. She looked up quickly and saw that the presence was the young man whose French novel was under her arm. He carried a raincoat thrown over his shoulder, and it was this that had brushed her.

He raised his hat, pretended to be surprised that they should
meet for the third time that day and blurted out that he thought
she was never going to come out. Then he was waiting for her? Of
course not, but why not let him take her home in a cab? He hailed
one, she settled back into a corner of the cab, he jumped in, threw
his raincoat into the corner opposite hers and sat in the middle,
edging a little closer as he talked and laughed.

The old taxi wheezed and jerked every time a gear was changed.
As they passed the National Gallery and she was wondering why
the driver wasn't turning towards Soho, her companion in the
most natural way, without warning, slipped an arm around her
waist and, drawing her close to him, kissed her. His fresh lips,
his delicate but greedy kiss made her nearly swoon with pleasure and surprise. Her hat had slipped and she immediately set to
straightening her appearance to help her mind recover from this
first encounter with Eros.

Why was he taking her to Leicester Square? She didn't live at
all in that direction. Her voice was supposed to be angry. But re-
ceiving no answer, she tried to convince herself that the driver had
been obliged to make a long detour. He finally drew up in Dover
Street. A commissionaire opened a door. Mé knew the restaurant
by name. The Maison Basque was small and exclusive. A girl she
went dancing with in Soho was engaged to one of its waiters. The
Prince of Wales frequently came here and so did famous actors
and actresses from the West End theatres. Mé was overcome with
panic. It wasn't fair to bring her here without warning. She was
certain that her hat, for instance, a homemade copy of a Paris original which had already suffered from the kiss in the cab, must look
miserably poor.

As soon as she entered the candlelit room she was confronted
with scores of adorable hats worn by beautifully dressed wom-
en. When a waiter pounced to help her take her coat off she was
ashamed of the plain black working dress she was wearing un-
derneath. Then came the choice of the food. Fear robbed her of
hunger. Her companion ordered tournedos and Béarnaise sauce
for them both. The burgundy arrived lying in a basket. The owner
of the place came over to talk to them.

Her companion naturally saw how nervous she was, but she
thought he interpreted it as a sort of tribute to himself and rather

enjoyed it. He said his name was Robert and that he would be twenty-six in August. His family called him Bob. She said she would be twenty-one on the thirteenth of August, he said his birthday was on the fourteenth. This seemed so unlikely that she implored him to stop joking, but he merely turned his limpid blue eyes on her and asked where she was born. On the banks of the Seine, in Paris. And he, said Bob, was born in London on the banks of the Thames.

Well, though he might not be intelligent, at least he was pleasant company. She ought to have expected he would have an answer to everything. He withdrew to call his office, while she slipped half a dozen little cakes into her bag, leaving enough on the silver dish for her theft not to be too obvious. Then they stood under the gas lamp in Stacey Street saying good night. Mé said it was late, her mother would be worried about her. He refused to leave until she put the key in the front door. She didn't want him to see the cakes in her bag when she took her key out. He said he would go if she gave him a kiss, a long goodnight kiss.

So it was that, standing close to each other under the gas lamp in deserted Stacey Street that midsummer's night in 1927, Mé and Bob sealed their fate. It was a magic moment that her memory would treasure. She found her key, opened the door and dashed upstairs.

Mathilde in her nightdress had a sombre look on her face. Her anger surged up, heaping on the anxiety she had felt for her daughter all evening. Rebellious and in love, Mé almost wished she was an orphan. Her mother remained silent. Her resentment had been nursed too long not to be cruel. Mé felt a very little girl. She told her mother she was sorry, but she had not been able to let her know, it had all happened so quickly. Mathilde snapped back that accidents also happened quickly. Who was the young man? The one Mé told her about at lunch. What? The one that insulted her? The one that looked at her like a cow over a fence? But Mathilde softened as she ate the little cakes, one after the other, and Mé fell asleep dreaming of her first real kiss in an old taxi as it wheezed and jolted past the National Gallery.

* * *

ALL THAT HOT JUNE, as the Savoy filled up with millionaires, Bob waited for Mé to finish work at lunchtime or in the evening. They walked and talked, watching themselves pass in the plate glass windows of the great stores. They argued, their different tastes clashed and fought, they gave ground, they discussed their favourite writers, the films they had seen, the paintings they liked. He bought her little presents at the Galeries Lafayette. Then she would imagine he had admired some passing female and hate the sights of her with all the hatred of her young heart. He too had his hates: her mother, her friends, even her cat, and scores of times quarrelling she left him, wrenching her arm out of his, flying off, leaving him surprised, furious, on the pavement. Half an hour later while reading or sewing at her cash desk, a shadow would fall across her field of vision. She didn't need to look up to know it was Bob. Then they would laugh and the quarrel would be quite forgotten.

Her colleague Scotty was never quite reconciled to their romance. She was suspicious of Bob chiefly because he was young and also because he never spoke about himself or his family. It was Scotty's opinion that nothing would come of his courtship and that one day he would suddenly disappear as mysteriously as he had arrived. Occasionally Mé did ask him where he lived or what his parents did, but he easily evaded her curiosity and in truth she didn't care. When they were together they two were the only people who mattered.

Her mother, like Scotty, was full of doubts. She wasn't accustomed to things turning out well. Never in her life had she been lucky. In her philosophy, though good might alternate with bad, the latter would assuredly triumph in the end. But Mé paid no heed. She and Bob spent every lunch hour running around the department stores and the evening meal became a thing of delightful importance. They dined regularly at Sovrani's in Jermyn Street, the Carlton Grill, and The Ivy. She had her first evening dress and an evening cloak of night blue velvet lined with pale silk, and silver lamé shoes. It was as if the shy young woman who had first pushed through the swing doors of the Savoy had undergone a magic transformation.

One evening when for once she was staying in to give her mother a hand with her dressmaking, their doorbell began suddenly to shake and splutter, as if the person downstairs was afraid of breaking the rusty wire. Mathilde, tight-lipped, annoyed by the disturbance, immediately feared who it might be and told her not to stay talking at the door for an hour. Mé ran downstairs and opened the door but saw nobody, not till peering right and left over the scrubbed white doorstep she discovered Bob standing right up against the wall. He said it was a bore they didn't have the telephone at home. Mé exclaimed that they hadn't even running water, or electricity, or anything else that other people had. He said that if she put on her hat and coat they'd just have time for dinner. She replied that she'd had dinner, besides she'd promised to stay in. As he was holding both her hands, and as he was no more anxious to go away than she was, she asked him if he'd like to come up, fully expecting him to refuse. Almost to her embarrassment, he said he'd love to.

There was no going back. Mé led him up the dark stairs, threw open the room door, and there was her mother sewing, with a mountain of pink flounces in front of her, her needle flying with incredible speed through the *crêpe de chine*, flying so fast that Mé knew she was trying to hide her emotion. 'Mother,' Mé said, 'here's Robert, he wouldn't go away.'[15] Mathilde rose and gave him her hand, then Mé made him sit on the edge of her bed while she went on with her work. He asked if he could light a cigarette and began to look with interest round the room. The cat opened her eyes, stretched, walked to the side of the table, looked at Bob and jumped into his lap. He showed no sign of gratitude.

They all spoke in jerks and mostly at the same time. Then Bob began to take up the flounces, admiring the material and the stitches, asking why the hems had to be stitched by hand. Mathilde explained that it was to make the flounces fall more naturally. Speaking of her work, which she alternately adored and loathed, her inborn timidity quite disappeared. They went on sewing and talking, and when eleven struck at St Giles's they were all surprised.

Mé took Bob down to the street door. They parted well pleased with one another, and Mé darted back upstairs, anxious to learn what impression he had made on her mother. Mathilde said it was funny, the way their cat took to him right away. She'd never seen her jump on a stranger's lap like that. Of course, Bob wasn't without charm, and he was so interested in things, and, in a way, rather good-looking. That was all Mé could get out of her for the moment.

The courtship continued. Every time Mé emerged from the Savoy she found Bob standing on the corner by the bank in his black hat. As always, they walked and talked, lunched and dined. He took her to a famous women's tailor's in Cork Street and had her measured for a two-piece by the senior partner, who told her she had one arm longer than the other, one hip higher than the other, and that her waist was smaller, her posterior larger than most English girls'. Bob bought her silk stockings and calf shoes from expensive shops. One Saturday afternoon in a West End cinema his hand touched her breast, his fingers closing over the silk of her blouse. She dared not move, the film didn't matter, only the feel of his hand on her breast.

Some evenings, when he was on the night shift at his paper, she waited for him in a taxi in Fleet Street until the first editions came off the press and he came out flustered, relieved, impatient, asking the driver to take them to the Carlton Grill. She would nestle up to him, careful not to ask any questions, for she had understood from the beginning that he was the sort of person to keep his worries to himself. His battles were all waged deep inside him, quite unlike Mé who as soon as she had a disappointment or worry had to share it with somebody else.

He finally told her he was being sent to Geneva to cover a conference.[16] He would be away for ten days or a fortnight. Over their dinner at The Ivy, he was loving but his thoughts seemed elsewhere. He had moods at times that she could never quite fathom. He played on the table with her hands. She felt something cold touch her wrist, a platinum watch set with sapphires and diamonds. She gave a gasp of pleasure and surprise.

They parted as usual under the lamppost on Stacey Street. Mé ran upstairs and bursting in showed her watch to her mother. Mathilde said it was far too beautiful to be just an ordinary present, it was the sort of present a man gave to a girl when he was leaving her. Mé shouted that it wasn't true, Bob wouldn't lie to her. Relenting slightly, Mathilde said she mustn't cry. Of course it would be better if he could make up his mind a little quicker, but she supposed they were both very young. She personally had never had any luck in life or in love. She said Mé got on people's nerves throwing her happiness about. When she, Mathilde, sat there alone, stitching, stitching, she sometimes thought that being in such high company had gone to her daughter's head. Mé blurted back that what her mother really meant was that she would be rather glad if Bob didn't come back.

Nonetheless it was true that Mé had reason to be pleased with herself. Her spontaneous charm and gaiety went down well at the Savoy with her colleagues and customers. Her male clients, not all of them elderly but all of them rich, found their vivacious and pretty manicurist a pleasure to meet and tipped her generously. Scotty advised her to open a savings account at the bank, the corner building on the Strand where Bob always stood waiting for her. But would he come back for her twenty-first birthday in August? Scotty thought not, and Mé was half-inclined to believe her.

In the meantime, an old count from Vienna pampered her with French novels and worldly-wise advice, and a wily Hollywood producer offered to turn her into an international film star like Mary Pickford. She was thrilled at this idea. One day, he invited her to meet him at the Café de Paris to discuss their contract. He was prepared to take her out to Hollywood with her mother. A box containing two superb orchids came that afternoon with a card from the producer reminding her of their rendezvous. Mé realised that he wasn't courting her but merely trying to make money out of her. She experienced the excitement of knowing that her life was about to change entirely. Success had come.

She left work that night late because the cashier she stood in for was on holiday. When she ran out into the Strand, she stopped suddenly, wondering if she was seeing a ghost. The black hat was there, by the bank, behind the evening paper. Her heart felt like bursting. He asked where they should have dinner. She said she couldn't, somebody was expecting her at the Café de Paris at eight. It was very important. And she showed him the orchids she was to wear. A young woman was hurrying past on her way to catch a bus. Bob stopped her, asked her to take the orchids and wear them to go out dancing that night, as they didn't suit his fiancée. The young woman blinked, took the box, said thank you, and ran to her bus which drew slowly away from the kerb. While still on the platform she waved to them, as if they were old friends, and they laughed so happily at the sight of her that, with Bob's arm tightly round her waist, they zigzagged down the Strand as if drunk.

Mé nonetheless did some stills for the Hollywood producer, who seemed unmoved by her not showing up at the Café de Paris, but when he noticed the engagement ring on her finger, he shrugged, muttered that he had no time for imbeciles, and stopped asking for her at the hotel. This didn't matter in the least, because Bob had decreed that she should leave the Savoy after Christmas. He had other plans for her, but for the moment he kept them to himself.

* * *

HE TOOK HER TREMBLING on a bus and tram to meet his parents at Brentford, warning her not to expect too much. The place didn't impress her, it seemed no better than Stacey Street or Clichy. At the foot of the vicarage slope, a girl in a white apron opened the door. A little dog barked. Mé's future mother-in-law appeared, tall, slightly bent, white-haired. 'Mother, this is Madeleine.'[17] Her serious, beautiful face under the neat white hair puzzled and fascinated Mé. All the women in the world in which she moved were relatively young. Her fiancé's mother on the other hand gave her the impression of having stepped down from another century. Her features, though soft, had a Quakerish determination. She wasn't the kind of woman with whom a girl like Mé would have dared take the slightest liberty. To give herself confidence, Mé bent down to make a great fuss of her Pekingese.

No less of a surprise than Bob's mother was her husband, a slightly stout, silent man whose ecclesiastical features and thinning white hair, his clerical suit and collar, caused Mé to revise her prior opinion that she should be able to charm him first. Clearly, she told herself, if her arrival into the family was to provoke doubts, it would be in the mind of this grave and taciturn man rather than in that of his brilliant and erudite wife. A polite coolness was to be foreseen.

At lunch Mé looked from her fiancé's mother to her son. The resemblance was striking: the same vivid blue eyes, the same slightly prominent nose that gave the eyes character and determination, the same thin lips but by no means cruel, though it would be unwise to oppose their will. Her mother-in-law had the loveliest of hands, and her fingers were covered with Victorian rings. She showed Mé around the house, her little room, the schoolroom. This tour of Bob's childhood home terrified Mé, it was so unlike anything she had ever seen. She felt inane and began to tell her mother-in-law that before leaving home she had washed her hair in her honour and it would not curl. Her guide appeared surprised to be let into this feminine secret but her expression changed, and for the first time she gave Mé an affectionate smile.

In spite of this, the ordeal of tea marked the low point in Mé's inept behaviour. The vicar emerged from his study. Mé was handed a cup of China tea which she had trouble pretending she liked. The little maid came in and out with hot buttered toast and thinly-cut bread and butter. Mé's throat was dry and she could eat nothing. When a cat appeared at the window, her fiancé's mother smiled and said that while she normally confined her affections for animals to Pekingese dogs because her mother had liked them, this cat appealed to her. At this, Mé's deplorable silences at the tea table led her to exclaim that her mother and she also owned a cat, and that one of the reasons she was so happy to have made her home in England was that English people loved animals. At this point, aware that her outburst had proved even more ridiculous than her silences, she became dumb again and felt the blood rushing up to her hairline.

Fortunately it was time for Bob and her to go back to town. On the tram back to Kew Bridge, she said she wished she hadn't come. She had made a dreadful fool of herself. Bob ignored her and began talking about his Aunt Harriet, Lady Wantage. She was like all the women in his mother's family. They painted pictures, wrote books, administered vast estates. All of them left big names. Mé said she understood why her arrival brought sorrow. 'Who can tell?' Bob answered.

* * *

Effie, as she learned to call her, invited her to spend a night at Brentford while Bob was away in Geneva. They knelt to pray together on the Persian carpet in Effie's little room, and Mé attended Effie's Bible Class in the church hall. By the end of the year, they got on very well together, but Bob's father remained aloof. As if to forewarn her, Effie told her the story of Hannah Mayer Rothschild's marriage to Henry FitzRoy, a love match forbidden and boycotted by the Rothschild clan, except by Hannah's mother who disobeyed the ban and drove her daughter to St George's, Hanover Square, in her coach and four before kissing her and driving off before the ceremony.

One day, Mé arrived back in Stacey Street to discover that Mathilde had received a surprise visit from Effie and her daughter, and that it had been very successful. However, for some time Mé had been feeling severe pains in her chest. A series of doctor's visits and X-rays discovered that she was potentially consumptive, not fatally so at present but soon to become so if she didn't get better air than in Stacey Street. A spell of mountain oxygen was indispensable. Bob received this bad news with his usual equanimity. After a wonderful Christmas Eve which Mé and he spent dancing together at the Berkeley Hotel, he took everything in hand. He gave orders not only to Mé but to her mother as well. Mé would leave the Savoy immediately, and she and her mother would spend the rest of the winter in the Pyrenees. When Mé was well again, Bob and she would be married. It all sounded very simple.

Mé's absence lasted much longer than they had foreseen. Shortly before Easter, Mathilde thought it would be wise to go back and renew contact with her customers in London. She wasn't even now at all sure that the marriage would take place. If Bob got tired of waiting, who could blame him? He was young and ambitious. Mé could go on believing him if she wanted to, but so much of what had happened to her, Mathilde, was so cruel that she felt duty bound to warn her daughter against a possible disappointment. She just sat there in the armchair at their lodgings, crying softly. Her skin was grey and she looked suddenly old.

It was late autumn when Mé finally returned to London, rested, happier, more confident, her eyes bright with a rediscovered desire for life. Effie had written her long, affectionate letters. Others less tender from her mother scarcely hid her continued anxiety. The long boat train drew up at the continental arrival platform at Victoria station. Bob was waiting for her, slim, smiling, his blue eyes full of tender love. How marvellous it all seemed! They fell into one another's arms and then she looked round for her mother. She wasn't there. Well, never mind, at least she had Bob.

But Mathilde *was* there with a woman friend from Stacey Street. When they saw Bob kissing Mé on the station platform, Mathilde said everything was all right now, they could leave.

* * *

Bob had taken a two-room furnished flat over the Ambassadors Club on Conduit Street. This address entitled him to get married, like his ancestor and *alter ego* Henry FitzRoy, at nearby St George's, Hanover Square. His father, disappointed and hurt, had refused to marry him at his own church in Brentford and said he would not attend the wedding in Hanover Square. Neither Bob nor Mé knew whether he loved them, was sorry for them, or hated them.

On Saturday 1 December 1928, they walked the two hundred-odd yards from Conduit Street to St George's. It was drizzling. Mé felt miserable. There would be no music, no flowers, no white dress. They climbed the stone steps and pushed the leather door open, advancing slowly into the dim interior. When Mé's eyes had become accustomed to the half-light she saw three women seated together in the centre of the church, with two others just in front of them. These last two were Bob's mother and his younger sister Blanche. Effie came forward to meet them, calm and impenetrable, alone with her daughter, Burr having remained as he had said in his study back at Brentford. The others were Mathilde, Scotty and the Savoy florist, whose white carnation smelt strongly in the buttonhole of Mé's black tailor-made. Mé thought her marriage looked more like a funeral than a wedding, nothing but women apart from Bob.

The clock in the rafters stuck two, and almost immediately the young curate came through the vestry door in his surplice. Then the rings were on their fingers, neither of them doubting that they would go all along the road together. Those present (except one, the Savoy florist) signed the marriage register with the curate in the vestry. As they walked down the side aisle, Mé felt a warm finger wriggling through the opening of her glove against her naked palm. She looked up, Robert was smiling at her with his blue eyes like a naughty schoolboy before suddenly going serious again.

The party reached the end of George Street, and they said a few

words about the drizzle. The two mothers shook hands rather coldly. Mé's sister-in-law took her mother's left arm, Bob the other.
Mé bade farewell to Mathilde and her two friends, who went off
together towards Regent Street. Effie muttered something about
getting back to Brentford to organise tea with her husband, and
quickly she and her daughter disappeared down Bond Street while
Bob and Mé, with no wedding cake and no arranged honeymoon,
stood together, hand in hand, on the edge of the pavement.

* * *

THEY STAYED ON IN CONDUIT STREET for a while, then found a
home in Knightsbridge, near Peli's old house in Hans Place, on the
third floor of a brand-new building still smelling of fresh paint and
plaster, on the corner of Brompton Road and Beauchamp Place.[18]
It was unfurnished and had no central heating, just gas fires. Car-
peting the bare boards cost a fortune, but Effie took Mé to Harrods
to buy her a bed, an armchair and the more necessary additional
pieces of furniture. She also sent over all Bob's books in three
large tea chests, a great pile of linen and some crockery, including
the remnants of a bone china tea set dating from Peli's days.

Mé, still officially convalescent, enjoyed her new role as a
Knightsbridge housewife, getting up late, not having Mathilde
just behind her shoulder to criticise, wandering off to Harrods'
food halls for the daily shopping, looking after Bob. He went off
to cover a four-day cruise on a Cunarder, met a fellow-reporter,
went to see this fellow's editor back in London and got a new job
as a reporter on the *Evening News*. He soon became the paper's
diarist, writing up to two columns a day for the leader page. This
gave him scope for displaying his talent as a writer, and he was
supremely happy. His 'Talk of the Day' column, unsigned like the
leader itself, was subtitled 'Men, Women and London'. These three
topics, together with the unnamed 'I' who wrote about them, were
to remain the principal matter of his many books, notably those in
which they gave examples of survival in the face of change.

A typical 'Talk of the Day' column published on 1 April 1935
(p. 8) picked up the front-page headline about the death of the Air
France chief pilot Robert Bajac in the first crash in his long flying
history. Bob's story told in short sub-headed paragraphs how 'I'

44

flew with his close friend on the morning newspaper runs from Croydon to Le Bourget in the early 1920s; took off with Bajac and an engineer in an open amphibian from the Seine in the heart of Paris and landed on the Thames at Hammersmith Bridge in 1925; dined with Bajac, Costes and Codos at Le Bourget to greet Lindbergh on his solo flight from New York in 1927; attended the pilot's engagement party in Chamonix at which Bajac danced at dinner with his fiancée with twenty stitches in his head after being half-scalped in a bob-sleigh accident the same afternoon. These sketches are accompanied by others (the legendary Christian Jakobsen Drakenberg; boy drummers at Wellington Barracks; the King George Jubilee Trust) and end with a two-line joke worthy of the vicar of Brentford's 'attic salt' back in 1913.

He decided to tutor Mé through his library and, having appreciated the attention to detail and the lively descriptions of places and people she had displayed in her long letters from the Pyrenees, he encouraged her to keep a diary of her own. Most mornings she sat up in bed by her breakfast tray once he had gone and dashed off a page or two in long lines of unhesitating French prose, never pausing to correct or refine. This would become a lifelong habit.

As she got better, he began asking her to accompany him on his assignments to picture shows, flower shows, first nights in the West End theatres, lunches here, teas there, suppers in expensive restaurants with a glimpse perhaps of the Prince of Wales dancing a blues or a tango, walks back through the park at 2 A.M., the first daffodils coming out in St James's Square, and so on. Their names appeared regularly in the Court Circular in the 'among those who accepted invitations' lists. It all went into the *Evening News* column. While he looked after the serious side, she provided the more feminine touches. What had the lucky girl who danced cheek-to-cheek with the Prince of Wales or Prince George worn at Quaglino's or the Savoy last night?

Whenever Mé went to Stacey Street now, she felt out of place, overdressed, not belonging any more. Mathilde was thinner, busier than ever, absorbed. Mé sat on the edge of her bed and wondered what to say. Mathilde told her that the French prostitutes she sewed for, by far the greater part of her clientele, were coming less often now that her daughter had married into money.

This was unfair, because Mé felt far from rich. Though Bob

could draw almost unlimited expenses on the *Evening News*, his salary was no higher than any other columnist's on a major British newspaper, which was nonetheless quite a lot at the time. He bought a second-hand 'Cloverleaf' Citroën for twenty pounds. The vehicle was old-maidish, a capricious starter, but she never broke

down and used up precious little petrol. They named her Totote.

They drove down to Biarritz and parked Totote next to the Hispano-Suizas, Rolls-Royces and Bentleys in front of the Chambre d'Amour or the Hôtel du Palais. During the apéritif hour they left her outside the Bar Basque while they tried to make their rose cocktail last while they noted the doings of the smart set bowing and curtsying to King Alfonso of Spain and Edward, Prince of Wales. Not being rich enough to plunge unheedingly into the gay life of Biarritz with Bob, Mé felt vaguely unfulfilled. Her only thought was to forget the black bread of her childhood and early youth. 'I wanted to dance, to see, to be seen, to wear beautiful dresses and go where the smart people went.'[19]

* * *

BUT IT WAS TO BRENTFORD that Bob and Mé went almost every

Saturday afternoon. Sundays were out because Bob had to be in Fleet Street for Monday's paper and the Brentford maids had to be free for church on the Lord's Day. The Saturday food was always overcooked mutton that would be religiously kept over for the morrow. They drove out for Burr's seventieth birthday on 2 August 1930 in sweltering heat. As usual, they had bought him a little toy that was sure to please his childish tastes, and something for Effie's Pekingese dog to which he was greatly attached. Effie was beginning to talk about retirement because the Ecclesiastical Commissioners were being offered fantastic sums for the vicarage by the gasworks and the brewery, both wanting to pull it down and expand. This was a great shame because the vicarage was all Burr's and Effie's life.

That particular Saturday, Mé ventured to see Burr in his study, leaving Effie and Bob in the dining room. Dressed as always in a shiny, threadbare black parson's suit with his hard clerical collar, he beamed a friendly welcome, as if he had never had any doubts about her. He was just one of those men, she told herself, who need to see you around the place for five or ten years before it strikes them to say good-morning. He said suddenly that his mother, a wonderful person, died at the age of ninety-two. He hoped to do the same. In his family, they all lived to be very old.

Try as she might, Mé could get nothing further out of him. The others came in and sat down. The oppressive heat seemed to weigh on him and several times he alarmed them by breaking into hiccups. Perhaps he had eaten too quickly. The weather was so threatening that Mé persuaded Bob to start for home rather earlier than usual. As the Cloverleaf was virtually an open car with only a light hood that gave no protection from the sides, she was anxious not to be out in what promised to be a tremendous August thunderstorm. As they drove home, she told Bob that his father seemed to consider her now as a member of his family. Effie had told her before supper that she had prayed and prayed that the family might keep together, saying they must keep together always, to the end of their lives. Mé said she took it that Effie was referring to her and Bob. 'Yes,' he said, 'she probably was.'[20]

They put Totote away in the tiny garage mews off Montpelier Street where she would not incur the wrath of the police, parking on open streets being at that time prohibited. As soon as the rain started it came down in torrents, and the thunder was like gunfire, but by morning everything was calm again, and only the rain-drops on the leaves of the plane trees, shimmering in another heat haze in the street below, spoke of the violence of the storm.

At about noon they received a telephone call from one of the maids at Brentford with a message from Effie saying that during the night Burr had suffered a serious stroke and was in bed with one side of his body completely paralysed.

They found Effie, generally so calm and full of quiet confidence, momentarily felled by despair. She felt responsible for the calam-ity. Shortly before ten o'clock the night before, as they were go-ing to bed, the Pekingese, indisposed by the heat, was violently sick in the middle of a Persian carpet, and Effie, exasperated, ex-claimed angrily against the animal while trying to clean up the mess. Burr, upset to hear her speaking roughly to the little dog he loved, arrived hurriedly on the scene in his dressing gown, fearful lest Effie, in her annoyance, should put the poor creature out in the storm. Great claps of thunder were shaking the house and the lightning was so vivid that it lit up the dining room where the oil lamp had already been extinguished.

Burr was terrified of lightning, having in his youth seen a man electrocuted while sheltering under a tree. He had put up compli-cated lightning conductors beyond the mulberry tree in his garden and something in his mind associated the sound of thunder with personal disaster. Effie blamed herself for her moment of anger.

Mé imagined that Bob, seeing his father inert in his white linen nightshirt in the big double bed, unable to utter a word, must have wondered whether it wasn't so much Effie and her dog that had brought on this virtual end to his father's long life, as Bob's own action in doing almost everything he could to disappoint him: Ox-ford, journalism, marriage to Mé. Such thoughts were not in Bob's nature, however. He was as hard as nails in everything concerning his father and in most things concerning his mother and sisters.

Burr recovered slightly. He shuffled around in his long dress-ing gown and slippers, supported by Effie. He no longer wore a clergyman's white collar and his expression had become pathetic and guileless, humiliated by his dependence on others. His sti-pend would cease, they would have to leave the vicarage and go off, just two more forgotten people, in search of a house for their retirement. But they were not without resources.

* * *

Effie found Westaway at Godalming, a large and handsome house built for a barrister in the 1890s with an extensive garden designed by Gertrude Jekyll. It belonged at the time to the famous chess personality Sir George Thomas. Effie gave it to Burr in case she died before him. It would also give him something to bequeath, because all that he had to his name was one thousand pounds saved from his annual stipend of four hundred.

Bob and Mé drove out there in Totote. After the modest vicarage at Brentford, the sudden display of wealth at Godalming took her by surprise. The estate struck her as far too large for Effie and Burr—the wood, the warren, the immense garden, the lawns and herbaceous borders. The house itself was a solid brick mansion in which there was more than enough space for a large Victorian family. But what put her in a paroxysm of jealousy was the discovery of a magnificent modern bungalow situated in the prettiest part of the garden and occupied by a young gardener and his wife—so much space, so much lovely country air for this couple of strangers to whom, because Burr and Effie admired them, she took an instant dislike. Thinking of her mother cooped up back in Stacey Street, she felt it was unfair for two young strangers to be so splendidly housed.

Since she had become Bob's wife, Mé somehow felt she owned a share in his family. She knew about the nest egg he had received on his twenty-first birthday, but she asked Effie one day why her husband wasn't heir to his grandfather's estate at Balcarres in Fife. She was told it had been sold back to the Crawfords, its original owners, after Sir Coutts Lindsay left Peli. Both Kitty and Blanche, Bob's sisters, clearly received allowances from their mother. Now that Effie's Harrods account had furnished Mé's flat quite nicely in Knightsbridge, Mé felt that something had to be done to help Mathilde.

Mother and daughter had fallen out over a trifle, as poor people perhaps tend to do even more often than others. Mé had sulked, Mathilde had not relented. The estrangement occurred just as Mé was having to cope with her first miscarriage. It was accidental af-

49

ter a bumpy car ride in the country, but the West End hospital staff thought they were dealing with yet another French wench who had botched a knitting-needle abortion. They treated her abominably. With no mother available, Mé in distress turned to Effie for comfort, but Effie wrote back saying she had torn up her letter and envelope and thought there was no need to worry. At this point Mathilde wrote to say she was sorry.

Mé wept on her mother's shoulder and decided that, although they could no longer live together as before, they should at least live close by. It was unthinkable to ask Effie directly for help. Mé decided to bring Bob by stealth round to the burning question. She accordingly began to make it clear that there was something on her mind. At a carefully chosen moment she would give a deep sigh, and even allow a tear to roll down her cheek. Though not exactly an honest way of achieving her ends, at least it proved an effective one. Perhaps Bob had never really understood how precarious Mathilde's situation had become.

He was no fool in any case, and when Mé told him about Mathilde's 'terrible adventure' at a ballet performance—she started losing blood and went home kneeling on the floor of a taxi—he said: 'Well, that settles it. Let's find an estate agent.'[21] As Mé had been meaning to do just that, they ran across the road to a firm that advertised flats to let. A pretty apartment at the top of a maisonette between their flat and Harrods was available. Two large, airy rooms overlooked the trees in Brompton Road, two others little private gardens at the back. Mé signed a five-year lease in her married name, and Bob's salary put down the first instalment.

The fact of having Mathilde not only so near to her but also of knowing her to be reasonably happy was a tremendous relief to Mé. Her mother came to see her almost every morning and began making her some of the loveliest dresses she ever possessed, repaying in kind the cost of her flat. Bob and Mé were constantly out for the *Evening News* at garden parties, first nights, operas, charity balls, receptions in London and Paris, weekends at Great Fosters with at least three of the royal princes. An abundance of new books, new plays, new inventions came their way. In 1934 and 1935 they sailed first class to Montreal for the *Evening News* on the P & O's new liner *Empress of Britain*.

The London evening papers had become almost as literary as

in Samuel Johnson's day. Arnold Bennett, Dean Inge, George Bernard Shaw and Lord Castlerosse replaced Addison, Steele and Swift. Bob was in his element. His column, with input from Mé, was highly successful, though it looks rather old-fashioned today. It earned him innumerable perks from tailors, shoemakers, shirtmakers, restaurants, hotels, night clubs, theatres, publishers, cruise organisers, trade events, debutante balls, society weddings. Wherever Bob and Mé went, Paris, Rome, Berlin, Cannes, Athens, Madrid, Brussels, Geneva, Montreal, New York, he never paid. Today he would be called an influencer. Mé herself was courted by the gossip papers. When she and Bob covered the inaugural cruise of the *Arandora Star* to the West Indies in 1932, the *Bystander* ('Holds up a Mirror to the Gay Life') recorded in June that she brought a new game back to London called the Yo-Yo. On another cruise to the Canaries she was photographed in wide-leg trousers doing a high-kick Charleston solo, with Bob and other passengers smiling in the background.

PART TWO

In Pursuit of Literature

The Norman Conquest

BOB MUST HAVE FELT, with his journalist's sense of epoch, that these foolish years, so like the pre–1914 decade, were building up yet again to a sinister finale. Reading the news pouring in from Germany, watching the workless processing down the Brompton Road towards their demonstrations in Trafalgar Square, he set out to celebrate in a book his family's continuity in the face of change.

It so happened that his mother's younger sister Helen Lindsay, a former missionary in China, now Mrs George Ramsay, had a store of family manuscripts and letters passed down by Peli. Effie also held some relics, notably a box handed down to Bob by his Aunt Helen. It had belonged to little Arthur FitzRoy, who died tragically at sixteen after a childhood riding accident. It was a square wooden box covered in leather, not unlike dispatch boxes used by Cabinet ministers. Arthur always kept it by him and it was just as he left it. Effie showed it to Bob just before he left for Canada in 1922. What was she to do with it? As the key turned and the lid sprang back, there were Arthur's books, his papers, his letters. 'Thanks,' Bob answered in 1922, 'I'll look at it when I come back.'[22]

A Century Between by Robert Henrey was published by Heinemann in September 1937 priced 15*s*.[23] The jacket reproducing a black-and-white miniature of Hannah Mayer Rothschild bore a copperplate advertisement at the foot of the front page: 'This book is the story of an English family since 1837. It starts with a romance famous in history. A hundred years ago two young people fell desperately in love. The girl was Hannah, beautiful daughter of the founder of the London House of Rothschild.'

Bob dedicated his first book to his mother, knowing she would see an ironic correspondence between the 'romance famous in history' and his own romance with Mé. Though Mé had little in common—to say the least—with Hannah Mayer Rothschild, Bob clearly saw in Henry FitzRoy an *alter ego*, quite as determined as he was to marry the girl he loved. Just as Hannah's and Henry's marriage was banned for solid religious and financial reasons by Nathan Mayer Rothschild, so was Bob's and Mé's by the vicar of Brentford out of sheer prejudice. Both engagements, when they prevailed, were subjected to a probationary period of several months. And both weddings, condoned by a loving mother but cold-shouldered by a forbidding patriarch, were eventually celebrated at St George's, Hanover Square, with a mere handful of people present. Where the irony becomes sublime, however, is that Bob's marriage isn't mentioned at all in this family story. He was married in 1928, but his narrative jumps straight from 1926 to 1930, then to 1937 where it ends.

This lacuna is all the more remarkable as the narrative dwells at length on the female side of Bob's ancestry: Hannah's mother, Hannah herself after her beloved Henry's premature death, Blanche FitzRoy as a child, as the unloved wife of Sir Coutts Lindsay of Balcarres, as Peli the rich Knightsbridge widow, young Effie Lindsay growing up in opulence among famous authors, artists and musicians before choosing to serve a modest Church of England parish and its truculent incumbent.

This celebration of womanhood told in the third person culminates unexpectedly in Bob's own story as 'I', suggesting that his existence somehow prolonged that of his female forebears.

The Madeleine figure does not appear here in any form, and neither does Mé as a person or as a writer. The stories transcribed from her pen in later books are lively factual chronicles—things said and done, pure day-to-day reporting with an acute sense of detail and human interest. But nowhere is it possible to find her writing this, for instance: 'The Dowager Lady Southampton was now growing old, and this spring she had taken to her bed. Nevertheless, until recently she had been active, going from place to place in a black poke bonnet, preaching and discoursing from the top of a barrel.' Or this: 'The Continent was full of kings in fine uniforms taking the salute on crowded parade grounds.' Or this: 'She [Anne Caroline FitzRoy] had married a minister called the Rev. Humphrey Allen. This man had a tall, conical, bald head, a sanctimonious drawl, and was often to be found leaning back in his chair with his hands placed together in the attitude of a praying saint.' Though Mé loved fun and games, her writing was usually gay or dramatic, even melodramatic, and rarely witty.

The clear motive behind this first book, which begins just after the coronation of Queen Victoria and ends just before the coronation of King George VI, is to establish a continuity between the old world and the new. Through trouble, sorrow and disappointment the true love of Henry FitzRoy and Hannah Mayer, as sung by their great-grandson, is rewarded by recognition and survival.

In the closing scene, probably imagined, a painting glimpsed on a table in the Speaker's house symbolises the world as it should be. 'It did me good to find him there where he would so much have liked to live, for the picture was that of Henry FitzRoy.' Henry's triumph is Robert Henrey's vindication: 'Time had avenged him. The FitzRoys had their Speaker after all.'[24] By the same token Robert Henrey, newspaperman, had joined the ranks of the people he admired above all others: the London literati, authors of books.

Considering this doubling up and the fact that Mé was definitely present alongside him at that reception in 1937, while she is totally absent from his story, this first literary object, in which facts and appearances yield to a universal subjective, is a prologue to a life in books, a *Le Temps retrouvé* in reverse. To celebrate its appearance, Effie gave Bob life membership in that temple of literature in the heart of clubland known as the London Library.

The *Sunday Times* wrote: 'Buy or borrow it: it is very nearly a model of all that a biography should be.' And the *Times Literary Supplement*: 'He has a romantic family history to tell, and the gift of a born writer in telling it.' Vernon Fane in the *Sphere* praised it as 'a love story that was really lived'. Richard King in the *Tatler* gave it two columns on 29 September 1937, stressing its readability: 'The diaries make it more than usually valuable, because they give so vividly scenes and personalities and impressions of a world which now seems almost as remote as the world of Queen Anne.' But King had the good sense to conclude: 'As a book [it is] far more interesting than a thousand novels, and far more valuable and exciting, simply for being fact instead of fiction.' At least there a reviewer was on the right track, except that he should have written 'as well as' and not 'instead of'.

* * *

THIS MODEST SUCCESS encouraged Robert Henrey of the *Evening News* to think of himself as an author. Newspaper gossip writing was all very well, it paid good money, but it was unstable. In his mid-thirties Bob felt a fit of disgust with the gay life and believed he should aim higher. Quite apart from Mé, his love of France was immense and for many years he had yearned after a place of his own across the Channel where he could build, grow, write. An actress's house on the Riviera seemed right during a week's Christmas holiday in 1937, but the deal fell through—in any case Roquebrune was too far from London to be of any practical use.

Now Bob remembered the Norman origins of his governess Mallalal, his day trips with Kitty and their father from Folkestone to Boulogne and back before the war, William the Conqueror, Flaubert, Proust. It was easy to get across the Channel to Normandy in a few hours by rail and steamer. On an impulse, as if he was off to America again after chucking Oxford and the *Daily Express* in the early 1920s, he took Mé by the hand just before Whitsun 1938 and trusted his luck. They got on the boat to Le Havre, carrying hardly any luggage, with no idea of where they would go. As soon as they stepped off the boat, they hailed a taxi and told the driver to follow the coastline past Trouville and Deauville until they asked him to stop.

Eventually they came to a row of houses, two or three small hotels and a low, white casino facing a vast expanse of golden sand. There was nothing in particular to commend the place, except that it looked pleasant and inexpensive. They paid off the car, took the best room in the main hotel and, five minutes later, were splashing in the sea. It was as warm as at Cannes. They lunched on the terrace from prawns and cider watching the giant liner *Normandie* come into sight off the harbour at Le Havre. For the next few days the sands occupied all their attention. When not actually in the water, they walked at low tide towards Deauville or Cabourg, remembering Proust and his Léa. One day they ran into the beauty of the rich pasture country inland. The hedges garlanded with honeysuckle and wild roses, a donkey in a field, a farm where they were offered a glass of milk—these were enough to awaken what

Bob called his 'sleeping lust for possession'.[25]

The wife of the local estate agent told him a small and inexpensive farm might soon be on the market. It stood on the plateau just above the village, a tiny sixteenth-century farmhouse in the middle of a six-acre field. There were a few more acres he could buy near it. She could show him over the place if he cared to come back before lunch the next day. Bob, never patient when his mind was set on something, determined to visit the farm the same evening.

He collected Mé from the sands where she was sunbathing and they set off. A bull, a few cows, several orchards, farmers, farmers' wives, farmers' children, farmers' applejack—two hours later

Bob had a clearer picture of what he wanted. He wanted an orchard and a kitchen garden and cows and hens, a place which might be self-supporting if anything went wrong in London. He might lose his job any day. Newspapers were becoming less essential than before. Almost every home in England had a wireless set by 1938, when only fifteen years before as a novice reporter he had been unable to pick up signals sent out only thirty miles away from the *Daily Express* office. Things were moving fast and the political forecast was gloomy. He needed land. And he trusted France.

It wasn't until late June that the deal was finally confirmed. He had decided to buy the old farmhouse and as much land as was available. He would build a cottage for his farmer and some stabling round a courtyard, creating an almost feudal establishment on the old Norman pattern. It even struck him that the farmer's rent and the vegetables they could grow in their garden would make them independent if the need arose. Everyone told him, he told him so himself, that his plan to build was foolish, money down the drain, impossible to recoup. Whoever would want to buy a farm with two houses side by side? He stuck to his plan, however. Mé received it with polite indifference. 'It's up to you.'[26]

He left her in London and crossed the Channel with the equivalent in French banknotes of nearly £1,000 sewn up in his inside jacket pocket, because the notary had told him by telephone that he was accustomed to doing business in cash. The legal papers were ready for signature, but they talked politics for a while. They agreed that it was a mistake to let the Germans rearm the Rhineland. War should have been declared immediately instead of shilly-shallying. The notary was courteous in his criticism of English politicians, but blamed his own country also and accepted the inevitability of another war with polite irony. He accepted it completely and coldly. Bob told him he had so much faith in France that he was buying a piece of her soil. The notary agreed that land was never a bad thing to buy. But he thought it was unwise to build when property values were falling, and Bob's plan to live beside a Norman farmer was in his opinion 'sheer madness'. The peasant and the townsman were in his opinion irreconcilable. When Bob objected that this was a sweeping statement, the notary just smiled and said: 'You'll see.'[27]

The documents were read through and duly signed. Bob guessed it was time he handed over the cash, but it was sewn so strongly in his inside pocket that he could make no impression on the thread.

He turned to the notary and asked for the loan of a pair of scissors, explaining that it wasn't every day he walked around with so much money. The clerk was called in. Bob was unsewn and the money placed on the table. He never saw it being counted, yet he was convinced it was done discreetly during a long discussion that ensued on trivial matters.

After that, he paid a visit to the farm. When he trod the grass of his orchard, when he saw the sun setting behind the house—his house—the clouds sailing gently past his Italian poplars, the apples growing on his trees, he knew that he was going to love the place. He dined with the estate agent, spent the night at the hotel and returned early the next morning to London.

* * *

THREE WEEKS LATER, Mé and he had to go to Paris for the state visit of the King and Queen. They decided to leave a couple of days beforehand to see what was happening at the farm. This time Bob brought enough money to buy three more fields. They signed the deed on arrival and went to inspect the building work. Mé gave her instructions for tearing down a lean-to stable, building a properly drained muck heap and extending the garden. Bob ordered 120 cider apple trees and two dozen Cox's. It was arranged that they would camp temporarily in one of the upstairs rooms, the farmer's family occupying the rest of the house.

That August, while on holiday at the farm after the royal visit, Bob heard that a nearby property had just been sold. Figuring that he could find the money by surrendering one of his endowment policies, he put in an offer for part of the sale and bought fourteen more acres and a wood, joining up his property with an extra hayfield and giving Mé her own supply of logs for the winter. He was now a farmer in a big way and felt quite pleased with himself. By some sort of miracle, a telephone line reached the farm on four posts, and only cost him the equivalent of £1.

In the first week of September he decided to go back to London, leaving Mé alone for another fortnight. But when the September crisis became more acute, he telephoned suggesting it might be wise for her to come back. The reservists had already been called up in France, and Londoners were frantically digging trenches in the parks, trying on gas masks and mounting overage anti-aircraft guns on the Thames bridges. Work on the farm came to an abrupt end. The thatcher had not yet done a quarter of the roof on the new cottage, the well sinkers had gone without finding water, and it was clear that everything would be left in the air for the duration.

Munich gave a respite, but the piece of paper that Chamberlain waved in his hand as he stepped out of his plane wasn't inspiring. They decided to go back to France and hasten the completion of the building work so that when war broke out, as it must do sooner or later, Mé might live there making herself useful on the land. Bob was determined to make the place independent of the outside world whatever happened. Mé had automatically acquired British nationality by marriage and considered London her home, but in wartime she would be as safe in France among her own people as in England, if not safer. And her mother, who was still French, might be restricted or even interned in England if the worst came to the worst. Normandy could be a refuge for them both, Bob thought, whatever happened to him.

The first people to make a reappearance at the farm in mid-October were the well sinkers, who almost immediately struck water eighteen metres down with a flow of nearly 200 gallons an hour. This was the best news they'd had for a long time, and an analysis showed that the water was crystal clear. The lack of electricity didn't worry Bob at all. It made their farm even more self-contained. The most immediate problem was how to get the water up from the well, for it was too deep for a hand pump. The local slater who had overhauled the roof of the old house doubled up as a plumber. He suggested a two-stroke engine housed in a little structure above the well under a thatched roof. The water would be driven up into two big reservoirs, one at the top of each house, so that they would have running water everywhere.

The weather was splendid that autumn. There was a bumper apple crop. The Devonshire cider firms took five tons from them because the home supply was poor owing to spring frosts. By the end of October the new cottage was almost ready and they were longing for the day they could get the farmer out of their house and into the one they had built for him. Mé complained that Bob had bought her a house that wasn't even her own. He was determined not to make a fuss that would let the notary say with his exasperating smile: 'I told you so.'[28]

Finally the day arrived. Their house seemed very large after the farmer's family had moved out, but at least they had it to themselves. The plumbers could begin installing the bathrooms and central heating, the carpenters could make new doors for the front of the house, the painters were ready to redo the inside. Mé ordered a Swedish Aga cooking range and a petrol-driven refrigerator for the kitchen, while oil lamps would be sent from Harrods for all the rooms. They handed over the keys to their friendly estate agent and left for England during the last week of November.

That winter was one of the most rigorous within living memory. Bob went over two or three times a month, mostly at weekends, to supervise the work, which took much longer than he expected. No sooner had the plumber installed all the water system than the fierce cold snap that covered the whole of Europe froze the pipes, many of which burst. As the workmen were still there, they went over the entire layout in the light of this experience and either relaid the pipes deeper or encased them in straw.

He took Mé over on 1 April, eager to show her the transformation scene. The house was now a little jewel, sparkling in new paint. The plumber had put on the central heating and lit the Aga stove in the kitchen. The village antique dealer had supplied most of the furniture: an old Norman grandfather clock that chimed every hour twice, a massive oak buffet, tables, chairs, beds, mattresses stuffed with local wool. All the tradesmen trooped through the house for Bob to pay them, thankful for having been given work during the winter when all the holiday villas were closed up.

* * *

THE POLICY OF APPEASEMENT HAD FAILED, and every week brought new crises. Bob and Mé wondered whether they would get through the summer without being involved in war, because something of immense importance was about to happen in their lives. Mé was going to have a child in July. She was convinced it would be a boy. He would be called Robert and Robert would be born on the farm. The local doctor was consulted and foresaw no complications, the midwife was alerted, a daily charwoman was hired, and Mathilde was brought over from London to be with her daughter for the happy event.

In the actual event Mé's labour was long and painful, so traumatic for her that she would write about it several times in the years ahead: the lack of proper anaesthetic, the nut falling off the forceps halfway through the delivery, the pain, the pain, the pain. The doctor, the midwife and Mathilde eventually produced a strapping boy, who turned the scales at seven pounds just as the village church was striking midday on 26 June 1939. Bob, who had moved into bachelor's quarters in Clarges Street after cancelling the Knightsbridge flats and selling the furniture (except Effie's bed which was put in storage), got a telegram from the doctor, spoke to him by telephone, flew to Paris as soon he was able, then jumped on a train to Deauville. The news seemed hardly credible, for he was expecting nothing to happen for at least another three weeks.

He stayed on at the farm until Mé was on her feet again, then simply had to go back to his office or lose his job. He managed nonetheless to get over several times during the phoney war in order to deal with the farmer. This fellow was becoming difficult, apparently because his wife was giving him a hard time out of jealousy of Mé. Bob liked him because he was so patently sly, a character straight out of Maupassant or Balzac, and in his heart of hearts he pitied him for having not one woman to cope with on the farm, but three. His wife was a shrew and neither Mé nor Mathilde, for reasons of their own, liked a man who drank, particularly in the proximity of their darling little Bobby.

In early June 1940, Bob was in London and not intending to go back to France for several weeks, but when there was no let-up to the aerial bombardment of Le Havre, he became nervous and applied for an exit permit. He never really expected to get one and had steeled himself to waiting until a front emerged. He would go back as soon as things quietened down. Most people at the time considered that the enemy would never pass beyond the Somme. Pulling all the strings he could, he got his exit permit by four o'clock and a ticket on the Channel service to St Malo, the only route still open. The train left Victoria at five. He made it with five minutes to spare. The boat took three days to reach St Malo from Southampton because it had to call at Jersey and Guernsey.

He was lucky to find a bus to Fougères, then a man willing to drive him to his farm. He walked down from the road just as Mé, Mathilde and the babe in arms were coming up the path.

The news was dreadful. All the coast from Le Havre to Honfleur was in flames. The petrol tanks at Port Jérôme, the largest in France, had been blown up by the French army so that they would not fall into enemy hands. The Germans were at Rouen, only fifty miles away. Bob decided that they would leave the farm the next

morning and head west. If things got really bad, he hoped to find a ship at St Malo to take them back to England.

His luck held out yet again. A young fellow they knew in the village agreed to drive them to St Malo. Mé emptied the bank account that Bob had opened for her, they said goodbye to a few people they met in the street, the notary, the doctor. Back at the farm, Mathilde had everything ready for their departure. They took a last look round their home. The bedroom was bathed in sunshine. Mé opened her wardrobes full of dresses, furs and hats, her linen cupboard, and tears came into her eyes. The books that Bob had taken a lifetime to collect glittered in their leather bindings. The bed was made, the room was tidied, Peli's pictures and

Hannah's gold candlesticks were dusted. Mé wanted everything to be trim when they left it. Downstairs there were roses decorating the big rooms, the table was laid for lunch, the Aga was still warm. Bob put the shutters up and locked the doors. The garden was a dream, a garden in June, it was theirs and they had made it out of grassland.

The farmer and his wife and their children were watching over their garden fence. Mé kissed the woman and the children, Bob took the farmer's hand and gripped it hard, saying he would be back just as soon as his family was safe, but they both knew he was lying. Bob, Mé, Bobby, Mathilde pushing the little pram full of baby linen, feeding bottles and tins of Nestlé's milk walked up to the gate where the car was waiting.

'I took a last look at my apple trees and my Italian poplars. It's terrible to be attached so much to a piece of land. It hurts to love.'[29]

* * *

BOB'S LUCK HELD OUT except for Mathilde. Their young driver got them without mishap to St Malo, where they found a couple of adjoining hotel rooms. There were stories of refugees on the roads being machine-gunned by German planes. A transport ship was standing by to repatriate Britishers. It had made the journey to Dunkirk seven times and once to St Valery en Caux. The crew had not slept in ten days. They had lived on their nerves, cigarettes and strong tea. Near the hotel, British soldiers continued until the last moment to fill sandbags which would never be used. Farther along, thousands of French soldiers, surly, unshaven, and with their tunics unbuttoned, lolled on the beach. Reynaud had already made his pathetic appeal for American help. Nobody had any faith in the future. Bob and Mé realised that they would never see their farm again. Their departure was a matter of urgency.

Bob went to the British Consulate, where the staff were already packing. A boy sat at a little desk giving out embarkation permits to British subjects. Bob received two for Mé and himself, Bobby included, but there remained Mathilde, whose passport was French. She had a properly stamped residence permit entitling her to live in England, she had come over merely to help her daughter with her child, her home was in London, but the rules said she

65

must stay. All pleading was in vain.

Bob felt a criminal in deciding to return and leave her behind. He told himself that staying would be pointless, that he and Mé would be interned by the Nazis and Bobby might die. But when they left her at the foot of the companionway to climb into the crowded transport ship, having given her all the French money they had left, he dared not look back to see her taking a last look at them.

The ship steamed out into the Channel. A steward passed with a cup of tea. The next morning they were in Southampton and that evening they were at the Savoy. The great hotel was virtually empty. All of its rich clients had deserted London. When Bob and Mé arrived in a cab looking tired and dishevelled, with no luggage but a bundle of linen and a small pram, the staff welcomed them as old friends and fussed over Bobby. They were given a large room overlooking the river. Bob decided to make the hotel his HQ while he reorganised their lives, his bachelor quarters in Clarges Street being unsuitable for the three of them.

He met a group of French journalists bewildered by their exile, most of them en route for New York, and saw General de Gaulle being glared at hatefully by members of the French embassy staff who were awaiting repatriation by the Pétain government. When news of the armistice was broadcast, the air raid siren sounded and Bob and Mé, who had seen and heard worse, went reluctantly down to the shelter. They found the ballroom, scene of so many brilliant banquets, shored up with steel girders, and there were bunks built between rows of damp sandbags. The wives of the senior members of the hotel staff had donned nurses' uniforms with big red crosses on their breasts, and were pouring out cups of tea for their friends in the gas-proof hospital. The orchestra from the supper room was grouped heroically in a corner playing subdued jazz to keep up everyone's spirits, and Bernstein, the playwright, his fine features ashen through fatigue, reclined on a bunk in a silk dressing gown, playing the banjo.

* * *

Bob immediately got his first wartime scoop when the evening papers announced on 2 July that the *Arandora Star* had been sunk by an enemy submarine off the west coast of Ireland. He knew that ship well. His coverage with Mé of the luxury liner's early cruises had done something to set her successfully on her glamorous career, and she had become synonymous with the picturesque,

happy, idle years that directly preceded the war. The evening press gave no details of her doom, and she was dismissed as yet another famous ship sent to the bottom of the sea.

The next morning as he handed in his key at the Savoy, the inquiry clerk told him he had just heard that the hotel's banqueting manager, Zavattoni, had lost his life in the ship. The implication was sensational, for if Zavattoni was on board, destined for internment in Canada, it was reasonable to suppose that the vessel was also carrying other famous Italian restaurateurs, quite a number of whom had been rounded up as enemy aliens in the same swoop as Zavattoni.

Bob called a taxi and drove to half a dozen of the chief hotels and restaurants. Everywhere there was consternation amongst the staff, and the tragedy was clearly more complete than he had guessed. The list of drowned grew larger every hour. There was Maggi of the Ritz, Benini of the Hungaria, Cavadini of the Berkeley, Boscani of Hatchetts, Zangiacomi of the Piccadilly, and Sovrani, the great Sovrani of Jermyn Street, the fame-giddy confidant of diplomats and newspaper proprietors. The death of any one of these would have hit the front page of the more popular national dailies in normal times. But the story was far more significant than the mere loss of a shipload of famous London night-life figures. It brought the curtain down on a decade of West-End restaurant glamour inaugurated by the Duke of Windsor when Prince of Wales and his brother the young Duke of Kent, an amazing period that Bob had described in his *Evening News* society column as the nearest thing to the court of Louis XVI.

He broke the *Arandora Star* story exclusively the next morning in the *Daily Sketch*, a Fleet Street tabloid that he had joined at the start of the war. Each evening he had to fill a given space with human-interest stories for his readers of the morrow. His space, though technically a column in length, worked out at just over a column and a half, with a picture in the middle of the first leg. He allowed himself two hours to write it each evening, regarding six P.M. as his deadline, though he could add and change at nine P.M. for the London edition. Never once did he find his task irksome or discover any difficulty in describing a dozen facets of the ever-changing London scene.

His desk in the features department on the third floor was of the roll-top variety that never closed, massive, full of pigeon holes. His typewriter stood squarely in the centre, with the telephone beside it, and a month's accumulated papers that nobody dared disturb. He shared a room with the film and stage critic Elspeth Grant, whose typewriter was hidden in masses of film publicity and back numbers of *Variety*. The wall behind her chair was decorated with film posters quoting her criticisms. Bob's part of the room was brightened murally by *New Yorker* cartoons deriding columnists as a race. On his right, level with his eyes when writing, was a photograph of Bobby.

In September 1940 he got a second scoop from 'a distinguished French deputy' who had been in Bordeaux on 16 June, an hour after President Reynaud resigned and was succeeded by Marshal Pétain. This man told him Pétain, with whom he had spoken before escaping from France, was 'rabidly anti-British' like his pro-German wife. He had seen Pétain holding Winston Churchill's offer to conclude a Franco-British Union for the duration of the war, which he had just received through the medium of the British ambassador Sir Ronald Campbell. This 'solemn act of union' would give every Frenchman citizenship of Britain and make every Briton a citizen of France. Pétain paced up and down the room, document in hand, speaking to two or three of his government colleagues. After a moment he turned and said gruffly: 'I will not accept this offer of Churchill's after the way I was treated by Great Britain in March 1918.'

In other words, the armistice signed by Pétain at Rethondes on 22 June, which handed over to Germany the French empire and its mighty fleet leaving France's ally Great Britain in the lurch, was partly due to the spite of a man who had never forgotten that the British had preferred Foch to him as generalissimo. Bob checked the facts with Lloyd George, who confirmed that he had prevailed on Clemenceau in Foch's favour at their meeting at Doullens, adding that he had 'no opinion of Pétain's resolution and resource in an emergency'.

Bob's story was picked up widely by the British and transatlantic press.[30] At a time when France was being foul-mouthed everywhere, it was his first shot at telling the English-speaking world that the true spirit of France was not defeatist, that there were French men and women who believed in her republican ideals and were ready to fight to defend them. How many of the *ex post facto* historians of the war spotted his scoop is a different story.

Writing in Wartime

C. B. COCHRAN, the impresario, ran into Bob in the Savoy lobby and said he was planning to leave the hotel and move into a flat in a great cement and steel building, relatively bomb-proof, just off Piccadilly. He suggested Bob should go and see if he also could find accommodation there. West-End flats were then at a discount. People had not yet the faintest idea of what would happen when London was raided from the air, and most Londoners who had money thought the best thing was to go into the country for a few months. Those who could not spend all their time away at least made arrangements to sleep a few miles out. Consequently, Bob had no difficulty in finding a choice of empty flats in Cochran's large block known as Carrington House on the corner of Shepherd Street and Hertford Street.

The original Carrington House, where Kitty Fisher and Lord Nelson once lived, and where Anthony Powell found lodgings matching his post-Oxonian mood of 'seedy chic' in the 1920s, had been knocked down and replaced by the great new U-shaped seven-storey block, but the area known as Shepherd's Market (officially Shepherd Market) kept vestiges of a Powellian 'old-world stylishness'.[31]

Bob chose a ground-floor apartment—one room and a bedroom—with three windows overlooking the entrance court. He casually offered half the normal rental and refused to sign a lease that tied him down to more than three months at a time. His offer was accepted within a few hours, and they moved in the following weekend. The place was so small that little furniture was needed. Effie's bed was brought out of storage. The owning company passed on as bait some fine carpets distrained from the previous occupant who left with debts, and the rest came from Harrods.

Most of the other tenants owned estates in the country, and only came up to town for a few days when they had to. The porters were tall, handsome, and admirably trained, and it was some time before they began to disappear one by one for national service. The building was practically self-contained. The company had its own carpenters, glaziers, electricians and plumbers. There were valets and maids equipped with electric sweepers of the most modern kind. The two lifts, one on either side of the entrance hall, went up to a passage on the sixth floor built like the covered promenade deck of a liner, with glass partitions leading out on a wide roof garden, from which there was a magnificent sweep over the roofs and spires of London. From their rooftop they could look down on Shepherd Street, the market's main street, which ran into the marketplace proper with its butcher's shop, its fishmonger, its greengrocer, the oil and candle store, and two pubs.

One afternoon Mé saw a carriage and pair swing into the Carrington House courtyard. The sight of this shining carriage drawn by two splendid bays seemed almost unreal at the height of the Blitz. The hall porters had by then been issued with tin hats and hatchets, and three of them hurried forward in this accoutrement to meet the fine equipage. Lord and Lady Portsea had come to pay a leisurely call on the Henreys' upstairs neighbour, the elderly Mrs Elinor Glyn. Lord Portsea and the famous red-haired novelist had played together as children on the sandy beaches of the island of Jersey.

Flat 2 on the ground floor to the left of the entrance hall had mirror-faced built-in wardrobes, central heating, and a kitchen that was typical of the luxury of West-End flats built only a few years before the war. Mé loved it. By the back door into Shepherd Street and White Horse Street, she was barely a five minutes' walk from Piccadilly and the Green Park. She began taking Bobby there almost every day with his Pekingese puppy Pouffy riding on the coverlet of his pushchair. When she was busy, a Carrington House maid who lived in a room on the first floor, Margaret, ensured the young pair's daily airing and sometimes gave the boy his evening bath, rationing the water on account of the war.

Bobby was an easy child, content to play on his own or with Pouffy, and when put to bed slept soundly even when his parents went out in the evening to the theatre or for a stroll down Piccadilly to inspect the war damage. The air raids which intensified as the year wore on never troubled his sleep. They placed his cot in the windowless hall, where there was no danger of flying glass, and left their bedroom window open to reduce the blast in the event of a nearby bomb. When the hits came closer, they huddled by his cot and once or twice threw themselves over it to protect him, but he just slept on.

One day the child was taken to Godalming to meet his paternal grandparents. The visit wasn't a success. Mé stood facing Effie and Burr feeling she was being judged, which was probably the case. Her humiliating position proved that Burr's misgivings at the time of their marriage were justified. The Surrey air was heavy with irony. France had lost the war, her armies were in flight and her politicians were making a dishonourable peace with the enemy. Bob and Mé had been married for ten years, and had nothing to show for their labours, literally not a penny in the bank and their farm abandoned. If Bob lost his job, their position would be hopeless. No charity was being asked for, and none would have been given, but Mé felt her old pangs of jealousy rise in her throat again, seeing the garden full of roses, the gardener's cottage with its chintz curtains and lupines, smelling the peaceful country air, feeling the indignity of her situation. Tea was served in the icy-cold dining room. Bobby bored, deprived of his usual environment, flew into tantrums and Effie, who had always had maids and nurses to deal with her children, didn't for once know what to say or do.

* * *

MÉ'S QUICK PEN supplied Bob that summer of 1940 with copy from her diaries for a book he thought they should write about their Normandy farm, adapting the picturesque manner they had used for their London column in the *Evening News*. No manuscript has survived, but it's fairly easy to distinguish her contributions from his. She provides simple free-flowing gossip, clumsily translated from French all too often, that jumps from person to person and place to place by a series of associations of ideas, almost always describing people's misfortunes. A spark sets it off—a name, an event, a feeling—and on it rolls until the momentum is lost or interrupted. The framing narrative with longer sentences and rarer words, together with the overall book structure, is clearly Bob's. His crisp, happy style stands out from her dramatic vivacity. Their 'I' is synthetic, identifiable from extraneous facts: now him, now her, now both, now either, but mainly him to begin with. This fluidity of gender, augmented by the composite 'Madeleine' figure that appears here for the first time, would remain a hallmark of their production right up to 1982.[32]

A Farm in Normandy was ready by Christmas 1940. Four nights later the Luftwaffe launched a devastating attack on the City of London. Over a hundred enemy bombers showered incendiaries on the area between St Paul's Cathedral and the Guildhall. The flames went on burning until practically nothing was left. Bob saw it all from the roof of Carrington House, where he was on fire-watching duty. From time to time he came down in his tin hat to tell Mé what was happening. She felt proud to be in London that night. In the early hours, Bob walked down White Horse Street. When he came back he said the whole town smelt of damp plaster and burning wood.

It was about six A.M. and Mé was starting to make coffee. Though the City was burning furiously, the West End was peaceful after the racket of the night and everybody was exhausted. Only Bobby had slept soundly and was now jumping up and down in his cot, making a terrible din. The telephone rang. Mé told Bob he had better answer it while she tried to keep Bobby quiet. He picked up the receiver and began listening. She saw the blood drain from his cheeks and he sat down limply on the edge of the bed. He turned towards her and said: 'Effie says that her Burr died in the night. In the small hours, peacefully.' She heard him say into the phone: 'I'll come just as soon as I can.'[33]

He came back the same night but said very little. Burr who was terrified of thunder and lightning had died at the end of the greatest explosions his beloved City had ever known.

Early in the New Year they hired a car and drove to Godalming. Effie had aged, found it difficult to climb the stairs, and Westaway was too big for her. Though she had given the place to Burr, she had decided to sell it. There was no provision in Burr's will for Bob or Bobby, and naturally nothing for Mé. When his safe was opened, that big old safe he always made such a fuss about, making sure it was shut at bedtime, it was found to contain nothing but a very worn teddy bear that Bob had loved as a child.

* * *

VIA THE LITERARY AGENT A. D. Peters, Bob sold *A Farm in Normandy* under his sole name to Dent. Mé contributed copy, but preferred not to cosign the book. The contract dated 26 January 1941 provided for no advance on royalties and contained no future preference clause, a freelance principle to which Bob would stick all his life. This is convenient for dating the corpus, as the contract date always coincides with the formal date of acceptance by the publisher.[34]

The book came out in July 1941 at 12*s.* 6*d.* The dedication reads:

> FOR MADELEINE
> BECAUSE THIS BOOK IS
> ALL THAT IS LEFT OF THE FARM
> THAT I GAVE HER

This 'Madeleine' is the first appearance of the literary persona, while this 'I' is a Proustian compound devised to celebrate Robert Henrey's ideal figure of femininity.

The story is told in chronological sequence spanning the months between Christmas 1937 and June 1940. Although most of the characters are named with their real names, the village where the narrative takes place (Villers-sur-Mer) is left unnamed, as if that could somehow save Madeleine's shrine from destruction during the war.

The reviewers didn't quite know what to make of *A Farm in Normandy*, because it belonged to no genre they were used to. What point was there in a book about obscure people in an obscure part of a country which had never been reliable and had just collapsed? Several reviewers (and library cataloguers) took it to be about French farm life, which of course it both was and wasn't.

The *Birmingham Daily Post* praised the 'highly coloured detail' that the author brought to his story, while the *Scotsman* wrote: 'He adds to the more personal story of his own and his family's experiences a really admirable background of the life of the Norman farmers, craftsmen, and peasants.' A long *Times Literary Supplement* review was more perceptive: 'Every fact emerging from the narrative has its own deep significance. That the roots of men are in the daily round is Mr. Henrey's firm conviction.'

A Farm in Normandy was reprinted in its first year and twice subsequently in 1944 and 1946 until it was eventually recast by Mé alone with unfortunate results.

* * *

DURING THE BATTLE OF BRITAIN in the summer and autumn of 1940, Bob lunched once a week with Anthony de Rothschild at New Court, the Rothschild HQ in the City. Anthony's charming Bischoffsheim wife Yvonne Cahen d'Anvers invited Bob with Mé to Ascott House in Buckinghamshire, where the splendid new library converted from the old Billiards Room contained a great many manuscripts from Napoleonic times. Over claret Anthony declared there were sheaves of letters in there from a man signing 'C. de B.' to the London house of Rothschild during the siege of Paris in 1870. Would they like to read a hundred or so and see if they would make a book?

They did. Bob entitled it *Letters from Paris 1870–1875* and published it as part of his personal war effort. His aim was to show that Paris in those years resisted and fought back against Prussia despite the collapse of a feeble French government and its incompetent Vieille France military. In other words, his second Rothschild opus was a Free French pamphlet. Its message was that France, though defeated and occupied in 1940 owing to 'mistakes, muddling and despair', would remain true to herself and recover. He wrote: 'These letters show the strength and resilience of France, and how it will rise again to new heights in spite of the errors of political and military leaders.'[35] His dedicatory epigraph '1870–1941' reads: 'In March 1941 a group of patriots defied death to circulate a typewritten newspaper called *Valmy* in Nazi-occupied France.' A note explains that this title commemorated the thousands of Frenchmen who answered the call 'The Nation is in danger!' and defeated the Prussian invaders at Valmy in 1792. *Valmy*'s existence wasn't generally known until Paul Simon's book *Un seul ennemi, l'envahisseur* was published in London prefaced by General de Gaulle in 1943, two years after Bob's initial propaganda piece was written.

The 270-odd extracts he selected from the thousand or so letters placed in his hands by Anthony de Rothschild reported day-to-day facts, sayings and happenings in a style very like his own 'Talk of the Day' column in the *Evening News*. Indeed, were it not for their pedigree, one might be tempted to say that Bob forged the lot. His own voice—defined stylistically by the autobiographical section in *A Century Between*—comes through clearly in his translations of the original French newsletters. Like Bob, Baron Lionel de Rothschild's informant 'C. de B.', whose identity remains unknown, showed an unusually broad outlook and was well-connected. His capacity for seeing things from a detached point of view made his information particularly valuable. Bob wrote: 'He sums up a situation in a few lines and foretells the future with extraordinary accuracy.'[36]

Dent's contract for *Letters from Paris 1870–1875. Written by C. de B. A Political Informant to the Head of the London House of Rothschild. Translated and Edited by Robert Henrey* is dated 4 September 1941. The book came out in April 1942 priced 15*s*.[37]

Though the first impression of 1942 wasn't reprinted, quite a number of reviews appeared over the next couple of years. Most of them harked on history. An 'A. G. P. T.' who must be Taylor frowned on its inexactitudes in the *Observer*. Only one reviewer, an anonymous contributor to the *Birmingham Daily Post*, seems to have spotted the real purport of Bob's story: 'It is useful to be reminded by how little the French republic escaped being still-born, to watch the 1870 struggle between a surrender and a resist-ance policy, to note the class conflict that has been so disastrous in recent times. But one sees also—and here there is a message of hope—how resilient is France, how swift to recover from what looks like complete ruin.'

This was the exact message Bob took it upon himself to propagate in his reviews of books by René Balbaud, Louis Lévy, Thomas Kerman and others for the *Spectator* in 1941 and 1942. Headed 'Facts About France' or 'Vive la France!' or 'Report on France' they were intended primarily to redress the negative image left in Britain by the collapse of France. All of his reviews condemned the weakness of the Popular Front and the Reynaud government, magnifying De Gaulle and the Free French movement while explaining how and why the ordinary French soldier, under-equipped and ill-trained, had been powerless against the Wehrmacht and had no sympathy for the Nazis.

* * *

BEFORE THE ROTHSCHILD LETTERS CAME OUT, work had begun on the first of the Henrey books about London. It's hard to say exactly how many are *about* London, for there's not a single one in the entire corpus that isn't set there at least in part. But at least twelve are focused on areas of what Bob and Mé considered, despite their love of other great cities, the heart of the world. They worshipped its every stone. Both were great walkers and curious onlookers, like Léon-Paul Fargue in his recent *Le Piéton de Paris* (1939), in which 'a man with time on his hands' rambles around the city he loves. They adapted Fargue's vein of erudite gossip to a London reduced to the scale of Paris, specifically their own brand of West End (Mayfair, Soho, Covent Garden, Hyde Park, Knightsbridge, Bloomsbury) and the City.

At a time when the content of mass newspapers was restricted by censorship and the rationing of newsprint, books and libraries mattered more than ever. In common with the BBC, the statutory public library system played a major institutional role in maintaining national unity. On 20 June 1940, the President of the Board of Education was asked in the House of Commons whether the public library services in Great Britain were regarded by the Government as services of national importance. The answer was yes. Virtually every British household had at least one free public library book 'on the go' at that time. Though no precise figures appear to be available for this period, publishers' sales to public libraries must have financed an appreciable percentage of first impressions and of course had significant spin-offs in bookshop sales. Many commercial libraries existed, too. W. H. Smith & Son's branches ran a day-by-day service for non-subscribers at 3*d.* a week or part thereof. Boots the Chemist branches also loaned books. 'Buy or borrow' wrote the reviewers. 'Light reading' was a catchword throughout the horrors of the war and the first print runs of 'light' titles quite commonly amounted to four thousand copies or more.

While setting the 'light reading' tone for the rest of the Henreys' London books, *A Village in Piccadilly* extends the propaganda element present in the Rothschild letters. The aim of the Nazi Blitz was to divide the British population by undermining their morale. It was therefore important to convey to the people—and the enemy—that life went on despite the Blitz, that common human decency continued despite the horror, in short that Britain would never surrender.

The idea was to show how a couple with a baby living by choice in the heart of blitzed London contrived to cope day by day with the onslaught on the life of their 'village'. Shepherd Market with its cultural tissue of customs, shops, characters and memories became a microcosm of Great Britain resisting Nazi Germany. Bob chose his tone carefully, avoiding grandiloquence and posture—understatement and irony had been his strong points since his Eton days. Coloured by Mé's continental sense of drama, his narrative became an imaginative weapon of war.

The contract with Dent is dated 9 May 1942. Delayed perhaps by censorship issues, the book didn't come out until December of the same year priced 12*s.* 6*d.*[38]

Seven of the book's sixteen photographs were specially commissioned from Kendrick showing parts of Shepherd Market in 1942. Of these, one has Bobby at the window of the ground floor flat in Carrington House, another has a view of Shepherd Street from the rooftop, yet another has Bobby out in his pram with Pouffy being pushed by Margaret, and finally one captioned 'Village Vista' seems to have Mé to the right of the picture, hatless with medium-length dark hair. (Normally long and naturally honey-coloured, her hair had just been bobbed for wartime convenience and died to follow fashion. She had cut it twice before, once as a child while staying with Marie-Thérèse in Paris, and once as a teenager in Soho. She would not cut it again until 1957.)

The better reviewers realised that *A Village in Piccadilly*, with its portrayal of a small community going about its business despite the bombs, was aimed essentially against the enemy. For instance, the *Irish Independent*'s reviewer wrote in December 1942:

> A well-known columnist on the staff of a big London daily, Robert Henrey writes with cool and easy competence. Unlike most of the authors who have described the great raids on London, he glosses over the horrors of those grim days and concentrates instead on how the people rose above all the sufferings and inconveniences.

Elizabeth Bowen in the *Tatler* in January 1943 welcomed its 'keen feeling for local atmosphere' during 'those strange months of 1940 and '41', and dubbed it 'a delightful bouquet that high explosives have hardly singed at all'.

* * *

A DIRECT COMMISSION for a further morale-booster came through as Bob was completing the manuscript of *A Village in Piccadilly*. Its final pages tell how a buff card fell through the letter box at the flat announcing that he would be de-reserved within the next few days. He took it to the staff manager at the *Daily Sketch* who said he must lose no time in filling up a form for deferment that would be countersigned by the editor. The idea was to prove to the authorities that his presence at the office was a matter of national importance, and that by no manner of means could his services be replaced. This was patently untrue, but it was clear, from previous experience, that the best he could hope for was a deferment of three months. A lot of people talked about getting good jobs as press or liaison officers, but Bob loved the smell of printer's ink and had no use for dodgers. The best thing, he thought, was to go on pounding out his column on the typewriter until he was taken off to peel potatoes or polish buttons.

One afternoon as he was about to leave home for the office, he received a telephone call from a government official whose department was eager to send him somewhere abroad. He went to a block of offices near the Strand where a quiet unassuming fellow in the thirties who spoke several languages fluently told him the details of his mission. It all sounded terribly exciting. If he passed certain language tests he would then meet the more important figures moving stealthily in the background. He would have to leave London almost immediately. His passport would be brought up to date, and he would not be called up for the rest of the war.

He was both thrilled and broken-hearted. What newspaperman in search of adventure could resist such an offer? But he also realised that it meant the temporary breakup of his little family. He was assured that Mé and Bobby would be taken care of whatever happened. He told himself that it was inevitable that he would be parted from them sooner or later, and that would be wise to choose his own way of going rather than just getting posted somewhere. But at heart he knew, right from the start, that he would accept.

He returned the next afternoon for the most informal examination he had ever sat. He was vaguely expecting to be given a seat in a classroom under the eye of a master in cap and gown. A woman handed him a sheaf of papers, led him into an empty office, and said if he needed anything, he could always give her a call on the telephone. As soon as he set pen to paper he discovered, to his horror, that he was overwhelmed by examination nerves. His hand was shaking. Then the click of typewriter keys in an adjoining office sang in his ears. He picked up the telephone and asked whether anyone would object if he used a typewriter. Of course not, she would send him one right away. As soon as his fingers felt the keys he forgot that he had ever been frightened.

When he heard that he had been accepted and must be prepared to leave for Lisbon by air within a fortnight, he had a sudden bout of depression. London had never seemed a better place to live in. Bobby, who would be three in June, was beginning to babble in two languages. He led his father by the hand, and told him where to go and what to do. They went shopping together, and when he was tired he knew how to put up a hand and hail a taxi. Would Bobby have forgotten what his father looked like by the time he returned? The child's third birthday was less than six weeks ahead, and his daddy would not be there. Bobby would probably ask for him for a few days and then take his absence for granted.

Mé and Bob, with only a few days ahead of them, felt an urge to live intensely. They put the boy to bed and plunged into the West End crowd. Both were tired after two years without a break, and Bob knew that in leaving her he wasn't the one to be pitied. She was the partner who would be faced with greater responsibilities and harder work.

At the office his resignation was taken philosophically. It taught him once more how little anybody mattered. People were disappearing every day. Contributors who were any good, especially women, were being bought up first by one paper and then by another. The office was in turmoil, and tempers were short. On the anniversary of the raid that had destroyed the City and set fire to Shepherd Market the Prime Minister made his great 'chicken' speech, partly in French about France, which was broadcast from Ottawa. There was vigorous optimism in his voice, but Londoners had no illusions about the seriousness of the situation.

Bob chose a sunny morning a few days before his departure to bid farewell to his mother. She now lived in a small house with a lovely garden called Leusdon on the road from Godalming to Portsmouth. That week she was celebrating her seventy-sixth birthday (15 May. They sat for a long moment on a wooden bench beside a border of tulips while an aged gardener, in the distance, bent over his spade digging a potato patch. 'You are right to go,' she said simply.[39] This unemotional statement was in keeping with her sense of duty. Her strong will masked her sensitiveness. She wished him to leave with as few regrets as possible, and hoped he would not see through the mask. But after lunch, when the sounds of a prehistoric taxicab that was to take him to the station became audible in the drive, she stooped to pick for him from a flower bed beside the porch three forget-me-nots, which she pressed into his hand. Her eyes were dimmed by tears, and she could not speak.

A few days later he was in Lisbon, having flown rapidly past, or over, the forbidden land of France. His mission was to gather information for a book, ostensibly a travel book, documenting life in Southern Europe and North Africa in wartime. On the eve of hush-hush Allied military operations in the region, his keen eye and ear would be valuable. His orders came presumably from the Ministry of Information in Senate House, but the operation was disguised as a business trip to neutral territory. His job was to report on prices, shortages, the German presence in Portugal, Spain and Morocco, the morale of the local population, and above all to pass on information gleaned here and there about occupied France.

He left in mid-May and returned 'at the end of a long hot summer'.[40] How he got back to London isn't told at this stage, as his story just peters out after a donkey ride at Tangier. He liked throwaway endings, but this one, unless the censor cropped it, is one of his most diffident. He was presumably debriefed at Senate House, though there's nothing to show that he was. His book was written fast from notes taken on tour. The contract with Dent is dated 3 October 1942, but the dedication bears the date December 1942, and the first reviews didn't appear until April 1943, suggesting there were production difficulties of one kind or another.

A Journey to Gibraltar is the first book in the Henrey canon to use an overtly mixed-gender 'I'. In the realm of real-life experiences, the narrator simply cannot be Mé when he writes: 'I had not seen anything quite like this since Victoria station during the Great War'.[41] Nor could Bob in real life enthuse about dresses in shop windows, inspect lace mantillas for two hours, or fix a tiny crucifix to a bracelet he was wearing. Here, 'I' is consciously impersonating Mé, who most definitely didn't go to Gibraltar in 1942.

This personality mix went back to their gossip column days. In short, a feminine viewpoint is mixed in the same narrative with a masculine viewpoint expressed by the same narrator. This peculiar device goes further than dual authorship. Its deliberate androgyny sets it quite apart from other male-female literary partnerships. Several passages, some with reconstructed dialogues, were recognizably penned by Mé from Bob's notes or her own recollections of cruise trips in the thirties.

The dedication must be read between the lines. Here it is in full:

My dear Captain Woodford,

There is no pleasanter place to take tea on a hot afternoon than the Garrison Library in Gibraltar, where well-filled bookshelves slumber in the shade of exotic foliage.

Will you, my dear Woodford, do me a favour? Will you take this book, which I dedicate to the officers and men of the Fortress, and place it in the hands of the Secretary of the Gibraltar Library? It will have to be classified as light reading. That which is noble, alas, and much that is grim has, by necessity, been omitted in deference to that unseen but all-powerful creature, the censor.

R. H.
December 1942
2 Carrington House,
Hertford Street,
W.1.

This manly epistle serves two purposes. Firstly, it certifies, complete with name and address, that the story relates (or relates to) the author's real-life experiences. Secondly, it indicates that the book's 'light reading' appearance cloaks a serious story with deep implications.

Bob would no doubt have laughed had someone suggested that this dedication in 1942 was tantamount to a literary manifesto. Yet no less a critic than W. J. Turner in the *Spectator* virtually said as much when reviewing *A Journey to Gibraltar*: 'Everywhere Mr. Henrey notes significant detail. He is interested in what I, for one, call the real things of the world—men and women, children, clothes, foods, shops, drinks, books, houses, fruits, and especially flowers.' Flowers in literature are, of course, poetry. Serious stuff.

The book came out in May 1943 priced 12*s*. 6*d*. and was reprinted the same year.[42] Most reviewers stressed its travelogue aspects. The *Manchester Evening News* wrote: 'The journey follows a course that has rather to do with people than opposing armies and navies. A brilliant observer to the minutest detail, Mr. Henrey gives an intimate picture of those among whom he mixes on his wartime journey to the Rock—their characteristics, the daily life led by neutrals who live on the border of this seething corner of Europe.' However, the *Birmingham Daily Post* picked up soberly that the trip was made 'primarily to discover something of conditions in France after two years of German occupation'.

* * *

THE SHIP BACK FROM GIBRALTAR that Bob boarded at the last moment in mid-September was officially nameless. Built for carrying passengers no farther than across the Irish Channel between Liverpool and Dublin, she had been three times to Dunkirk, had evacuated British nationals from Bordeaux, and had made innumerable trips across the Atlantic and to Iceland. She was sufficiently modern to be a liner in miniature. The cabins were clean but small, with four bunks in each and life belts laid out on the pillows bearing the names and home towns of hundreds of former passengers. Her skipper was from Dublin, her chief engineer from Glasgow. Anti-aircraft guns were mounted on the promenade deck. A Royal Navy destroyer zigzagged in front of her 'like a hound on a lost scent'.

She carried a unit of a famous British regiment returning to England, some Allied officers, some foreign civilians and a few women and children. Bob saw in her voyage a symbol of Britain at war. Her passengers and crew, unknown to one another when she weighed anchor, grew closer as the days went by, drawn together under one flag by the daily round of drills and social activities, sharing experiences and helping others in the face of danger. With no newspaper job to go back to, Bob realised that the story of this togetherness could provide a happy sequel to *A Village in Piccadilly*. His beloved London was like this ship after all, a haven for many nationalities and social classes, an icon of good defying evil, a place beyond belief.

He would call his new book *The Incredible City*. Rather than sketch a sequence of mainly isolated London characters observed haphazardly as before, he decided this time to follow a group of foreigners recurrently as they adapted to London. The voyage from Gibraltar gave him all he needed in this respect. As was usual on shipboard, the normal social requirement of being introduced was relaxed and all those hailing from Europe were known by pseudonyms. He was particularly attracted to a small group of French-speaking refugees among the passengers. He saw at once that the story of their bravery against the Nazis and Vichy could help to redress the shameful image left in wartime Britain by the collapse of their countries. No questions were ever asked. When they spoke of their own experiences in order to sort things out in their minds, never mentioning any friends or family, he took notes soon afterwards, trying to reproduce their words as he heard them.

'Charles' was a genial Belgian giant who had spent several months in a Spanish concentration camp at Miranda, near Madrid. He was writing a book about the place.[43] 'The Millionaire' was a quiet young officer who had escaped from a prisoner of war camp in Prussia. 'Scissors' the surgeon had studied under Thierry de Martel, a renowned professor who committed suicide when he saw the Nazis marching up the Champs Elysées. 'The Lady from Paris', alias 'The Lady of the Red Hair', whose real name wasn't known to anyone on board, held salon in the lounge every evening. Her daughter 'Marie' and son 'Arthur' were travelling with her. It was understood that her husband had left occupied France by a different route. 'The Breton girl', also known as 'Anne', was often at her side. Scarcely over twenty, Anne rarely spoke. She had come all the way from Brittany in a cotton dress after a boy under torture had given her name. All were heading for London to join the fight against Germany in whatever capacity they could.

He saw most of them fairly regularly during the months after their arrival. He and Mé helped them with their English, showed them the town, took 'Anne' to Eton for the Fourth of June, a group of them to Kew opposite Bob's childhood paradise at Brentford, now demolished. They met the mysterious husband of 'The Lady from Paris' known as 'Lavoisier', a Scarlet Pimpernel figure in the Free French movement, a socialist with whom Bob, a born conservative, discovered more political affinities than he expected. His true identity wasn't revealed until his death in France was confirmed. He was Pierre Brossolette.

As the refugees drop in at the Carrington House flat or pop up in various parts of London, the reader of *The Incredible City* gradually pieces together the puzzle of their exile. In between come picturesque scenes of London life, visits, conversations, gossip sessions in the Green Park among women neighbours told month by month. Bob generally wrote the more thoughtful passages, while Mé penned the more picturesque. But their roles were interchangeable, especially as Mé's contributions were generally jotted down in French in the first instance and subsequently translated, either by herself or more frequently by Bob.

It's perhaps time to give examples of their writing to allow comparisons to be made.

This is by Bob in St James's Park on 3 September 1943:

I had just reached the suspension bridge over the lake when an Admiral of the Fleet whose sleeves were richly caparisoned with gold—a little man with a wind-buffeted skin and heavy eyebrows—surveyed the water to larboard, where a great number of ducks were riding to anchor. The Admiral leaned over the parapet at the very centre of the bridge, and taking a piece of bread from his pocket, started to distribute this largesse with rapid thrusts of the hand. Pursuing my way, I turned left by the fig tree and looked back at the Admiral from the southern bank. He stood there, as on the bridge of his flagship, oblivious to the passing crowds. The feathered community of the lake, warned by the excited cries of their fellows, was sailing down upon the Admiral from every direction. Soon he had a full regatta, while above him the sky was darkened by an air cover of seagulls. In the distance Buckingham Palace, framed by the weeping willows of the lake, stood in all the glory of its dazzling whiteness. The Royal Standard floated gently in the wind. A moment later the Park was filled with the music of the Guards as they marched down the Mall behind a policeman riding a white horse. This was the London that men dream of all over the world. When I looked back at the bridge the Admiral had gone.[44]

And this is by Mé:

The wave of influenza which swept the country over the holidays was not particularly malignant, but it left tiresome ailments in its wake which were the more difficult to cure because of the shortage of doctors and the fact that many people were unable to get away for a change of air during the summer. Yet Londoners remained extraordinarily good-tempered. Their politeness was what struck foreigners most forcibly. 'When one is jostled in an omnibus it is hardly ever by a Londoner,' Mme Lavoisier remarked to me at lunch one day. The London bus often put into relief the Cockney philosophy. The best example was in a No. 19 bus in which I was travelling early in the year. An old lady had joined us at Piccadilly Circus and, after being escorted to her seat by the conductress, discovered that she ought really to have mounted a No. 14. 'How very tiresome!' she exclaimed. 'My daughter *did* say I should get into a number fourteen. A moment ago all I could remember was that there was a 'teen in it.' The conductress told her that she could change at the next stop, and when the time came to get off, the old lady said to the conductress, 'I'm afraid I've been wasting a lot of your time. Still, I have had the pleasure of meeting you!' 'Oh, it's a pleasure for me, madam,' answered the conductress.[45]

Computer analysis helps to identify the two styles. It must be said, however, that only a reasonable degree of probability can be established in this respect, as on a number of tested occasions not connected with translation issues, Bob can be observed writing like Mé and vice versa. A good example of their stylistic cohabitation is found in chapter 8 of *The Incredible City*. The first three pages written by Bob describe a lunch with 'Charles' at which Mé wasn't present. After a scene break, an editorial transition reads: 'We had lunched in Soho, and, having said farewell to our friends, we decided to walk home through Berwick Market.'[46] The rest of the chapter describing the walk, fictionalised from facts, was penned by Mé.

The contract for *The Incredible City* is dated 8 October 1943, six months after the publication of *A Journey to Gibraltar*. The book came out from Dent in June 1944 at 12*s.* 6*d*.[47] Thirteen of the eighteen photographs (one representing Bobby with Mé in the Green Park) are credited to Kendrick, who took most of the pictures included in *A Village in Piccadilly*. The epistolary dedication similar to the one in *A Village in Piccadilly* reads as follows:

My dear Richmond,

If I may lay any claim to your friendship, it is not only because of the many proofs you have given me of it, but also because of our mutual attachment to the city of our birth. We who loved London in the easy pre-war days loved her better still during the days and nights of her suffering; and now we see her as the magic city which shines over Europe in bondage. I ask you, therefore, to accept this book, knowing that you will appreciate its meaning and forgive its shortcomings.

There is, perhaps, another reason. Like myself, you were born along that lovely stretch of the Thames (as Mary Russell Mitford put it, the pleasantest highway in his Majesty's dominions), near Pope's grotto and Strawberry Hill. The few lines about my youth you will find in this volume may possibly recall memories of yours—the lime trees, fragrant with blossom and musical with bees, that screen Kew Palace from the river.

R. H.

2, CARRINGTON HOUSE,
HERTFORD STREET, W.1.

April, 1944

Who this 'Richmond' was is anybody's guess. Freddie, the ninth duke, was at Eton with Bob, but nothing else would appear to connect them, not even Twickenham.

The *Birmingham Daily Post* reviewer (June 13 1944) resented the persistent portrayal of French people in a book purportedly about London: 'It is not these people whose adventures read like fiction that make the incredible city; rather it is because London is incredible that they are there.' But Elizabeth Bowen in the *Tatler* wrote (July 5 1944):

> At intervals throughout *The Incredible City*, Anne, Charles and Mme Lavoisier reappear, and we watch them adjust, by degrees, to their life with us. I think this part of the book needs especial study—it may be a key, for many of us, to problems and conflicts faced by our ally-guests, by friends we should like to help without always knowing how.

* * *

INSOFAR AS IT WAS MEANT to help the Free French in London, *The Incredible City* was overtaken by events, as De Gaulle was in Algiers by the end of May 1943 and Paris was liberated by the Division Leclerc barely six weeks after the book came out in 1944. Notwithstanding this time gap, Bob signed a contract with Dent on 25 May 1945, a fortnight after VE Day, for a sequel entit*led The Siege of London.*

It was published in February 1946 priced 12*s.* 6*d.* as the final volume of 'a trilogy' presenting 'an eyewitness account of London during the war'. A fourth impression of *A Village in Piccadilly* and an unchanged reissue of *The Incredible City* (already reprinted in 1945) came out simultaneously at the same price in the same format with similar jackets. Dent's *Siege* blurb vaunted the trilogy in these terms: 'The great value of Robert Henrey's writing is that it

88

describes how life went on in detail, leaving the political and military movements behind the scenes. From these vivid pages we are reminded, and future historians will learn, how ordinary people behaved and felt during these extraordinary years.'

An undated dedication in *The Siege of London* to the memory of Pierre Brossolette signed 'R. H.' explains that the pseudonym of 'Lavoisier', whose identity could not be revealed in *The Incredible City*, has been retained in the text of *The Siege of London* for the sake of continuity.[48] Starting with a flashback to Gibraltar, the Lavoisier-Charles-Anne saga is told intermingled month by month with other people's stories and picturesque portrayals of London life spanning the period from the February–March raids of 1944 to the end of the war with Germany.

Mé contributed quite a lot of copy to this title, notably about an American called Dorothy Berker and other Americans in town, while Bob wrote the Free French material and a few visits to parts of London.

The reviewers were kind about *The Siege of London* although it covered much the same ground in much the same style as its two predecessors. It's a token of Bob's skill as an editor that there's no apparent flagging of interest or repetition of material. He takes the reader quickly from one topic to the next using time tricks such as 'A few days later I took a bus down Baker Street', or 'We were in Soho and it was the eleventh of November', or 'In the afternoon (it was Saturday)', or conniving nudges such as 'You will remember', or 'As you know'. The *Times Literary Supplement* noted 'the same quick eye' and 'the same lively glimpses of the insides of other people's houses and other people's lives' as in *The Incredible City*, adding: 'Not that he needs the contrasts and tragedies of war to stir him to write. Put him in the most somnolent of little towns, sunk in perpetual peace, and he would find it exciting.'

* * *

SHORTLY AFTER HIS RETURN from Gibraltar, Bob was given a writer's job at the Ministry of Production near Storey Gate in Whitehall. His functions there have left next to no trace. There's just one mention in *The Incredible City* of an official visit to a Clydebank shipyard and another mention *in The Siege of London* of Sunday morning walks to his office with Bobby. When his son asked him later on what Daddy did during the war, he answered flatly: 'Propaganda.[49] The job definitely left him with time to spare. Between his return to town in 1942 and his departure from the MoP in 1946, he published no fewer than seven books adding up to something like half a million words. Mé certainly did her stint, but a great deal of the writing and all of the editing were done by Bob. He also handled the business correspondence and the accounts. Considering the labour involved, the fact that the reviewers continued to praise the quality of the output is remarkable.

* * *

ONE OF THE BEST of the Henreys' seven wartime books isn't about the war but about the years that led up to it. The contract for *The Foolish Decade* was signed with Dent on 17 August 1944 and the book came out priced 12*s.* 6*d.* in July the following year between *The Incredible City* and *The Siege of London*.[50] Covering from 1922 to the end of the war, it's the first of three novelised third-person narratives that tell the story of 'Philip' and 'Madeleine' before the official autobiographical sequence began publication in 1951. Like all the Madeleine books, it's an honest story told from selected facts in order to gain public recognition and earn a decent living. It isn't history, though Mé sometimes liked to think it was. Neither is it fiction. There can be little doubt that in Bob's mind it was poetry, an extended metaphor for what he believed in devoutly: continuance, survival.

The title translated from the French cliché '*les années folles*' is a misnomer. It suggests a critique, or at least an account, of an epoch. This isn't what the book does. Most of the narrative concerns Madeleine's life with 'Mrs Bernard' and her romance with 'Philip', a young man from a vicarage overlooking the Thames with parents called 'Reyhen' and no known skill apart from spending money. Nothing is said about the newspaper world, quite a lot about Soho and Mayfair. Normandy is barely sketched in. The act of writing here is selective. Its aim is to involve the reader in a story of human survival in an indecisive world.

In hindsight *The Foolish Decade* looks like a blueprint for the books to come. We first get Madeleine's life with her moth-

90

er in Soho till 'Philip came into her life like a whirlwind, and everything changed from the moment she saw him.' Then we read of the couple's married life in the thirties up to the departure for Normandy. At this point 'she was clearly starting a new and very different phase in her life.' The remaining chapters bring the story up to the end of the war, when 'in many ways it appeared to Madeleine that her life had completed a cycle'.

In truth *The Foolish Decade* sketches the saga of a woman on her way through life. Its telling of mundane facts from a feminine viewpoint was a new departure, particularly as its Madeleine, described as 'furiously ambitious, anxious to expand in every way—to think clearly, to read well and usefully', is no English lily. Yet few reviews appeared and the book does not appear to have been reprinted. The *Times Literary Supplement* dismissed it in a few lines while praising its pages on Soho. Herself a novelist writing on London, Elizabeth Bowen in the *Tatler* read it as a novel about London: 'Mr. Henrey can paint with his pen.'

It took a poet no doubt to perceive its true worth, as in John Betjeman's review in the left-wing *Daily Herald* of 25 July 1945. The future Poet Laureate confesses that for him 'the trivial has always had a fatal fascination', because its 'accumulated evidence' can bring understanding about 'how people lived rather than what sort of treaties their leaders signed'. Betjeman continues: '*The Foolish Decade* is a significant record of the trivial. It is a biography of London in the nineteen-twenties and thirties, symbolised in an attractive girl called Madeleine.' And he concludes: 'Forgive my pomposity in saying this is not only a good book, but a good *social document*.'

* * *

ONLY A YEAR OLDER THAN THE WAR, Bobby grew up with it. He gurgled with pleasure to see a building on fire, was wheeled down Bond Street when pavement and road were strewn with broken glass. It seemed normal for people to place their furniture in rooms without walls, light bonfires for public amusement, and let off sirens at bedtime. The flying bomb was a reality, and he knew from experience that when the engine cut out, it would glide down and explode, after which a pillar of black smoke would gush into the sky. But this phenomenon was as natural to him as the sight of a bus or the roar of the Tube. When a flying bomb buzzed overhead he plotted its direction and reassured his mother.

The child of the new generation lived soberly, and contented himself with little. When his cot became too short, the end was sawn off, because not even Harrods had children's beds for sale during the Blitz. Lacking companions to play with (so many children were evacuated) he had become, at the age of six, a sophisticated but romantic little Londoner, who knew Piccadilly from end to end and went on occasion to films and plays. His lessons were taken from real life and by necessity were taught at home. In any case Bob remembering his own childhood didn't believe in schools for little children.

It was perhaps easier for him, who went off most days to fish stories for his column, than for Mé. Carrington House had no governess, no nurse, no parlour maid, no cook, no scullery maid. She woke Bobby in the morning, cooked his breakfast, left his pram on the kerb when she did her shopping, made the lunch, did the washing-up and put him to bed at night. She did alone the work that five people were paid to do in the gracious past. At times she felt envious of Effie, whose life had always been so leisurely, so sensitive.

Bob went to see his mother regularly, but for Mé it was more difficult. They had so little in common and travelling was complicated. After Burr's death they kept in touch mainly by letter. True affection grew on both sides, however. While Bob was away in the Mediterranean, Mé and Bobby spent a week at a hotel in Godalming and went to see Effie every day. Mé remembered in *The Foolish Decade* that they picked lavender from the long hedges in front of the sitting room, then sat down at a little square table to make muslin sachets for the dried flowers. Having run about the garden all morning, Bobby was tired. His grandmother put him in a green velvet chair and ordered: 'Now, young man, you must sleep.' And he slept.

The next day was Mé's birthday. When she arrived at Leusdon from the hotel, Effie gave her a letter that had just been forwarded from her former home Westaway on the opposite hill. It was a regulation Red Cross letter from Mathilde saying that she was safe in German-occupied Versailles. Both women wept.

In the final stages of the war, Effie wrote a long letter to 'her dearest Madeleine' signed 'Mother.' Among other things it said:

There is so much I would like to say to you, but it is difficult to know how to say it. I think you may be quite sure of one thing, and that is that Bob really loves you very dearly; he is like his father in many ways, and Dad was a very faithful friend—if he once loved, he never altered. [...]

Bob talks a great deal more than Dad ever did, but I don't think he talks much about himself, does he? And you probably have to take a good deal for granted, as I had to do. Then you have an added difficulty to deal with, and that is that Bob has an uncertain temper, and is often very irritable. [...]

One small bit of comfort I can offer you, and that is that Bob certainly is more even tempered and happier since you and he married. Also I am sure that the child gives him a sense of responsibility that is good for him; and he is so fond and proud of the youngster.

Mé cherished this letter, and it was published in full in 1976 at the end of her autobiographical memoir *Green Leaves*.[51]

* * *

THE KING OF BRENTFORD, the second of the three 'Philip' and 'Madeleine' narratives, was published in October 1946, not by Dent, but by an imprint set up in 1926 by J. M. Barrie for his ward Peter Davies, the original Peter Pan. Peter's youngest brother Nico, who worked for the firm as an editor, was a contemporary of Bob's at Eton, and Peter too was an Old Etonian, so the old school tie may have had something to do with the deal.

Why Bob dropped Dent for this book and three that followed, also published by Peter Davies, may well be related to the disappointing performance of *The Foolish Decade*. No advertisements for this title have been traced in Dent's usual publicity channels, and most of the reviews obtained were concomitantly lukewarm as has just been seen. Another explanation may be an incipient disagreement between Dent, Bob and Mé concerning the attribution of authorship or the payment of royalties or both. This disagreement reached its first crux in 1949 and underwent a great upheaval in 1952 as we shall see. The move from Dent to Davies also

93

eliminated the A. D. Peters literary agency, who handled the titles from *A Farm in Normandy* to *The Siege of London*. For the next thirty-six years all the paperwork would land on Bob's desk. This didn't make his life with Mé any easier as will become apparent.

For the moment, 'Philip' and 'Madeleine' went to Brentford to meet the vicar and his wife. *The King of Brentford* has one foot in Georgian England, the other in wartime Europe. It illustrates Philip's remark to Madeleine: 'You were brought up in the present. I was brought up in the past. With a little care the two may be persuaded to meet.'[52] Told in the third person in 1943, fifteen years after Madeleine's marriage to Philip, the story is a blend of memoir (Bob's upper-class childhood as Philip) and chronicle (Mé's wartime motherhood as Madeleine). In between stands a portrait of Mr and Mrs Reyhen, Philip's parents (Burr and Effie), poised on the brink of extinction like their vicarage, soon to become a coke tip.

The publishing agreement was signed on 1 November 1945 and the book came out in October 1946 priced 12*s*. 6*d*.[53] The dedicatee was the novelist Elizabeth Bowen, whose name occurs four times in admiring terms elsewhere in the corpus. Her books pages in the *Tatler* were invariably kind to the Henreys.

The King of Brentford presents itself as an unassuming entertainment like the rest of the Madeleine canon. To an attentive reader, however, these stories for everyone often suggest more than what they say. This one in particular shows genius in its structure and writing, combining the old-fashioned and the modern in accordance with the book's theme, joining present and past with poetic panache. In literary terms, this urban comedy marries the sentimental satire of Goldsmith's day to the modernist prose poem, reproducing the grammar of each. This feat is summed up in just three consecutive lines while Philip and his child are shown walking to Eel Pie Island: 'But what was this strange growth with the mauvish tint of Scotch heather on yonder arbour jutting out from the wall? "That's no arbour," said the child. "It's a blockhouse."'[54]

The parodic combinations are effortless and effective. Chapter 10, for instance, is a memoir of Bob's father in Goldsmithian style (down to the initial capitals on Vicar of Brentford), while the Great Ormond Street episode of chapter 17 with its gossipy stuff from everyday life is successful as a piece of modernist writing. Regarding the rather odd title, though the jacket blurb pointed to Matthew Prior's *Alma* and its kings of Brentford 'discreet and wise', the allusion to Thackeray's absurd Gorgius IV from *Punch* and *The Book of Snobs* cannot have been lost on the better-versed class of reader.

Imagination is always needed to translate recollected events and speech into readable narrative and dialogue, and the facts of a story may remain true or become deformed depending on its telling. Mé, being French, liked facts. Bob, being English, liked stories. Her memory was phenomenal in every respect, her pen raced on the pad from left to right with no margins and no corrections. His typewriter and blue pencil curbed and shaped this brilliant impetuosity. In their best books from now on they would write truly with one voice (in spite of angry quarrels that their son remembers), and the impulsion resulting from her dash and his restraint would make many of their texts worthy of high praise, which they sometimes obtained.

Elizabeth Bowen gave the book two columns in the *Tatler* of 30 October 1946. She must have seen a proof copy before the dedication to her was added (unusually on an even page), as her sense of professional propriety would not have allowed her to review it otherwise. Her treatment of *The King of Brentford* was generous, referring as it did to 'Robert Henrey by now, I think, acceptedly placed in the small first rank of our contemporary writers about London'. Coming from a distinguished writer who was herself writing about life in wartime London (*The Demon Lover* collection in 1945, *The Heat of the Day* in 1948), that was praise indeed. Her view of the book was characteristically perceptive: 'Mr. Henrey's gift for construction, his power of interleaving past and present, is here put to brilliant, effective use.' The *Times Literary Supplement* reviewer on 12 October found it 'a better and fuller book than either *The Foolish Decade* or *The Siege of London*', adding 'the best of it is Mr Henrey's own memories of Brentford more than thirty years ago'.

Further Farm Stories

MATHILDE, LEFT ALONE on the quay at St Malo during the German invasion in 1940, envisaged jumping off the cliffs to end it all. Instead, she contrived to find a means of survival as she always did. This time he was called Louis Soilly, widower of her sister Marie-Thérèse. Somehow Mathilde dug him out in Versailles and found a cramped roof under his, where she eventually received a Red Cross message informing her that her grandson and his parents were safe in London. When Louis started talking about marriage, she moved out and worked as a seamstress at a Vichy government patchwork factory in Viroflay, living in hostels.

After VE Day, she made her way back to the farm. Bob had given her a key but she didn't really need it, because the house had been broken into. Its books, pictures, family heirlooms, manuscripts, papers, furs, dresses, furniture had been looted, smashed or defiled. The New Testament that Effie had given Mé lay in the lavatory used as toilet paper. Even the Aga had gone. Mathilde discovered Bobby's little white chair in the Goguets' house next door, but she didn't dare to object because Mme Goguet was aggressive, visibly resenting her return. From other neighbours she borrowed a mattress, cutlery, utensils, and set to cleaning the place up.

As soon as Bob and Mé heard that she was back at the old house and that it was still standing, they began planning a sequel to *A Farm in Normandy*, which was selling well in its third impression with a fourth on the way. There was a flurry of correspondence on this subject between Peter Davies and Bob as early as October 1945. Mé of course wanted to join her mother immediately, but it seems women civilians were barred from travel to France for some time after VE Day. Bob obtained with great difficulty a travel permit for himself. He got leave from the MoP, where his job was drying up anyway, and boarded a crowded boat train at Victoria in mid-June 1945.

After a difficult journey via Paris and Lisieux, he spent a night at the farm on a wicker chair in an empty room, until a friendly couple living nearby took him in for the rest of his stay. He met Mlle Lefranc, the Villers midwife, who told him she had suggested removing the more valuable contents from the house for safekeeping just after their departure, but Mme Goguet had refused saying she had no key. Some time later, the midwife had found Bobby's cot and a drawer full of English nappies, linen and ointments at the Goguets' house when their twins were born. Nobody seemed to know where Goguet himself was, though there were sombre hints that a Judas had betrayed him.

It soon turned out that Mme Goguet had been arrested at the farm that April and had not returned. A friendly gendarme told Bob that her son Roger, who was in semi hiding after doing business with the German occupants, had also been arrested, while her father Eugène Hommet, Bob's water diviner, had slit his own throat when they came to arrest him at his house in Annebault. Deeply upset about all this, Bob went to see the examining magistrate in Pont L'Évêque and learned that Roger and Hommet had denounced Goguet for hiding a shotgun and that Goguet had been arrested by the Gestapo in November 1943. He had died of dysentery at the Austrian camp of Ebensee on 29 December 1944 after dictating a letter to a fellow prisoner asking for justice to be done. This letter had just come to light. There would be a trial in September.

Young Mathieu, who had driven the Henreys part of the way to St Malo in 1940, tipped Bob off that Mé's Aga and refrigerator had been requisitioned by the local *Kommandantur* in Blonville and were still in the villa where the Germans had left them. Bob arranged for them to be brought back by Mathieu with a crew of six humpers. Other objects came back mysteriously. Renée Goguet returned the grandfather clock without its winder, which was later replaced by the local locksmith. Friends in the village told sad stories of the occupation years and the liberation. Towards the end of the conflict, two British planes had hit the railway station bang on with a single bomb, when twenty-five Allied planes had missed it previously with two bombs apiece, destroying the cemetery, a number of cows and several orchards. No damage had been done to the village itself, as Canadian and Belgian troops had taken it on 9 July 1944 with little or no fighting.

Bob dined with the Duprez in their new house. Since his father's retirement, Victor had been buying up as much property as he could get his hands on. Maître Vincent, the sarcastic notary, was inconsolably depressed: he had sent his wife and two youngest children to Caen for their safety and they had been killed in the Allied bombing that destroyed the town. Dr Lehérissey was still around, getting old but holding on.

Two months after Bob's return, Mé finally got her travel permit and went to join Mathilde in Normandy, leaving six-year-old Bobby delighted in the care of his father. She herself was torn between the anguish of leaving her child for the first time and the joy of seeing her mother again. She filled a linen bag with all the small things she had forgotten at the last moment, and then realised that it was the one she had brought away with her when leaving the farm in 1940. It had contained the baby's feeding bottle and some tins of Nestlé's milk. Now it was scorched on one side where she had laid it over the lamp on her writing table during one of the worst raids in the war, wondering whether they would live to see morning.

At the trial in Caen on 4 September 1945, Roger was sentenced to hard labour for life but Mme Goguet and her mother were acquitted. Arriving three days later, Mé learned from Mathilde that the two women were back at the farm, where young Renée had been in charge while they were awaiting trial in prison. The farming lease was due for renewal at Christmas, but Mme Goguet had already decided to sell up and leave. She told Mé she never wanted to see a cow again as long as she lived. She emptied the cottage barrow load by barrow load to a small house she had taken in the village, where Maître Vincent would hold an auction. The day she handed in the keys at the farm, she brought Mé a bowl of cream so thick that the spoon stood upright in it. 'It's the last one,' she said without showing the slightest emotion. It was Mé who felt like crying.

The apple crop that year was the worst in living memory. Having taken away more than her share of the cider casks stored in the press, Mme Goguet didn't concern herself with the pear crop, which Mé had to dispose of as best she could. A replacement farmer for the grass, which was among the richest in the neighbourhood, had to be chosen too. The decision to exclude the cottage from the lease had already been taken. A non-resident farmer willing to pay a good price for the hay and grazing rights, the fruit crops, use of the cider press, felling rights on dead fruit trees and so on, and not be a pain in the backside into the bargain wasn't all that easy to find. The matter was put into abeyance.

The following spring, when the apple trees were in bloom, Mé came over to reunite her son with his grandmother and open a new chapter in the farm's four centuries of existence. Bobby took to the place where he was born as if he had never left it. What he called 'the funny old house half way down a field full of milking cows and bent-over apple trees' was heaven compared to living in a two-roomed flat in Mayfair. His Grand'mère (pronounced the French way) was just over sixty, still alert and active though beginning to suffer from rheumatic pain in her hands. She intimidated him to begin with, and instead of using the familiar '*tu*', he addressed her with the formal '*vous*', which left her crestfallen. But it didn't last. She soon became his confidant, always taking his side as he always took hers. They were natural allies against all that was unfair in the world.

Bob left the MoP on 1 June and came over to fix things on the farm, do some writing and play his part in Bobby's education. All he asked of the boy was a daily essay in English on what he had done the day before. Mé was more demanding. She required multiplication tables, dictations in French with the correct agreements and concordances and all that, and she easily lost her temper. Bobby remembers: 'There were fireworks aplenty. Tempers often flared between my mother and my grandmother, and my parents were among themselves practiced quarrellers. I had become used to these grand shows and assumed that this was how all families operated. I was hardly in a position to make comparisons.'[55] After a while, Mé went back to London to get some peace and quiet and enjoy a little freedom. There was also some writing to do for the two books on the stocks at Peter Davies.

* * *

Two unhappy things happened that hot summer. Firstly, Effie died peacefully on a couch in her sitting room at Leusdon on 9 August 1946. Bob had seen his mother for the last time just before setting out for Normandy. In ill health, she told him that, at eighty, she was looking forward to joining her Burr and their Pekingese in the better world. Secondly, Mé was frightened by a burglar who got into their ground-floor flat at Carrington House through an open window while she was sleeping. She was woken up by the creak of her bedroom door, which she always kept shut, and saw the burglar, a good-looking dark-haired young man she felt sure she had seen somewhere before. She screamed, the man leapt out of the window and the old night porter didn't dare to intervene. The thief got away with a bracelet and some gold coins from Spink in King Street. She was still shaken when Bob got back to London.

On 1 September, he joined *Radio Times* as a features editor. In the thirties, this big BBC weekly had used leading writers and illustrators in the same vein as the *New Yorker*. It had slumped during the war, but a revamp was under way. It failed to come up to Bob's expectations, but what matter: his consuming interest at present was his books with Mé.

* * *

The Return to the Farm by Robert Henrey came out from Peter Davies in January 1947 at 12*s*. 6*d*. It bore the following dedication dated October 1946 at Villers-sur-Mer, Calvados: 'This sequel to *A Farm in Normandy* is dedicated to our notary Me Vincent, who was called upon to suffer more than his share during the great invasion. His lovely wife and two of his children having left Villers to spend the summer at Caen were never heard of again. May this book be a tribute to them.[56]

For no apparent reason corresponding to a coherent artistic plan, *The Return to the Farm* is a narrative mess, jumping from place to place, person to person, moment to moment in a most confusing manner. It's often hard to know when something is happening, who is concerned, where they are, and what they are up to. This text breaks all the rules. Why? Heaven knows, perhaps even Bob didn't.

The illustrations are uncoordinated as in a family scrapbook, odd photographs picked up here and there, some perhaps illegally from personal sources. One of them is disgraceful. Its caption reads: 'The spot where old Hommet cut his throat, showing the knife on the table.'

Bob's inputs and Mé's seem to have been pasted together almost haphazardly, in utter disregard of their reader. This uncharacteristic muddle seems terribly peevish. It would be too charitable to regard it as an early experiment in deconstruction. Was Bob peeved by having to produce what looks like a potboiler? Or was Mé mad at him for some reason? Judging from later developments, it may be surmised that he was keen on writing fiction, whereas she wanted to stick to their reality vein.

Not much came in the way of reviews. Faithful Elizabeth Bowen in the *Tatler* philosophised about the return to 'a beloved place, a house, a stretch of countryside, a lane-corner fraught with associations', thinking no doubt of her own dear lost Bowen House. Her article spoke mainly of the wartime London trilogy and its value as a document, adding 'one cannot have too many'. Identifying the present book as autobiography, she wished 'the author and his wife' had dropped their Reyhen mask: 'No possible confusion with fiction need have been risked—for, *The Return to the Farm*'s being true, its dealing with real-life happenings *is* important.' But the narrative muddle got the better of even such a brilliant reader as Elizabeth Bowen: she thought Goguet had been betrayed by his wife.

* * *

A MERE FOUR MONTHS LATER, in May 1947, Peter Davies published *Delphine and Other Stories* by Robert Henrey at 8*s.* *6d.*[57]

This volume may have been the first cause of ructions in the Henrey literary ménage. Mé's narrative style, governed among other things by brusque asides, branching associations of ideas and extended dialogue in the French manner (quoting successive speakers in short separate paragraphs), is perceptible in most of this volume's twenty-three stories. However, other stylistic evidence (sentences, vocabulary...) suggests that the volume as a whole was largely worked up by Bob and contains copy by him alone ('The Dead Man's Box' for instance).

101

Apparently Mé was not happy to let him publish straight stories. A note on the copyright page reads: 'This is a work of fiction and there is no reference to any living person.' This disclaimer is misleading. Most of the stories are set in Piccadilly or Soho, some in Normandy, all in the immediate time frame. There's much talk of the war. Seventeen are told in the first person by a woman who makes much of 'the Green Park', 'my mother', 'my husband', 'my baby', 'my Pekingese' in a familiar tonality. Madeleine is actually named on page sixty-nine. Other characters (manicurist Mme Neroda, former Gaiety Girl Nefertiti) appear in other 'true' books. So what the copyright page really means is that this 'work of fiction' isn't a proper Madeleine book. Years later, Mé would disown all such 'fictions' associated with her name, and to respect her wishes Bob would exclude them from the official canon listed in her *Who's Who* entry.

Obviously a lot of thought went into the composition of the *Delphine* volume. Yet the press coverage was meagre. *Delphine* tended to end up in the 'Books Received' lists with a bare sentence of comment, or was completely passed over. The reason isn't hard to find. A plethora of new books came out in 1947, and people were fed up with reading about the war. In the twenty-three *Delphine* stories the dreaded three-letter word occurs forty times. Only John Betjeman in the *Daily Herald* gave the book a pat on the back. After wondering if anyone still read 'that Victorian writer of London poverty, Edwin Pugh', Betjeman wrote: 'Robert Henrey is the champion of modern Soho. He specialises in character studies of glamorous ladies of French extraction with West End flats. If he will prune his style down to Pugh's telling brevity, he will do something even better than this good collection of Soho stories. He will be the Edwin Pugh of Soho.' To those critics of Pugh who find him melodramatic and repetitive, this may sound like a back-handed compliment. To those who admire Pugh's prose, it will seem perfectly appropriate.

* * *

WHATEVER THE DISAGREEMENTS between Mé and Bob, they rarely lasted for long. On 17 July 1947 a new contract was signed with Dent, who would remain their publisher for the rest of their career after their four-volume excursion to Peter Davies. The Dent contract concerned a novel, *An Attic in Jermyn Street*, which reached the bookshops priced 10*s*. 6*d*. in March 1948 as by Robert Henrey.[58] Elizabeth Bowen identified it as 'his first straight novel' after 'his famous wartime trilogy, his Thames-side chronicle and his Normandy farmhouse series'. It was written almost wholly by Bob from Mé's drafts, which have not survived. Though the narrative is centred on a young woman, the writing bears little trace of Mé's idiosyncrasies and remains crisp and witty for most of the time.

The contents of Bembridge House, a symbol of Victorian grandeur in Piccadilly overlooking the Green Park, are being auctioned off before the building is pulled down. Twenty-year-old Corinne Gay, an upper-class country girl, is determined to clear out of boring old Worcestershire. Her mother, 'a strange mixture of harshness and sensibility', dominates her father and sister as in a Jane Austen novel. 'For some curious reason the women in her family had always ruled, not merely by strength of character, but because by a strange turn of events most of them had been provided with large dowries, and it was Mrs Gay who on her marriage settlement had brought the Worcestershire estate.'

Having secretly answered an advertisement for 'a young woman reporter', Corinne has just been engaged on three weeks' trial by a national morning daily with a million and a quarter net sale. On this her first day, she has been sent off to report on the auction taking place in the Bembridge ballroom, where her mother when young danced after being presented at court by the lady of the house.

As the story opens, Corinne reflects on the fading grandeur of her class epitomised by the event she is covering. 'The war of 1914 had shaken everything to do with the society to which by birth she belonged.' Having been told to bring back a human interest story, she absorbs the atmosphere rather than the detail of 'the striking down of one of the old and mighty houses of the town', then lunches quickly at a sandwich counter in Jermyn Street. She rather likes this part of town. Returning to the bustling newsroom in the City, she presents her typed report to the news editor and, after making friends with Angela, a nice young staff writer who covers the fashion shows, she is sent off to the West End again to cover a celebrity scandal in theatreland. And so on.

This is clearly Bob's world rather than Mé's. The novel contains many allusions to his life before he met her: his passion for the Ballets Russes at the Alhambra in 1921; his coverage that same year of the 'Midnight Follies' cabaret show at the Metropole in Northumberland Avenue, which London County Council were trying to ban under the 1914 Defence of the Realm Act; the predemolition auction sale at Devonshire House on Piccadilly where his Rothschild cousins danced before the Great War; the country house in Wiltshire called Everleigh that the FitzRoys rented in 1857, etc.

On the other hand, there are plenty of echoes of Mé's life too (the difficult birth of her son, her village in France, Blois, her block of flats during the war, her little boy saying his prayers for his Grand'mère), and the indispensable feminine viewpoint is firmly expressed here also: a room of one's own, freedom of choice, independence, ambition... Corinne's attic in Jermyn Street represented ideals that many young English women cherished in 1948. But the novel argues that the war had changed fewer aspects of their lives than people liked to think. What Corinne really wanted, according to this story, was a husband. When she got one—a handsome young baronet's son who painted pictures—she had to cope with herself to keep him, and she was full of contradictions. Her town self could somehow not agree with her country self.

Elizabeth Bowen summed up her predicament in the *Tatler* on 21 April: 'Corinne who, at the start, had looked on, wondering, at the pitiful sexual dramas of Jermyn Street, is to find herself taken by the throat, shaken, by the demon of her own capacity for jealousy.' Bowen reckoned *An Attic in Jermyn Street* 'a remarkable novel—remarkable most of all in its alternations between the joys of the senses, at their most innocent, and the dire extremities of the soul'.

All the same Bowen was no longer young, and Mé herself had turned forty. It seems likely that many women readers in their twenties would feel uncomfortable with the novel's concluding sentence. Corinne's husband, driven away by her violent contradictions, has just come home after a misery-fraught separation: 'He laughed, but it was clear that he meant to rule, and she felt once again that the thing she needed most in the world was to be subjugated.' Perhaps an apter judgement of this novel for the younger class of reader in 1948 would be that voiced by a country critic in the *Western Morning News* on 25 May: 'A meandering love story, naïve and faintly snobbish.'

The book was dedicated to Edith Shackleton, a highly regarded bisexual feminist journalist and writer who had worked with the Henreys at the *Daily Sketch* in the late 1930s. She was the mistress of W.B. Yeats for the two years before his death in 1939 and in 1948 was living in London with her lover Hannah Gluckstein. Apart from the remunerative fact that Shackleton regularly reviewed the Henrey books favourably in the *Observer*, this dedication placed a modernist key signature at the head of a tale which in some ways looked back to Dickens, notably with its picturesque gallery of characters called Mrs Beaupré (a prostitute with a prominent bosom), Growler (a pipe-smoking crime reporter), Bert Gandergast, Kerrigrew, Yendal (a predatory impresario), Riverfold, Graffington, Mrs Rugyard, or the smooth Sir Max Everleigh of Everleigh. *An Attic in Jermyn Street* is a contradictory novel. Torn between vice and virtue, comedy and drama, love and violence, it's a remnant of a former age striving to be up-to-date like its heroine and hero, Corinne and Claud.

The Fallen Idol

THE AUTHORS' EVENINGS AT HOME in Carrington House were spent reading aloud to each other alternately in English and French, while Bobby read or mused on his side of the room until late at night. Mé wondered what sense he made of Enid Starkie's *Arthur Rimbaud* or Maurice Sachs's *Le Sabbat*. However, the rule was that he did just as he liked until lights out and could listen or not.

The flat was really small for the three of them. By now Bobby had a proper bed of his own in his parents' room and an 'office' with a small table and a row of bookshelves in the windowless hall, where his cot had stood during the Blitz. In the daytime, he played on the living room floor or in the Green Park. Mé worked in bed, Bob at his paper. Mathilde was in Normandy, where she gardened and looked after the house, her hens and her rabbits, reconciled and even content with life in the country. Pouffy was with her now and she kept a bevy of cats. She did chafe, it seems, at feeling a financial burden, though she more than earned her keep at the farm. It was in her nature to chafe, anyway.

Bobby and she loved each other dearly, and that solved part of the living space problem as he chose to spend as much time as he could in Normandy. He helped Grand'mère in the garden dressed in overalls, rubber boots and a floppy hat, followed the odd-job man and neighbours through the woods and fields, watched Mathilde kill and pluck her hens, admired how she slit the jugular vein of her rabbits and skinned them for the pot with a matter-of-factness far beyond his mother and even more so his father. When they came over to check up on his essay writing and arithmetic, he was rarely sorry to see them go. One of his jobs was to fetch the cider from the press in a pitcher for lunch, and he kept losing the key and spilling or even breaking the pitcher to his parents' despair.

Hay making was the time he enjoyed most. During the breaks for chunks of bread and Camembert cheese he sometimes got to dip a lump of sugar in the men's mixture of black coffee and applejack. Perhaps the best of all was to be allowed to ride at the top of the hay carts. Each cart was drawn by two horses and moved slowly along the rutted hedge-lined lanes. Many years later he would remember lying on his back gazing up into the sky as low-lying branches from the oaks, wild cherry trees and hazelnut bushes brushed over him. 'On a warm July evening when the sun was still high in the sky this was indeed a foretaste of heaven. I would rush home, tell my grandmother about my day's adventures, secure in the knowledge that the next morning I would have plenty to write about.'[59] He could actually speak Norman dialect, and still can.

* * *

TOWARDS THE MIDDLE OF JULY 1947, Mé received a note pushed through the door of the Hertford Street flat. It asked whether she could possibly agree to let Bobby play a leading part in a film due to be made in London starting in September. She thought it was a hoax, but Bob suggested writing back noncommittally that the boy was in Normandy. Two days later, a production executive from London Films in Piccadilly invited her to meet Carol Reed, the film's producer and director. He explained that he wanted a boy aged eight, with no acting experience and a foreign accent, to play an ambassador's son left alone for a dramatic weekend at his father's embassy in Belgrave Square.

The main actors were Ralph Richardson as the butler, Sonia Dresdel as his wife the housekeeper, and Michèle Morgan as an embassy typist in love with the butler. London Films had spotted Bobby on the cover of *A Village in Piccadilly* and allowing for the five year age difference between the photo and now he looked just right for the part. If his parents agreed to let him take a film test, they were ready to fly him over and back the same day in a private plane from Deauville. Bob thought the experience could be interesting both for Mé, remembering how she had longed to go into films while working at the Savoy, and for the boy. The money would be useful for him later on, and she could always draft a book about it. Let him do the test and see how things worked out.

It seems nobody asked Bobby how he felt about any of all this. Mé came to fetch him, and the trip from Deauville was fun. The young French pilot let him sit beside him in the small plane, pointing out the places they flew over. On the way back from Croydon they made room for a bicycle Mé had bought for the farm. Two weeks went by, then Bob called to say the contract had been signed. Shooting was to start in Belgrave Square on 15 September, then continue at Shepperton Studios for ten weeks in all, with possible extensions. Bobby would be paid £1,000 down and £100 for every week beyond the ten. He would stay at the studios with his mother and a governess from Monday to Friday. Weekends would be spent at home with Bob.

Dr Lehérissey having decided that Bobby had to have his tonsils and adenoids out, he started work two days late after leaving the farm in tears. September is the loveliest month in Normandy. Sadly he did the rounds of the neighbours, packed up the toy village he had made with the local carpenter, and went back to England for the first time in many months.

On Carol Reed's instructions, he was dressed in the white short-sleeved shirt and sleeveless red home-knitted pullover, short black trousers, white ankle socks and black oxfords he would wear throughout the film. Mé and he were driven straight from Croydon Airport to Belgrave Square. The 'embassy' building on the corner of Wilton Crescent and Grosvenor Crescent was at that time occupied by the British Red Cross and St John libraries. Bobby shot his first scene running across the street towards the square that same afternoon.

The film, adapted by Graham Greene and Carol Reed from Greene's story *The Basement Room*, was to be called '*The Lost Illusion*', but the title was changed at the last moment to *The Fallen Idol*. This change focused the drama on Ralph Richardson, the disgraced butler, rather than on Bobby, the disillusioned boy. In either case the subject is the same, a familiar tandem in Greene's work: secrecy and belief.

The lonely little Phillipe—with two lls and one p according to the title cards and the continuity script—worships the rascally butler Baines, who invents stories about himself to entertain the child, who believes them. The embassy housekeeper, the butler's puritanical wife, is obsessed with dirt and falsehood. She finds out about the secret Phillipe shares with her husband, a pet snake, which she destroys as 'vermin'. Then she discovers, by accusing the boy of lying, that her husband secretly meets a 'niece' Julie on the embassy staff. Mrs Baines lays a trap to catch them out, but falls from a window ledge and is killed. Baines spins a tale about the death to protect Julie. Believing Baines has murdered his wife, Phillipe lies repeatedly to protect him, despite Julie's pleas with him to tell the truth. The police veer from one 'truth' to another, until the forensic scientists discover a 'truth' that has nothing to do with Mrs Baines's death, and decide the death was an accident—which it was—despite Phillipe's belief that the forensics trace was caused by him—which it was also. When the Chief Inspector leaves the building asking the boy if he can tell him a secret, Phillipe answers vehemently in his Court of St James's accent: 'No!'

The 'embassy' building was used solely for the exteriors, which were shot first. The famous night scenes on the fire escape and in the street were shot with a stand-in, fifteen-year-old Eric, at the rear of Seaford House on the south-east corner of the square. Bobby and Mé lived at home, almost around the corner, during this initial stage. A unit car drove them four times a day between Hertford Street and Belgrave Square, and Bob joined them each evening after his day at *Radio Times*. A caravan in the square, guarded by a policeman, was available for resting between shots. Bobby and his governess, Mrs Cleverley, used it for their three R's. Mé wrote and knitted there when it was free. It was clear from the outset that she was writing a book about the filming. Everyone in the unit knew this. They all addressed her as Mrs Robert Henrey in recognition of her professional writer's status, rather than as a real-life Madeleine, Bobby's mother.

The idea for the book seems to have been a kind of literary 'making-of', if the term could have existed at the time, an anecdotal bonus to the film in keeping with the documentary aspects of the Henreys' earlier publications. Basically, the Madeleine figure is presented as a female Candide, an innocent abroad in a matter-of-fact world dedicated to producing make-believe. This paradox provides some good stories at Mé's expense, such as her performance as the mink-coated ambassador's wife in the final scene— she had one line to say in French and botched it—or the weekend she trimmed Bobby's hair between two shots and held up filming for several days. There are glimpses also of the family universe at home, Carrington House seen as an extension of Shepperton Stu-

dios: Bob reading *The Three Musketeers* aloud from a first French edition, Bobby's teddy bears and so on.

The film book may have been commissioned by London Films as an implicit clause of Bobby's movie contract, as no publisher's contract has been found. Several reasons support this hypothesis. When Alexander Korda visited the unit towards the end of the shooting at Belgrave Square, he told Madeleine: 'Carol lent me the first part of your book to read over the weekend.' To Bobby he said: 'I see in your mother's book you are very pleased with the caravan.' After the unit moved to Shepperton Studios for the interiors, Mé was given a director's chair on Stage C with her name on it, and the jacket and end papers for her book were drawn by a London Films set decorator.

Whether the writing of the book was sponsored by Korda or not, a marketing deal between Peter Davies and London Films definitely took place. The book's storyline ends at Christmas 1947, when Mé turned her attention to other titles as will be seen. However, publication of *A Film Star in Belgrave Square* was held back by Davies to coincide with *The Fallen Idol*'s grand premiere at the end of September 1948. This simultaneity was obviously a promotional tool for both media and may explain why this title wasn't included in the official Henrey bibliography drawn up in the 1970s.

A Film Star in Belgrave Square is nonetheless an honest piece of journalism, a lively chronicle of events and conversations taking the lid off a world unknown to the general reader. Its particular interest as literature is that it's part of a developing corpus, an œuvre with its own rules and originalities. Overlaid with autobiographical elements like its two full-length predecessors (*The King of Brentford* and *The Return to the Farm*) and some of the *Delphine* stories, all published by Peter Davies, it adds an imaginary dimension to a factual narrative which otherwise might have been written by any talented journalist. By involving the reader in the life of its main characters, who also happen to be its authors, the joint Henrey mix in these works transforms chronicle into poetry.

Like its two predecessors, *A Film Star in Belgrave Square* is a third-person narrative about Madeleine, Philip and their child, but here the child is by necessity named for the first time and only Philip-the-husband keeps his mask on to avoid confusion with the poet, the nominal author of the book, Robert Henrey. The Madeleine figure is greatly expanded here to reveal feminine strengths and frailties that were barely suggested in the earlier books. In fact one begins to wonder who the star in the title really is. Just as Bobby features in almost every shot in the movie, Madeleine appears on just about every page in the book. The Madeleine character is actually seizing power in the corpus at this point, and there's a distinct gender shift in the tone of the narratives from now on as the author becomes an authoress. In later books, as Mé increasingly takes control of the narrative process, it will be seen how the corpus focused on Madeleine will become principally—and sometimes exclusively—an unpoetical diary of her daily life.

Stylistic evidence suggests that the usual authorial method—Mé's French draft followed by Bob's English fair copy—wasn't followed for this book. The text is full of technical terms which Mé couldn't have known the French for. Additionally, it abounds in gallicisms. The conclusion must be that Mé wrote it in English or that Bob did, imitating her English. To be on the safe side, let's say it was a bit of the two.

Elizabeth Bowen blew the gaff about the authorship in the *Tatler* on 13 October 1948:

A Film Star in Belgrave Square is nominally written by Robert Henrey—the 'Philip' of the dialogue, Bobby's father. I am, however, allowed to reveal that the book is, actually, *Mrs* Robert Henrey's work; and more, that the Robert Henreys have been engaged in a happy conspiracy for some time—part authorship of a few, sole authorship of the other now famous 'Robert Henrey' books has, now, been admitted by Madeleine Henrey. A charm, and I think virtue, of all the books is their effect of being a blend of two personalities, two experiences—of the London wartime trilogy, the other London chronicles and the novels, it *had* struck me that they might have been written, equally, by either husband or wife.

Bowen knew the Henreys personally, and she had reviewed all their books. Her cautious 'revelation' allows for some leeway in what Mé regarded as 'authorship'. Helping to write a book by researching facts or sorting papers or providing copy isn't the same as being an author, especially when the copy provided is in French or faulty English. Bowen's 'blend of two personalities' is a correct representation of their 'happy conspiracy', but speaking of the authorship she should have written '*claimed* by Madeleine Henrey' rather than '*admitted* by Madeleine Henrey'.

Bob was no usurper like Colette's Willy. In his Higgins role, he did everything he could to lift his Eliza to independence, but he took things a step further by actually becoming Eliza himself as well as her. Quite logically he suggested they author their books in future as 'Mrs Robert Henrey', adopting a slightly old-fashioned form of address commonly used professionally in publishing and the theatre as well as in ordinary life: authoress Mrs Humphrey Ward, actress Mrs Patrick Campbell, etc. Mé wasn't quite ready for this, apparently, and the papers got wind of her irritation. The 'Londoner's Diary' columnist on the *Evening Standard* wrote under the catty innuendo 'ROBERT IS A WOMAN' (6 November 1948):

Here disclosed is the secret of an author who earns £8,000 a year. It is the story of a changed personality. Robert Henrey, a former London journalist, used to write books. [...] In 1940 his wife Madeleine collaborated with him on a book, *A Farm in Normandy*, which told of their escape from the farm when the Germans came. Mrs Henrey dictated the book to her husband; his part was to edit it. It was published as by Robert Henrey, and was more successful than those the husband had written alone. [...] His only part in the next book, *A Village in Piccadilly*, was to provide his wife with some notes. Since then Mrs Henrey has been the sole author of nearly a dozen books; but all appeared under her husband's name.

Mé herself used the phrase 'Robert Henrey is a woman' a year later (5 November 1949) in a letter to the *Somerset County Herald* signed 'Madeleine Henrey' claiming sole authorship of the pre– Mrs Robert Henrey books.[60]

Though Bob was probably amused by this exaggerated gossip and may even have encouraged it for publicity reasons and because he was increasingly projecting himself into the Madeleine persona, Mé's bid for authorial emancipation led to considerable bibliographical confusion. When *A Film Star in Belgrave Square* reached the London Library on 30 September 1948, the spidery hand of the cataloguer amended the title page by pencilling under the printed name of the author Robert Henrey: '[i.e. Madeleine Henrey, wife of R. H.]'. Subsequently, especially after the publication of *The Little Madeleine* in 1951, libraries throughout the world re-attributed all their Robert Henrey holdings to 'Mrs Robert Henrey'. The British Library even tagged them '[or rather, by Madeleine Henrey]'.This was bibliographically inexact, as only two titles—reissues that came out after Bob's death—were ever published during Mé's long lifetime as by 'Madeleine Henrey'.[61]

The shortest title in the corpus, copiously illustrated, *A Film Star in Belgrave Square* is dedicated

To
'Alex'
(Sir Alexander Korda)
and to
W. J. O'Bryen
who had a hunch
and to
Everybody in the Unit from
Carol Reed to Bobby's stand-in.[62]

The jacket shows a Bobby figure in red pyjamas floating dream-like, lit by two studio arc lamps, above Belgrave Square in the dead of night. The visual pun on Peter Pan cannot have escaped Peter Davies, the book's publisher, who as a child inspired the character in J.M. Barrie's play and novel. Mé herself, solicitous and talkative in Bobby's orbit, must have struck the film unit as a sort of Wendy figure. She mixed with them freely on and off the set, and wrote most of them into her stories whether they liked it or not.

The reviewers talked about the film rather than about the book. Poet John Betjeman, amused by the jacket pun no doubt and perceiving its projection of the film world as a kind of Neverland, wrote in the *Daily Herald* that 'this wide-eyed and enthusiastic story' by 'Madame Robert Henrey' about her son's 'fairy-tale life' making the film made everyone seem to have been 'radiantly happy'. More prosaically, Vernon Fane's 'The World of Books' column in the *Sphere* thought that 'this day-by-day account of the making of a new English film' was 'one way of learning how a story is filmed, and what goes on on the floor'.

* * *

THIS ISN'T THE PLACE to tell about the fallout of the movie, which marked Bobby's life much more deeply than anyone realised at the time. Robert Henrey, as Bobby Henrey preferred to be known in later life, published his own memoir of the experience (and what followed) in 2013, *Through Grown-up Eyes: Living with Childhood Fame*. Suffice it to say here that the film money encouraged his father to leave *Radio Times* and his mother to buy a pearl necklace.

Complacency wasn't in their nature, however. Thanks to a great deal of hard work, they brought out three books in 1948, completed one more the same year and began work on three further titles which would be contracted (i.e. completed, given Bob's commitment to on-delivery contracts) in 1949. The end of wartime paper rationing and a constant demand for their books from a faithful reader base identifying with their lifestyle was clearly beginning to make their production a viable enterprise. A portrait in oils done by Wilfrid de Glehn R.A. at his home in Salisbury that summer of 1948 celebrated a pert Mé seated in three-quarter profile wearing a dark blue Breton hat with a feather, clearly on top of the world.

114

Hard on the heels of *A Film Star in Belgrave Square* from Peter Davies in September 1948, *London* came out from Dent in November. For the first time the contract was drawn up in Mé's own name followed by her pseudonym, viz. 'Mrs Madeleine Henrey (Mrs Robert Henrey)'. It's dated 20 September 1947, meaning as usual that the text had already been completed and accepted at that date. There's just a six-line update to 'the summer of 1948' that was probably added to the final proof.[63]

London is a pot-pourri of historical anecdotes, personal reminiscences, quotations from the Shakespeare-Pepys-Evelyn literary contingent, borrowings from the London Library's Topography shelves, guided walks, reportages, interviews, a full-blown prose poem entitled 'Nocturne'—the whole interspersed with twenty full-page colour illustrations by Phyllis Ginger, a young watercolourist who had worked for the wartime *Recording Britain* scheme. Greatly admired by Bob in particular, she became the preferred artist of the Henreys' jackets for the next thirty years.

Her work for this book, reduced from her original formats and printed on the same paper as the text, may have been an early shot by Dent's own Temple Press (later known as the Aldine Press) at using the recent sheet-fed offset process. The result is unworthy of the artist's talent. The jacket produced by traditional lithography, showing the same view of Piccadilly Circus as the picture within, is far more satisfactory than its counterpart pictorially speaking.

A varied entertainment volume with informative captions in italics facing Ginger's illustrations, *London* frequently echoes the authors' previous London books—there's even a straight twenty-five-line block quotation on page fifty-one from *The Incredible City*. At the high price of 20*s.* it was obviously timed to cash in on the Christmas market. It was what the Victorians and Edwardians called a 'parlour-window book'. Meant for browsing rather than studied reading—it has no index—and brimming with anecdotes as well as curious facts and images, it prefigures (in a smaller format and with more text) the coffee-table book of the 1960s onwards. It was the first of the Henreys' books to come out in America—from Dutton in New York in 1949.

Dedicated to women's journalist Dorothy Sutherland, with two stanzas entitled 'The Londoner in the Country' by Richard Church as its epigraph, it went down well with almost all the reviewers. The *Scotsman* thought that 'the charm of the writing' was enhanced by 'the delightful watercolours of present-day London by Phyllis Ginger'. Novelist Howard Spring in *Country Life*, praising the book's factual side pointed out that the book slipped up 'on one point of fact' concerning ruling monarchs during the war, and observed that Mrs Robert Henrey was becoming 'a most prolific writer' as if that in itself was a defect. More relevantly from a literary point of view, Rupert Croft-Cooke in the *Sketch* admired Mé's 'contemporary portraits', particularly the one concerning 'a Mrs Montrose Cloete, a hostess of Edwardian days, whom Mrs Henrey found alone in a house in Berkeley Square from which all but a few pieces of furniture had been stripped, but who could recall building the stables for £2,800 and keeping eight horses'. Croft-Cooke produced a crisp definition of such portraits in Mé's work at this time: 'nostalgic without mawkishness'. That sounds rather French actually—'*nostalgique sans mièvrerie*'—and it's spot on.

A few days after the 1948 end-of-year gift season, Elizabeth Bowen wrote in the *Tatler*: 'Finely printed and produced, *London* suggests itself, I should say, as the ideal exchange for a book token.'

* * *

A NEW HENREY NOVEL, *Philippa*, came out while the general release of *The Fallen Idol* was breaking box-office records in 1949. Bob signed the contract with Dent on 29 October 1948, the date of Bobby's grand premiere. The publication date was 11 August 1949, a day before Mé's forty-third birthday and two days before Bob's forty-eighth. It was the first book to bear the author name Mrs Robert Henrey on its title page. With such astral conjunctions, how could it fail? Alas, it did.

Despite the fact that it was new and nicely expressed, *Philippa* didn't get beyond its first impression and was apparently remaindered at 5*s*. in November 1951. Only five (tepid) reviews and a single advertisement have been traced. It was excluded from the official bibliography—indeed Mé wrote in 1974 that it should be destroyed.[64] It's a poetic out-of-the-world novel, doubly so in fact—out of its own world and out of the world it was written for. Its symbolism is baffling by any standards, and its chart of a young woman's heart set on being true and loving in a grim post-war world was definitely off-key in 1949 to judge from the lurid best-seller lists found in the press of the day.

We are in the country somewhere. An expanding Research Centre threatens the survival of the little Saxon church and its Queen Anne rectory. The parish has already been engulfed by an artificial lake. All but a few inhabitants have been moved away into town. A small rural community remains: a few children, the school mistress housed in a caravan with her truck-driver husband, the local builder, an old churchwarden, the learned rector's family. Philippa, a 'daughter at home' neglected in the good old way for a male sibling at Oxford, is far from dull: she has taught herself Italian and French, and her father's rich library has nourished her thoughts and dreams.

Meeting no potential husband of her own class, Philippa falls in love with Johnny, the builder's boy back from the war in Burma, her childhood playmate. Their two worlds are far apart, as her mother points out—not just socially, which doesn't matter all that much in the postwar world, but intellectually. Feeling inferior, Johnny resolves to make money for her, gets into the black market, is found out. Philippa wants him nonetheless, goes through deep water for him, brings him back from the brink of despair. And they go off to face the music together.[65]

The first question has to be: Why 'Philippa'? Philip was the codename used for Bob in the three Reyhen books. So who does this Philippa stand for? The answer is a sort-of Mé plus Bob, of course. Much of this novel reflects motifs from their joint life story: Philippa's rectory corresponds to the Henrey vicarage, the red pillar box to the Stacey Street lamppost, her brother's meningitis to Bébert's diphtheria, Mrs Dale's grief to Mathilde's bitterness, Philippa's longing for Johnny to Mé's yearning for Bob and vice versa. Yet *Philippa* isn't a disguised autobiography. Its metaphors—the crime, the flight, the ferry, the mystical marriage—take it beyond an ordinary life narrative. Not for nothing does the term 'romantic' occur fifteen times in the tale.

There's just one important point at which Mrs Robert Henrey draws attention to herself as an authoress. It comes on page eleven: 'Philippa deliberately chose from her father's shelves books written by women. What a great number had lived excitedly! Perhaps, after all, it wasn't such an unfortunate thing to be born a woman? It might even be turned to advantage.' Then follows a reading list of women writers, quite out of place in any ordinary novel: Mrs Aphra Behn, Mme de La Fayette, Mme de Sévigné, Mme d'Aulnoy, Lady Mary Wortley Montagu, Mme de Grafigny, Lady Coke, Mrs Delany, the Misses Berry, Mme du Deffand, Mme Campan, Mme de La Rochejacquelin, Mme de Genlis, the Duchess of Abrantès, the Countess of Boigne, Mme de Staël, Jane Austen, George Sand, George Eliot, Colette, Virginia Woolf, Margaret Mitchell, Elizabeth Bowen.

Was a pen poised to add Madeleine Henrey to the list? Perhaps not yet. It would probably have been Bob's pen in any case, not hers. He was by now her most fervent admirer.

The volume is dedicated to Julia Cairns, a women's journalist known for her broadcasts on fashion and furnishing—her book *Home Making* would be a big hit in the 1950s. In 1948, as president of the Women's Press Club and editor-in-chief of Weldon's publications on knitting and needlework, she liked addressing Women's Institutes and Business Women's Clubs on 'the red light of materialism' and the need for 'heart' in the life of the postwar nation, saying: 'So much rests on the shoulders of the women today.' This wasn't feminism, but it was an assertion of women's social importance and their right to autonomy. The author of *Philippa* most certainly agreed with this point of view. The name of Philippa's mother Mrs Dale suggests, perhaps coincidentally, the heroine of the popular radio serial 'Mrs Dale's Diary' about a woman's role in ordinary domestic life. However, Philippa is more modern than her mother. She has no experience, but she has devoured her father's library and is sensually aware of her wants and needs, with the result that an idea of sophisticated womanhood coexists in her psyche with her housewifely convictions.

Elizabeth Bowen in the *Tatler* had two shots at commending *Philippa*, the first time with a nice photograph of the author merely announcing the publication, the second with a full review underlining the novel's 'important theme', asking romantically: 'What *is* to become of the gently-born girls of England, daughters of a now so-called "dying class", who, isolated in the country or in unpropitious neighbourhoods, have no chance to marry into what should have been their own world?'

The other reviewers would have none of Bowen's social poetry. The *Illustrated London News* 'Fiction of the Week' column found Philippa and her predicament 'unexciting', and stated that Johnny's desperate flight could not be believed and spoiled the story. The *Aberdeen Press and Journal* also found his envisaged suicide 'not in character'. The *Western Morning News* labelled the novel 'a disappointment' and stated: 'It never completely impresses one that it is real.' Of course not, it's a tale, and a delightful one.

* * *

It suddenly turned out that the employment of child actors in British films was illegal under the Children and Young Persons Act 1933, art. 33, sect. 22. This provided that 'No child under twelve years of age may be permitted to entertain.' An amendment to the Cinematograph Films Act 1938 allowing children to be employed in films with appropriate safeguards was unexpectedly thrown out on a point of order at its second reading in February 1948.

By this time David Lean's *Oliver Twist* with nine-year-old John Howard Davies and Carol Reed's '*The Lost Illusion*' with Bobby were in an advanced stage of production. The Conservative opposition accused the Home Secretary of closing his eyes on the law in order to accommodate his colleague at the Board of Trade, who was losing a bitter war with Hollywood. The Home Secretary responded in the usual manner: he set up a departmental inquiry to consider 'under what safeguards, as to health, welfare and ed-

119

ucation, the employment of children as film actors could properly be allowed.' Nothing further happened until *Oliver Twist* and *The Fallen Idol* came out and met with considerable success.

A week after *The Fallen Idol* premiere Alexander Korda stoked the controversy by announcing that he had signed Bobby on a £30,000 four-year contract for films that would have to be made abroad owing to the current legislation in England. Bob mischievously told a *Daily Herald* reporter on 6 October that the deal was actually worth £60,000—half guaranteed, half expected from the loan of the boy to France and Hollywood. Bobby would probably make two films for Korda: one at his father's farm in Normandy and one in Technicolor in the West Indies.

In fact Bobby's film career never brought in more than £5,000 which went straight into the Carrington House everyday expenses account. In the meantime, the hoo-ha pumped into the papers by London Films and British Lion made life in London fairly intolerable. The family moved to the Ritz in Paris to allow Bobby to dub his part in French. They came back briefly for the Royal Command Film Show on 29 November at which Bobby was filmed for Pathé News presenting the Queen with a bouquet of orchids. Then they settled for Christmas and the winter at the farm in Normandy.

Everyone locally knew about the film, which had been in all the papers. But nobody gave it more than a passing mention, whereas in London Mé could not buy a ribbon or a pair of stockings without the sales girls flocking around them. Bobby returned to the farm with such enthusiasm that Mé could only think the place flowed in his blood. He embraced his Grand'mère, who smiled imperceptibly, for she wasn't demonstrative, even a little bitter on account of her rheumatic pains. She lived alone in the thatched cottage, except for her cats and Pouffy the Pekingese.

The place was by now what Mé, in her bookish idiom stretching from Shakespeare to Elizabeth Bowen, described as 'commodious'. They had electricity, gas, central heating and running hot water as well as the Aga and the fireplaces. It wasn't long before Mé found Bobby disguised as Don Quixote, mounted on a broomstick with a lance in his hand, charging the apple trees. He had pined for the farm during their last days in London. His father's genes were beginning to assert themselves, and the chubby little eight-year-old who had meekly listened to Carol Reed telling him over and again what words to speak and what faces to make was developing into a lanky pre-teenager with a mind of his own. Mé thought his dreaminess and sudden irascible moods were traits of herself: 'I had the feeling of a mirror being held up to my own soul, laying it uncomfortably bare.'[66] Perhaps. Her mini-portrait of Bobby reads awfully like Effie's descriptions of Bob, however.

Apart from the retreat from Kordaland, the idea of course was to write a book. Bob was no good at anything else, and Mé was full of her new-found authorial independence as Mrs Robert Henrey. They decided to foreground their Madeleine character, dropping the third-person disguises they had used previously—Reyhen and so on—in order to promote 'I' as a French girl of humble extraction living an elegant modern life as a woman writer in English with a flat in Mayfair, a farm in Normandy, a mother, a son, and many acquaintances. A husband would become a vague adjunct, a nameless background figure, almost an afterthought in the different worlds gravitating round the pervading presence of Madeleine.

This was Bob's choice as a professional. The fan mail received at Carrington House came mainly from women captured by the feminine side of the Henrey stories, curious to know more, wanting to be involved. Some actually turned up in Villers and tried to find Madeleine's farm. The Pygmalion in Bob was quite content to leave the limelight on Mé while he got on with the job. The sound of his typewriter clicking away filled the old house all day. It actually got on Mé's nerves. *'Ah! Ton père et sa machine!'* she often complained to Bobby, who says he never saw her use one. Indeed, the term 'typewriter' referring to her activity as a writer occurs only three times in the entire corpus. She preferred her fountain pen and a foolscap pad or school exercise book, usually in bed, though she refers once or twice to her 'writing room' and 'writing table' for more solemnity when answering her mail by hand or correcting proofs.

Bobby's schooling seems to have been neglected that winter, and that suited the boy perfectly. His parents wrote all day, Grand'mère made the meals, a char did the cleaning, Bobby did as he pleased until Mé collared him at milking time to go down to the village or to do the rounds of the neighbours. After supper, once Mathilde had locked herself up in the cottage after shooing in her fowls and turning out her cats, the other three read aloud by the fire in the old house. They grilled rump steaks on the hot embers and toasted long strips of French bread which they spread thickly with butter. All three felt, probably in different ways, that this period was as good as they were ever likely to have. Their readings were *Treasure Island* which they all enjoyed, *Kidnapped* which soon bored them with its endless brigs, pistols, bludgeons, grimaces and oaths, and *King Solomon's Mines* which had insufficient feminine interest for Mé—it was abandoned after fifty pages in favour of *Pride and Prejudice* and *Evelina*, both of which enchanted Bobby.

One evening their tenant farmer Déliquaire came round with his lantern to listen to a recorded interview by Bobby talking about the farm on the BBC French wavelength. When it came to the part about Mme Déliquaire teaching Bobby how to milk the cows and how the cow known as Bouboule was the boy's favourite, Déliquaire leaned forward excitedly. 'Bouboule!' he exclaimed, much impressed. 'Fancy M. Bobby mentioning Bouboule! I was going to sell her because she's hard to milk, but now she's famous we'll have to keep her!'

* * *

THIS DÉLIQUAIRE WAS TO BE THE STAR of that winter's Madeleine book. Entitled *Matilda and the Chickens*, it was undertaken—perhaps partly for tax purposes—to show Madeleine performing as an *exploitante agricole* with Mathilde as her *aide familiale* in charge of house, garden and basse-cour. This produced another muddle alongside the authorship confusion. Bob had bought the farm, but Mé must be perceived as owning it. Consequently, Madeleine had to be shown dealing with the tenants, lawyers, suppliers, tradesmen, journeymen and all the rest connected with working the farm.

To anyone acquainted with peasant life in France around 1950, this was and remains totally implausible. Men dealt with men. There can be no doubt whatsoever that in 1949 the person in charge at the farm, objectively speaking, was Bob, though he encouraged Mé to think—and write—that *she* was. This suited her, just as the pretense of her being the sole author of their books suited her, though that too may have been prompted initially by

122

tax considerations, a bugbear for them both..

From the outset Bob, who liked to see himself as an astute businessman but wasn't, had entertained the thought of making the farm a viable economic unit. He had enlarged the estate several times as land and cash became available and would continue to do so with part of the film money in 1951. An idealist with a sound biblical and capitalistic foundation, he had an edenic vision of nature that his childhood memories reinforced. Why shouldn't the farm be his vicarage garden, indeed his Gunnersbury in miniature? He had always been lucky, self-sufficient by the grace of God. Autarky in Normandy had seemed a good bet in 1938 and the idea still attracted him. He began talking about having livestock of his own—a cow to begin with, a few sheep to graze the orchards. His bucolic vision was pure Horace Walpole, his notion of sheep grazing the orchards positively heretical—sheep ruin grass as every proper Norman farmer knows.

Mé shared his love of nature, but in town. The beauty of the Green Park overwhelmed her and her heart melted at the sight of little animals (except mice), particularly when they were injured or newborn. However, Bob's talk about the farm's future alarmed her. Mathilde had adapted to country life because she had been brought up to it in Blois. Mé her daughter was a city girl. She could be content at the farm, but she just could not see herself being tied down to an economy of orchards and cattle in what she called a bog.

Rather than confront her husband on the issue at a time when they had important literary business in hand she went to see Maître Vincent, the notary, in whom she knew Bob had every confidence. Pretending the livestock idea was hers, she received a blunt reply, which she put down in writing in *Matilda and the Chickens*: 'Townsfolk and farmers do not mix. You are tempted to re-create a little Trianon. Like Marie-Antoinette, you want to play at being a country woman. You will rue this day, madame. I tell you, it cannot work.'[67] (That it was she rather than Bob who recorded this incident is clear from the grammar in the previous sentence: 'How clearly did the notary warn me at the time, so distant now, of the giving to Goguet of that cow.' Bob was good at forging her style, but that particular construction seems beyond even his imagination.) Having ignored the notary's warnings on two previous occasions and had cause to regret it, Bob bowed to his advice this time with good grace.

There was a great fuss when Mathilde found out that she was being put in books. Shy to the point of self-effacement, she regarded the literary invasion of her private life as an intolerable liberty taken with her person. She was right, of course. Bob and Mé were quite callous about writing real people into their stories, considering that frankness and sincerity were synonymous with truth and that truth was necessary in literature. Fair enough. But did literature matter more than privacy? The debate is an old one and the answers have varied from one period to another. Bobby sided with his Grand'mère when she exploded.

Yet there's nothing in *Matilda and the Chickens* that seems clearly objectionable—deeper indiscretions were to come in later books (twelve altogether featuring Mathilde, uncritical as long as she lived). 'Matilda' isn't even Mathilde. Who in Normandy would identify her in a book in English published in England? Who in England would remember her from her Soho days? The chances were slim. The problem would become potentially acute in Normandy when the first two volumes of the Madeleine sequence appeared in French from a Paris publisher identifying 'Mathilde' as '*ma mère*'. Even then, however, possible embarrassment was mitigated by the fact that Mathilde was known in Villers under her second married name (Mme Thibert), when the books in French called her by her first one (Mme Gal). In the novelised wartime Reyhen books, unpublished in France, she was called Mrs Bernard, a modification of her maiden name.

Regarding *Matilda and the Chickens*, the title is, not for the first or last time in the corpus, a misnomer—eye-catching but inaccurately descriptive. Neither Matilda nor the chickens play a major part in it. The story's principal characters are people speaking about themselves—mainly Madeleine naturally in this piece of autobiography—and various members of the Déliquaire family, who were the Henreys' tenant farmers and close neighbours on the other side of the stream via the cider press. A more accurate title would therefore have been '*Madeleine and the Déliquaires*', a pretty rotten title if ever there was one. In any case, the reference to Madeleine was reserved for another title as will be seen.

Bob was fond of old Déliquaire—*le Pé* in Norman French

(meaning *le père*), hence *la Mé* (*la mère*), Bob's mock-Norman nickname for his own wife—as he had been fond of Goguet, and for similar reasons. Both were typical Norman peasants, crafty and unreliable but bound by ancient lore to standards of behaviour that had allowed their kind to survive against the odds—climate, lords, war, feuds, pestilence—and continue on the land from one generation to the next.

Continuance and survival were Bob's particular field of study, and he knew or felt, as these peasants themselves knew or felt, that their days were numbered. The god Progress had decreed their doom. There was even a government programme for their extinction called *le remembrement* which was destroying their orchards and forcing them to clear out of their farmhouses. In addition, beach villages like Villers were threatened by the proliferation of holiday villas and *résidences secondaires* promoted by postwar prosperity and businessmen like Victor Duprez. Mé recorded all this in her diaries as it happened. Bob's concern was with telling the tale.

Their book opens with a wedding and closes with a funeral. The two-day wedding feast recorded by Mé in picturesque detail[68] is marred by the fact that Roger Déliquaire, born and bred by his father to succeed him on the family farm, is marrying a town girl and has got a job as a truck driver for a cider factory. That thread is broken. Mé's factual account shows, with no voices off, how the wedding feast has lost its meaning and become a piece of mechanical folklore. The funeral in the closing pages is heartbreaking, a fine piece of writing that must be in part reproduced here in case it's never reproduced anywhere else.

Along the white road, with the rhythmical sound of the horse's hooves and the slow steps of the black-clothed mourners. The hot sun made everything shine and sparkle—the tricolour flag unfurled, the brass pieces on the ornate tawdry hearse with its dusty black feathers, but on all sides covered with red and white roses, which filled the dusty road with their magnificent perfume, scenting the hot day as if one were in a garden.

Clop... clop... clop... clop... went the hooves of M. Fournier's white horse, the grizzled, white-haired carter who had delivered my coal and drunk in my cider press dozing in the hot sun. Clop... clop... clop... clop. On either side of the hearse softly trod the strong men who at the cemetery would lift the coffin, strong men, none stronger than one with curly pieces of hair encircling his baldness—the woodcutter Rettol; another, tall, rather gawky in a Sunday set of strange-fitting clothes—his son-in-law Bouveau.

Clop... clop... clop... clop. Here, on the outskirts of the marshland, was Mlle Lefranc's small villa, where the elder Bouveau, with bullets in his thighs, leaving a long trail of blood, dragged himself after the battle in the doll's house where he had hidden the British parachutists. On the other side of the road was the mean row of houses in one of which lived the Goguette, widow of my first farmer, reduced to penury after being rich, obliged as part of her rent to milk the owner's cow night and morning.

Clop... clop... clop... clop. Magnificent plane trees with boughs trained to form six-armed candlesticks, not yet in leaf but proclaiming amazingly the art of the expert gardener. How sweet smelt the roses from Nice and Monte Carlo where today, why yes, today, there is carnival! It is mid-Lent. He died on the first day of spring. He is being buried on carnival day. Something in this thought made me less sad. One is more certain of resurrection on a feast day.[69]

Going back to the authorship issue, Mé assumed in *Matilda and the Chickens* that her entitlement to the sole authorship of *A Farm in Normandy* and *The Return to the Farm* was proven, though this wasn't at all the case. Here is what she writes:

My first books I had asked my husband to sign because I was bashful. In *A Farm in Normandy* I made it appear that I was the narrator and I even composed a dedication from him to me. [...] Though I continued this rather stupid subterfuge in *A Village in Piccadilly* [...] I soon found it impossible to prevent my femininity from coming out. I was never comfortable writing like my distinguished compatriot George Sand in the masculine gender. Now that on each new title page the prefix Mrs preceded my name an immense thankfulness had taken hold of me. I had never been so proud of being a woman. I felt immediately capable of deeper thought and altogether more serious work.[70]

The mix of past tenses in this passage masks the strict truth of the situation. Bob wrote those early books partly from her drafts and partly from his, she didn't write them on her own. What is more, the female prefix appeared for the first time on the title page of *Philippa* published as recently as July 1949, not in some distant past as suggested by her pluperfect 'had'. The only book produced since *Philippa* was *A Film Star in Belgrave Square*, which can hardly qualify as 'deeper thought and more serious work' despite its many qualities.

Neither can *Matilda and the Chickens*, which is a fairly typical Henrey mixture of portraits, topographical descriptions, reconstructed dialogues and (auto)biographical information. To this basic brew are adjoined unexpectedly for the first time a number of earthy conversations concerning price fluctuations, leases, manure, woodcutting, hay making, artificial insemination, tree felling, animal traction, cider making, farm machinery etc. Madeleine is supposed to have had these palavers with the local males. Yet as has already been pointed out such man-to-woman talk, particularly with monetary implications, was inconceivable anywhere in the French countryside in 1949. It would not have been condoned in a Norman village by the menfolk and even less by their wives before the 1980s at the earliest. One is forced to conclude that these discussions took place with Bob and were transposed by him writing as Madeleine.

This being so, the reference to 'deeper thought and more serious work' becomes comprehensible. Elsewhere one reads, and this is Mé writing:

> I had put down in a notebook some scenes of my girlhood in Paris, and they suddenly struck me with their background of apaches and burning-eyed girls, fights and passionate love scenes as splashes of hot, human colour of some value to record. I decided to call this *The Little Madeleine* and to tell the whole of my girlhood courageously and in detail, through all our picturesque poverty and tribulations, till we left Montmartre and the bastion walls of Paris for a new life in Soho, and this book, which I would make long and exciting and vital, because true, I started immediately to write before this one was finished, so intent was I on the idea.[71]

What this means is that while Bob was polishing off *Matilda and the Chickens* on his typewriter at one end of the upstairs corridor, Mé in bed at the other end—with Bobby running wild outdoors not far from the benevolent eye of his Grand'mère and the old gardener—was busily penning the big book of reminiscences for which she would become world famous.

Meanwhile *Matilda and the Chickens* was delivered and contracted on 10 September 1949 and came out in May 1950 at 15s. Mé dedicated it in a letter from the Carrington House address to 'My dear Jean Lorimer' stating: 'You and I are both women who earn our living from the pen, I by writing, you on the executive side of our great magazines.' In fact they had known each other when Mé and Bob were writing *The Siege of London* and Lorimer was a Condé-Nast features editor at the *Tatler*. Mé claimed in the *Matilda* dedication that she had 'long promised' Lorimer a book, and hoped that 'our Norman orchards' would give her sophisticated fashion friend—who would later ghostwrite the memoirs of Helena Rubinstein—'a few happy hours of relaxation', which seems rather doubtful all things considered.

There weren't many reviews of *Matilda*. Vernon Fane in the *Sphere* liked it, writing: 'It reveals her own personality just as surely as the characters of the countryside she describes in every chapter.' The *Scotsman* wrote: 'Mrs Henrey takes the unusual line of drawing her characters direct from life, so that visitors to her neighbourhood can see the originals for themselves if they care. She writes naively, apparently just as topics come into her mind, trivialities jostling for room with matters of life and death. But if her book rambles, it rambles pleasantly and is enhanced by Diana Stanley's telling little studies in black and white.'[72]

Madeleine in the Spotlight

THE FAMILY RETURNED to Carrington House in August 1949 to discover that London Films didn't quite know what to do with Bobby. Korda had a problem with his old friend Karl Hartl, whose unsuccessful *Der Engel mit der Posaune* was to be remade in English with a different director. The equation was solved when Korda got wind of a story, said to be by Hartl, about a musical child prodigy exploited by an unscrupulous impresario. In the context of the child performer controversy, it had interesting political overtones as well as its obvious moral issues. Hartl was hired to direct it in Austria starring Bobby.

The script was concocted by Hollywood screenwriter Gene Markey, latest husband of the actress Myrna Loy. The title he suggested—*The Wonder Kid,* along '*Wunderkind*' lines—wasn't inspired, but neither was his screenplay, and much of the acting was over-dramatic or downright bad. Bobby was no longer the cute little boy audiences had loved in *The Fallen Idol*—like Lewis Carroll's Alice he had grown and grown—and Hartl was no Carol Reed capable of coaxing an untrained juvenile into giving an unforgettable performance.

The adults were Elwyn Brook-Jones, an all-purpose repertory actor who had played Butcher Cumberland in Korda's epic flop *Bonnie Prince Charlie,* the elderly Muriel Aked known in the trade for her innumerable supporting roles, and young Oskar Werner with ten years to go till he became Truffaut's Jules alongside Henri Serre as Jim. There was also a young couple played by Robert Shackleton, a Broadway musical comedy actor who was trying to make it in movies, and a novice girl journalist from Vienna called Anne-Marie who was billed as Christa Winter. Under Hartl's direction, this cast produced an early attempt at a children's adventure movie featuring a pantomime villain, two young lovers, a gang of lovable scoundrels, a pair of old codgers and a Rintintin dog. Today it's rather embarrassing to watch except for its splendid photography of Tyrolean landscapes.

The deal for Bobby was the same as for *The Fallen Idol*: salary, upkeep, expenses and a governess. Via Gabbitas & Thring, familiar to W. H. Auden readers ('Letter to Lord Byron', IV, 19, 7) as Rabbitarse & String, Mé engaged Margaret Duncan—a twenty-five-year-old Aberdeen graduate who had taught at Heathfield girls' school at Ascot. Miss Duncan's unenviable job was to tutor the boy, who had been growing like an untended weed among the cattle in Normandy for over a year, to the standard required for the Eton entrance examination in 1952, for which he had naturally been 'down' since birth.

The book Mé penned about their trip was entitled *A Journey to Vienna*, a not-so-distant echo of Bob's title *A Journey to Gibraltar* written in 1942. Mé stated that she undertook the book for women less fortunate than herself, 'women who so long for adventure and yet, through no fault of their own, are tied down to dull surroundings'.[73] It was dedicated 'To my fellow members of the Society of Women Journalists'. This reads as if the Mrs Robert Henrey on the title page was a long-standing member of this institution, when in fact she had only just been admitted at the instigation of Julia Cairns.

All that 'my husband' does in this book is see his wife and Bobby off at Victoria and get sent a letter or two. However, family documents prove that Bob joined Mé and Bobby in Thiersee and Vienna for Christmas 1949 and that they all flew back together from Vienna to Paris and London once the Austrian footage was in the can. This surprising first-time exclusion of the writer's husband from the narrative, in which other women's husbands are mentioned over forty times, was presumably due to Mé's new posture as an independent authoress.

The acceptance contract was signed on 30 March 1950 and the book came out the following November as a Christmas gift offer.[74] Few reviewers bothered with it, none at all in London it seems. The *Irish Independent* gave it two columns, unexpectedly. *Country Life* in Bath just said: 'Like all Mrs Henrey's travel books, this one is full of vitality and clear seeing.'

As a travelogue it's not a non-book, but it *is* encumbered with self-centred trivialities. It didn't sell. Presumably the housebound housewives for whom it was written felt little sympathy for a puffed-up authoress swanning about Mittel-Europa with her £30,000 wonder kid. To be fair on Mé, she did try to get the film's title changed to avoid criticism and was nicely told to mind her own business. The movie flopped anyway when it was eventually released in 1952, and this was most unfair on Bobby, who did a pretty good job on the whole in unfavourable circumstances. Korda's contract, however much it was really worth, was never heard of again, and Bobby's brief film career was over except for the lasting damage he felt it did to his life.

On 5 December 1950 Mé took part in a 'Vista of Fashion Through 200 Years' pageant organised at the New Theatre by Doris Langley Moore to publicise her Museum of Costume in the presence of the Queen and Princess Margaret. The detective novelist Dorothy Sayers walked on at the show dressed as a suffragette, but almost all the other participants except Mé were famous actresses—Edith Evans, Claire Bloom, Dorothy Dickson, Margaret Rawlings, Irene Worth.

According to *Country Life*: 'The early Victorian blonde satin worn by Mrs Robert Henrey with the long-sleeved bodice draped with a white lace pelerine and a lace "fall" over the hair recalled the illustrations of Dearest in *Little Lord Fauntleroy*.'[75] Reading this, one wonders whether there wasn't some kind of ladies' tea party scheme to haul Bobby on to the stage in his Fauntleroy concert outfit from *The Wonder Kid*. If this was so, it's to be hoped that Bob, who had just joined the London *Star* as features editor after a spell at the farm and a bout of chicken pox, said no.

* * *

In Elizabeth Bowen, who had covered all their titles up to *Philippa* in her weekly book pages in the *Tatler*, the Henreys had lost a trusted ally. She had ceased reviewing at the end of March 1950 in order to give more time to writing books of her own. As her editor wrote when she left after nine years on the paper, its staff and readers were losing the company of 'a good woman, an erudite and kindly reviewer, and a great contemporary novelist'.

There's no way of knowing what this most secretive of autobiographers, almost the opposite of Mé, would have made of the Bobby film star business and Mé's new self-conscious authoress pose. However, there's every chance that the three stories that were to come out in rapid succession from the House of Henrey in 1951 would have met with her approval because, like her own art, they are true records of places and people. She had for some time been urging her Henrey friends to abandon their novelised third-person Reyhen narratives and go for straight autobiography.

So *The Little Madeleine* came back from Villers in the first person and was immediately accepted by Dent on 10 September 1949. Contractually speaking, the story should have been published within twelve months, taking things to September 1950 at the latest. However, when news of a second Bobby Henrey film broke in October 1949, *A Journey to Vienna* was set in motion for Christmas 1950 instead of *The Little Madeleine*, which was held over to the following spring. More than likely Bob was also anxious, while Mé and Bobby were away in Austria, to give Madeleine a final polish before she went to the printer's.

* * *

THE LITTLE MADELEINE eventually came out in March 1951.[76] The dedication page carried the inscription:

> This is the story of my girlhood.
> No fact has been altered.
> Each character bears his, or her, own name.

Well, this isn't quite exact. There are quite a few fibs in the book. Some were intended to spare her mother's feelings. For instance, Mathilde was unmarried when Mé/Madeleine was born, and her marriage to Émile two years later was an expedient to raise her daughter, who probably wasn't his. The book says quite the opposite. Other fibs belong to the domain of poetic licence: Mé was born in Paris and grew up in grotty Clichy, not in picturesque Montmartre as the book states Madeleine was. Fibs like these don't count as untruths, though, because they are accessories to a story that is essentially true.

As for the names, Mathilde is called 'Matilda' because some camouflage was deemed necessary to save her face. That was how her Alsatian father pronounced her name anyway. She disliked it, perhaps for that reason. Her sister Marguerite is named 'Margaret' on page twenty-six, but this error is later corrected. (Names do at times get irritatingly translated in the Henreys' books, Pierre into Peter and so on, just as foreign monetary values are invariably expressed in sterling and 'Madame Henrey' for instance is translated as 'Ma'am Henrey' for local colour.) Other names in *The Little Madeleine* are withheld, such as that of the Belgian count who introduces Madeleine to the Savoy. This omission is exceptional, however, and one is constantly astonished by the way the Henreys portray and name people in their books as imperturbably as they did in their newspaper days.

Considering its profession of authenticity, perhaps the most striking artifice in this book, as in them all, is the use of reconstructed dialogue. For instance, the scene in which Marie-Thérèse reappears in Rue Marcadet carrying her baby Rolande in her shawl is told as follows:

'Is he up there?' queried Marie-Thérèse in a whisper.
　'Yes,' answered Matilda.
　'I know,' said Marie-Thérèse. 'Mme Berthier came out of the café to warn me. It was she who called out to you.'
　Matilda looked round, and in spite of the stifling night she was as nervous, as trembling, as her sister.
　'Wait!' she exclaimed. 'I'll go and see what I can do!'
　My mother came back very white, her lips twitching, and as she stood in the doorway, not yet brave enough to speak, Émile said sharply, looking up from his paper:
　'What a time you've been! Gossiping again?'
　'Émile, listen to me! Marie-Thérèse is downstairs.'
　'I told you I never wanted to see her again!' said Émile, throwing down his paper and getting ready to roll up his sleeves.[77]

This episode must have occurred while in actual fact little Madeleine aged less than two was still in foster care in Soissons. How can the reader accept that the narrator, being Madeleine, knew what happened and what was said as recounted here? The ready answer is because her mother, Marie-Thérèse, Mme Berthier or

Émile told her these things when she was old enough to record them in her memory or write them down. But could these details have resurfaced accurately more than forty years later? Probably not. Though the gift of memory in some people—actors, musicians, doctors, lawyers—can give astounding results, the real answer regarding the authenticity of stories isn't in the writing but in the reading. The reader, caught up in the narrative, is prepared to grant the narrator the benefit of the doubt.

'No facts have been altered' doesn't in any case mean that no details have been imagined. The Marie-Thérèse episode is actually commented by the narrator in these terms: 'No happy turn of events had yet come in the novel of Marie-Thérèse's existence and indeed it seemed that the story might that same evening end in a suicide.' Novel, story: the poetic intention is announced clearly enough. When a way with words transmutes facts into emotions it surely doesn't exclude the pursuit of truth.

On the factual level, the timeline in *The Little Madeleine* is as difficult to retrace as in the rest of the Henrey books. A wedding day recorded as a Saturday turns out to have been a Tuesday when checked on a perpetual calendar. Years rarely figure in the dates they give and have to be worked out from other indications such as characters' age or time elapsed between two events. Months have sometimes to be deduced from seasonal information. Historicity—the way facts come about and their status in time—isn't the Henreys' subject. What they are interested in is the higher reality of themselves and other people relative to each other and their environment, in the way they contrive to survive or not in the face of misfortune, illness or age.

Roughly speaking, *The Little Madeleine* spans the years 1906 to 1926, from Madeleine's birth to the death of her aunt Marie-Thérèse. There's some fudging at the start, middle and end of this period. Madeleine is said on page five to have been born before her cousin Rolande. Rolande was in fact born in 1907, a year after Mé, when Émile was supposedly married to Mathilde and when in fact Émile and Mathilde got married in 1908. This intricate fudge has a sole purpose: it conceals Mathilde's unmarried status at the birth of Madeleine in 1906. The middle fudge hides Mathilde's failed second marriage in London, which isn't even hinted at. (It was portrayed in the spin-off *An Exile in Soho* a few months later.) And the end fudge states that Madeleine started at the Savoy in October 1926, when the real date was February the following year. This final fudge masks the fact (revealed in *A Girl at Twenty*) that she got engaged and nearly married to a young Italian in Soho before she was swept off her feet by her Savoy millionaires and intrepid Robert Henrey. But honestly who cares? What the reader of Madeleine wants is the story of a life, not its history.

The biographer, critic and occasional detective novelist C. E. Vulliamy went to town on *The Little Madeleine* in the 9 March number of the *Spectator*. He began by denouncing the 'splendid mediocrity' of books in his day: 'They represent, one may say, a high level of utility goods.' (That grumble sounds rather familiar seventy years on.) He continued:

> This fine book, written by a Frenchwoman in English, transcends by many degrees the common level; it is a work of considerable art, revealing many of the qualities of great literature and among them a control of the English vocabulary such as few modern writers possess. The acute eye may perceive an occasional Gallicism, the use of a word that is no longer current and even slightly archaic, but there can be no question of making allowance for Mrs Henrey's nationality; her book has the vivid immediacy of direct observation, with all the grace, insight and accomplishment of a practiced writer.

Vulliamy reckoned that the book had a dual nature. 'By some curious mastery the book seems to combine the skills of two languages. The medium is English; the vision and experience and the characteristic vitality of detail are French. It is a translation of French thought into English literature of extraordinary aptitude. Only an amazing degree of bilingual competence could have produced this brilliant and entirely satisfying result.'

On reflection, this remark is less trite than it sounds. Vulliamy, a veteran of the London publishing scene, was aware that Bob and Mé worked together and that of the two the real wordsmith was Bob ('By some curious mastery...'). So one can but wholeheartedly concur when he writes: 'What is particularly delightful and remarkable in this book is the union of imaginative reconstruction with authentic record.' Vulliamy's final judgement must nonetheless remain his own responsibility, however much one would like to agree with him: 'In many ways, if not in every way, a great book.' Lavish praise indeed from a respected reviewer.

E. V. Knox, editor of *Punch* magazine from 1932 to 1949, who had just taken over his friend Elizabeth Bowen's books pages in the *Tatler*, wrote: 'Mrs Robert Henrey has a prodigious memory, and one so vivid that scenes, conversations and characters, known in early youth, appear to be the product of immediate observation by an onlooker, or a brilliant reconstruction, rather than that strange confusion which is all that most of us can summon up from the mist of childhood's years.' Knox's conclusion was that 'the number of people who come into the book, their ailments and their enjoyments, their deaths would be baffling and even tiresome, if they were not so excellently seen, and so unforgettably described.'

The *Listener*'s 'Books Chronicle' wrote:

> From the first page of this long autobiography the reader is netted, is emotionally and imaginatively involved in another world, another time. Nobody, confronted with such aliveness, is going to bother much with the faults of Mrs Henrey's account of her childhood in France, for faults it has. It is surely too long, too crowded, confused, cumbersome, too cluttered up with detail and not really well-written. Mrs Henrey is writing—as few of us could—in a language not her own; and her English is sometimes (excusably) unsure, involved, inapt. The French keeps coming through with odd effects. Strange words creep in now and again. But all this is dimmed, swept aside by the book's extraordinary power to convey pictures and call up feeling.

The *Times Literary Supplement*'s anonymous reviewer (identified today as David Tylden-Wright) thought much the same as the *Listener*'s:

> Frequently Mrs Henrey is sorry for herself, often she is sentimental, nor does she spare the reader any detail, however intimate or insignificant, of her daily life. She thus tells not only how her tonsils were cut out without an anaesthetic but of her sufferings from scabies. [...] Yet with all her faults, and few successful writers have more, she gives a vivid impression of the strength needed to struggle against the contagion of a life that is too cramped and confined.

Several of the many articles on record found Madeleine's encyclopedic recollections tiresome, such as this one in the *Sunday Times* by Margaret Lane, biographer of Beatrix Potter and several other writers:

> Even if this 'total recall' is real and not embroidered, is it not, for our friends, the least little bit of a bore? Mrs Henrey has an enviable gift for making friends with her reader. [...] If one is so disobliging as to object at all to her artless and sometimes moving tale in *The Little Madeleine*, she does run on. Scores of characters are introduced, named, described, followed for a page or two and then forgotten. Neighbours, sempstresses, blanchisseuses, road sweepers, shopkeepers, concierges, prostitutes flit in and out of her packed, conversational page, so that one is constantly trying to remember who Uncle Louis is, or Mme Laparge, or whether Louise is any relation of Ernestine.

Perfectly true, particularly as this reviewer picked up the fundamental nature of the Madeleine books: 'Her attitude to life is warm, inquisitive and uncensorious—very un-English, in fact—and she has the poet's essential delirium that every detail of life is a separate marvel.'

Even when they missed that the book's Frenchness and its apparent artlessness are part of its meaning, reviews such as these were gratifying no doubt. However, there were hints among the pack that Mrs Robert Henrey's prolific output was beginning to grate. Novelist Howard Spring salted his favourable critique in *Country Life* with this small sarcasm: 'There appears to be nothing that comes amiss to Mrs Henrey as material for a readable book: a farm in France, a parson's life in England, a journey to Vienna, the making of a film. It was inevitable that sooner or later her own early days would be used, and here the book is at last.'

The ultimate accolade came when *The Little Madeleine* was made a Book Society choice. This meant an extra order of at least 10,000 copies for the Society's members plus a celebrity guarantee in bookshops, libraries and the press. The title was reprinted twice within a month of publication, adapted for radio, serialised, translated. In its first year in Britain alone it sold 40,000 copies. It went through eight impressions and remained constantly in print until 1985. The BBC Home Service broadcast a radio adaptation by Mollie Greenhaighe read by Cecile Chevreau in fifteen weekly instalments starting 9 February 1961.

* * *

WHEN THE HENREYS CAME BACK FROM VIENNA in 1950, Bobby was almost eleven. A reporter from the *Sunday Mirror* came to interview him on 26 February and found him in a pretty pickle:

> Bobby struck me as being shy, although that didn't hinder our talk, for Mrs Henrey was never lost for his reply. [...] Mrs Henrey, a widely travelled, intelligent woman, has very definite ideas on the way a boy should be brought up. Are her ideas right? I don't think so. Bobby Henrey is a nice kid. But he needs the companionship of other children. Nice, rough, noisy kids who will knock the smooth edges off him. Otherwise, when he grows up and finds his own feet, he's going to find this a cruel and unfriendly world.

As it happened, that was exactly what fate had in store for him. His parents had no intention of leaving their Mayfair flat. Its address was known worldwide thanks to their books. It was also cheap, flattering and convenient. Partly because there was literally no room there for Bobby, partly because he needed serious cramming if he was to get through the Eton entrance examination in 1952, as his father expected of him without having done all that much to prepare him for it, he was abruptly enrolled at Northaw preparatory school at Surrenden Dering near Pluckley in Kent.[78] The place was run on military lines by a Major Reynolds, an army chum of Field Marshal Lord Montgomery of Alamein. Monty regularly turned up on sports day from Switzerland laden with Toblerone chocolates for the prize winners and was entertained at lunch by the school singing 'Lili Marlene' while he ate his pudding. Bobby's ineptitude at sports due to his short-sightedness didn't endear him to the gym instructor, Sergeant-Major Sandal. Having grown up among intelligent adults, he was unprepared for the apple pie beds and shrieks of mirth of boarding school life. His difference from the prep school culture, not to mention his movie fame, let him in for ragging and scragging by the tribal majority. When he fought back, his flailings only compounded his difficulties.

In later life, he wrote that this was one of the most unpleasant periods of his life. He felt abandoned by his parents but kept his spirits up knowing that there were holidays. At the end of each term he was sent immediately back to Normandy. His Grand'mère always welcomed him and made him feel he was the most important person in the world. Each of his returns to the farm was a reprieve, a journey back to his roots. He dreaded having to go back to London. He wrote: 'There was a routine to the miserable business of having to go back to school that included the night spent on a mattress in the Mayfair flat and being taken to Waterloo station for the afternoon train.'[79] When the time came for him to sit the elaborate written exam for Eton, he failed it, and his parents were told he would not be given a second chance. Bob was deeply hurt. He felt that his beloved Eton had let him down.

By a stroke of luck, Mé had a Mayfair friend who was in a position to pull strings at Downside School in Somerset. The monks agreed to take Bobby in Lent Term 1953 if he continued at Northaw and passed the common entrance exam in November. Fair enough, but two weeks after the autumn term started at Northaw, on 10 October 1952, the old manor house went up in flames with the whole school looking on in the dead of night. Those boys who, like Bobby, were due to sit Common Entrance were billeted out among the local inhabitants and taught in what had been the stables. He remembered it as a thoroughly enjoyable experience without the irksomeness that had made the school a misery. He did well enough in the exam and was duly entrained at Paddington the following January to join the fourth form at his new school in rural Somerset, where he settled down in Smythe House until it was time for his pre-Oxford in-between year in 1957. His true home during this whole period was the farm.

Mé had always been a possessive mother coupled with a caustic critic, unconsciously reproducing her own love-hate relationship with Mathilde. Bob was far more relaxed about the educational process. All he asked was that his son should go to Eton and afterwards earn his living somewhere somehow, preferably as a journalist. Bobby wasn't given any choice in this or any other matter. One cannot help thinking that, on the whole, it was probably a good thing he was sent away to barbarian Northaw. His parents were so preoccupied with their writing—the next few years were to be their heyday—that they had little time to guide him. Downside turned out to be a godsend in this respect, and there was always the nurturing presence back at the farm.

It so happened that Maître Vincent telephoned to Bob and Mé in London that Mme Victor Duprez's model farm Berlequet had come on the market in 1951 as part of her divorce settlement. The house itself was long and low, set in a hedged field by the lane at the top of their land with its outbuildings and kitchen garden. Two separate fields to the south adjoined the Henreys' land straddling the stream. Maître Vincent thought they should buy. The whole amounting to some seven hectares would increase their holding to over eighteen, which was quite sizable in the Vallée d'Auge. Above all, it would bring in a separate farmhouse. Mé immediately thought it would be ideal for Jacques Déliquaire to live in with his pretty half-Ukrainian wife Georgette. The young couple were still housed following the old Norman peasant tradition by the husband's parents in their farm beyond the stream. Reinstalled at Berlequet as the Henreys' farmers they could be independent while keeping an eye on the other house and on arthritic Mathilde when Bobby wasn't around.

So Bob and Mé bought Berlequet. They also bought a diamond solitaire to celebrate the success of *The Little Madeleine*. As Dent like all publishers paid out royalties six months (or more) in arrears, these splurges along with Bobby's school fees hit their savings quite hard. In the terse end of year review Bob was in the habit of writing to himself, he noted gloomily for 1951: 'Only £3,000 in the bank.'

* * *

PALOMA CAME OUT FROM DENT in November 1951 at 15*s*.[80] Nothing quite like it had been done before. The only reviewers of note—E. V. Knox, Vernon Fane, Marghanita Laski—found it 'almost impossible to convey the quality of this remarkable work', judged its 'feminine and intuitive approach' difficult to describe, granted it 'a charm of its own', declared it 'convincing and entertaining', praised its 'frequent felicity of phrase' and left things at that. Nancy Spain enthused about it inaccurately in *Good Housekeeping*, but she was a friend. Dent's adverts alone struck the right note: 'In Paloma the author turns from her autobiographical *The Little*

Madeleine, revealing a new facet of her literary skill.'

Literary skill indeed. The story is told as a series of short conversation scenes in two acts—first in the Green Park and two or three Mayfair apartments, then in Saulieu in Burgundy—linked by sparse narrative passages with a long central chapter. The unfolding investigative technique sets out to answer the question: 'Who is this mystery woman called Paloma encountered by chance in the Green Park in 1944?' The narrator is a feminine 'I' copiously referred to as Madeleine. She has a husband who is conveniently 'away'. Her child has a walk-on part with one short line to say. Her farm and her mother are mentioned in one word once each. The usual 'I' is on stage, then, but not lavishly so, and the reader is intriguingly baffled by her nipping around the set as the lights go up and down on one zone after another as in a modern scenography.

The real heroine is this Paloma, an odd old character about whom Madeleine and the reader discover successive life details as they are hinted at. One's first impression, quickly mitigated, is that Paloma is a mythomaniac, supposedly raised from peasant origins in Burgundy to a life of pampered luxury as a Gaiety Girl in Edwardian London, loved and lodged by a succession of amusing Stage-Door Johnnies, dukes and such—one of whom, she says, remembered her in his most considerable and highly considerate pre–1914 will. She still has a doting old bachelor who visits, wines, dines, and takes her to the theatre every Thursday when in town. Rich, with a flat in Bloomsbury (condescendingly referred to by Mayfair 'I' as 'a district which at the beginning of the century was very fashionable for having a flat'), she is both thrifty and spendthrift, dressing in a kind of sack with zips except on her nights out, throwing pound notes and cheques around though squabbling about the price of a trifle. Her language is affected, old-fashioned, outspoken and quaintly French.

The narrative reveals, checks and records every fact learned about this fascinating creature and her constellation of snobs and humble folk, whose own lives are sketched in as they appear: Emma, Gabrielle, Mr Stephen and the rest. 'I' herself gradually finds out, even going down to Burgundy to investigate, that 'the things she had told me were true', that Paloma 'never told an untruth'.[81] The final chapters in Saulieu after Paloma's death are

movingly elegiac, a sensitive woman's farewell to a woman she
loved—probably because she found so much in her that she found
also in herself.

There's an epigraphical inscription, strangely composed by the
Temple Press typographers. It sets a preliminary emotional tone,
rather like a key signature at the head of a musical score, presumably at Mé's behest:

If ever
you go to Saulieu (Côte d'Or) on
the fringe of the Burgundy country,
and climb the hill above the grey
town with its crooked streets, ask
to see the tomb of Marie Siller
(Saquet was her maiden name)
whose strange story, because I loved
her, I here tell.

After this, some people might regret the dedication:

Very affectionately for
YAKY
the
Begum Aga Khan

But that sort of stuff was Madeleine, too. Begum Yaky, formerly
Yvette Labrousse, Miss France 1929, climbed from obscurity to
luxury by being a lovely woman and by getting loved. Her kinship
with Paloma and indeed with Madeleine herself must have been
obvious in 1950.

More meaningfully for style-minded readers, the first sentence
in *Paloma* is remarkable for being the longest in the corpus:

Towards the end of one of those interminable days in 1944, when we
were expecting the invasion of France, hot, windy, keyed-up days
spent queuing at food shops, and uselessly discussing the varying
merits of opposing armies, I looked up from my sewing, and meeting
the lifted eyes of my restless pekinese, thrust needle and stuff aside,
unhooked the harness from a nail in the kitchen, and fastening it on
the overjoyed animal led him through Shepherd Market, up that dark
narrow alley known as Whitehorse Street, across almost deserted

Piccadilly, into the freshness of the Green Park.

As for the book's relationship with truth, it has to be said that all the facts recorded in the story, when checked, turn out to match history, except that the Saquet family's Marie, aka 'Paloma Garcia' of the pre–1914 Adelphi Girls lineup ('seventh from the left'), had two sisters, both of whom met their destiny with rich men in Paris as she did. The adorable Louise was really called Marie-Louise. She liked wine too much and had to be rescued by her sisters. The magnificent Joséphine was known to the registry of births and deaths as Reine ('Queen'), which somehow seems apt—she was the pampered mistress of the famous actor Benoît-Constant Coquelin, the original Cyrano de Bergerac. Back in Saulieu the three sisters' father was a clog maker.

* * *

A LONG SEQUEL to *The Little Madeleine* came out from Dent in May 1952 entitled *Madeleine Grown Up*. The contract was signed on 21 May 1951.[82] The jacket reproduced a watercolour drawing by Phyllis Ginger showing Mé in a black tailor-made and a little black hat crossing the busy Strand from Southampton Street to start work at the Savoy in 1927. Bob loved this picture and asked

Ginger to redraw it several times, which wasn't easy. Though hard to make out, the news vendor's board in the doorway of number 378 Strand seems to read anachronistically: 'Starring BOBBY HENREY' next to an *Evening News* poster.

Like the reissues to be discussed later, *Madeleine Grown Up* bore a dedicatory message 'From the Authoress to the Reader' explaining that it carried on the story of her life from her going to the Savoy as a manicurist in February 1927 to her marriage at St George's, Hanover Square, on 1 December 1928. For the first time this dedication was signed, not 'Mrs Robert Henrey' as usual, but 'Madeleine Henrey'.

Perhaps to boost her sales, she made a sortie into the feminist arena at this time, writing to the papers and speaking in radio interviews about her belief that women should remain 'womanly' while asserting their independence. Her viewpoint was applauded in the 17 May 1951 issue of the *Spectator* as 'admirable and true' by Angus Wilson, who wrote:

Women have too often been chasing a *fata morgana*, and in the effort to assume the position of men are imperilling their own future happiness. [...] In their own field—which is different from a man's—they are far more capable than he is, but the home, with all the lovely things that should surround it, is a woman's natural place, and she will never find full satisfaction in any other field. She should refuse to surrender her true liberty for the demands of the so-called Welfare State.

The *Illustrated London News* reviewer of *Madeleine Grown Up* played along with the new Madeleine: 'What strikes one most is the femininity. This writer is professionally feminine. She values all success, but her ideal and passion is success in womanhood. And she regards it as a job of work.' E. V. Knox in the *Tatler* wrote: 'Perhaps what attracts us most is that anyone so profoundly interested in every trifle of dress and deportment, of gaiety and luxurious living, should also be so deeply and tenderly sympathetic towards the little sorrows and troubles of her friends.' Vernon Fane in the *Sphere* contributed what was expected of him: 'It will amaze none of her admiring readers that the author has managed to colour her tale with humour, with great vitality and with that most disarming honesty of hers. Recommended with enthusiasm.'

Humour? Perhaps Fame had special spectacles.

C. E. Vulliamy in the *Spectator* of 5 May 1952 back-pedalled slightly on his eulogy of *The Little Madeleine*: 'I think it may be doubted whether Mrs Henrey has again risen to the same level. [...] Something has been subtracted; something is disturbingly absent. Perhaps it is the reassuring touch of satire that would have put the pomps and vanities of this wicked world in their proper place.' Of course Vulliamy the insider knew that the 'something subtracted' and 'disturbingly absent' was the wit and social malice of 'the masterful, blue-eyed Robert' mentioned earlier in his review.

Madeleine Grown Up was read by Rosemary Davies in fourteen daily instalments on the BBC Home Service 'Morning Serial' programme starting on 5 August 1952.

Mé and little Bobby in bombed Stacey Street, 1945

PART THREE

Playing the Market

The Authorship Issue

THE YEAR 1952 marked a watershed in the Henreys' literary partnership. It coincided with Mé's first big bout of bibliographical revisionism. A smaller convulsion (with deplorable results in library catalogues) had occurred in 1949 with the addition of the 'Mrs' prefix to Robert Henrey's name. A bigger one came this year with a new impression of *A Village in Piccadilly* and a combined edition of the farm books. A still bigger one would come in New York in 1954 (and in London in 1960) with an omnibus reissue of what Dent had taken to calling 'Her London Trilogy'. The amazing aim on all these occasions was to expunge pre-existing indications of joint authorship, i.e. to oust Bob from the books: a literary 'Kill Bill'-like operation half a century ahead of time, or perhaps more aptly Mé doing a latter-day Colette on Willy.

The first revisionary demonstration came in March 1952 with the sixth impression of *A Village in Piccadilly*. Here is the message that Dent printed on a new page vii:

From the Authoress to the Reader

This book, originally published under the male pseudonym 'Robert Henrey', was written by me during the summer of 1942, partly from my own experiences, partly as the result of conversations with my husband on the eve of his departure for the Middle East. On reading these pages again before the printing of the sixth impression my chief problem was to explain how I, a woman writer, had come to choose this curious form of self-expression. The truth is that both *A Village in Piccadilly* and its predecessor by a few months *A Farm in Normandy* were experiments in writing. Then a harassed refugee mother with a baby child, I had no desire for my own name to come before the public. Later these two books tended to impede my rise as an authoress. In allowing this volume to go out once more into the world, I think it is only fair that I should add this explanation. The Madeleine of this book is myself, the 'I' was my husband. The only excuse I can find for its reissue is that it was written in the heat of the moment with an atmosphere that today I could not hope to recapture.

Mrs Robert Henrey.
  2 Carrington House,
  Hertford Street,
  Piccadilly, W.1.
  February 1952.

Mé was clearly not on top of things when she wrote this strange harangue. The facts are known, and they just don't support her assertions. Only part of *A Village in Piccadilly* and even less of *A Farm in Normandy* were written by her, most of the finished job having been done by Bob from her drafts and his. He never went to the Middle East, unless Gibraltar qualifies as such. By posing as 'a harassed refugee mother with a baby child' Mé is laying it on—there were plenty of people around to help her. Professionally speaking, these two books could surely not have 'tended to impede [her] rise as an authoress' any more than George Sand's pseudonym impeded hers. The crux comes no doubt in the penultimate sentence: 'The Madeleine of this book is myself, the 'I' was my husband'. These 'is' and 'was' verbs are sure signs of disarray, symptoms of an identity crisis.

Confirmation of this diagnosis is found in a second revisionary message published in October of the same year in the combined farm books volume:

From the Authoress to the Reader

A Farm in Normandy and *The Return to the Farm* are here published in one volume. The first was written after my flight from France in 1940: the second in the full joy of my reunion with my mother and the Norman soil at the end of the war. Originally produced under the pseudonym 'Robert Henrey' they now appear in feminine form to take their rightful place amongst my other works.
  Madeleine Henrey.
  London, 1952

Four times 'my', not once 'our'—and the signature 'Madeleine Henrey' used only once elsewhere in the corpus (in the dedication to *Madeleine Grown Up* the same year) and never used again in their books until after Bob's death.[83]

Paradoxically, each of these disputed reissues appeared under the usual author name 'Mrs Robert Henrey' and not the market unknown 'Madeleine Henrey'. Dent presumably shoved the contracts across the table when the authorship question was raised. In business terms, Martin Dent must have said, the author's name was the same as a product brand: it had been invested in, advertised, had sales value, and could not be changed without at least partially destroying it.

Anyway, the March 1952 edition of *A Village in Piccadilly* was reprinted from the original with two extra pages in the preliminaries for the harangue and its blank verso. This created some nonsense between the harangue and the text, as when Madeleine, who never had an office, is supposed to have written: 'On my way to the office...' There's more of this inconsequence elsewhere.

Additionally, the illustrations originally placed in a single signature were tipped in separately among the text with modified captions and imperfect punctuation, but somebody forgot to edit the Illustrations list accordingly. Bob would never have allowed these blunders to pass. The jacket reproduced the original scrapbook design with modified flaps. The front flap blurb made slight amends for the outspoken harangue by mentioning 'her husband'

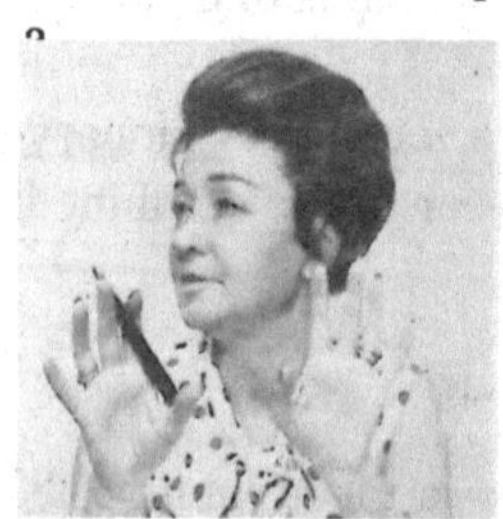

and 'the family'. The back flap author profile written almost certainly by Mé proclaimed immodestly and illogically that her early books as Robert Henrey 'placed her in the forefront of women writers'. To prove it Dent stuck in a head shot of the authoress 'Mrs Robert Henrey' looking forefrontedly feminine.

The jacket profile alleged (in rather strange English): 'The love of London flowed in her blood and resulted in her trilogy of London through the Battle of Britain and the flying bombs.' It continued clumsily in a transparently first-person third person:

The most famous of these books [...] was originally written under the male pseudonym "Robert Henrey", but later she wrote: "I was never comfortable writing in the masculine gender," and it was with a sense of immense relief that she agreed to the feminine prefix "Mrs" being added to the title pages of her books.

In April she wrote rather confusedly to the Editor of the *Sunday Times* to position herself as a 'womanly woman' in response to an article by the *ST*'s women's columnist Mary Dunbar:

SIR,—Mary Dunbar's plea ['Don't Blame the Men', 13 April 1952] that women should cease to accept the absurd position of being imitation men raises a question of immense social significance. In her brilliant article she points out that it was inevitable that during the struggle for emancipation we adopted many of the men's standards as our own. Alas, that is true, but during the Victorian and Edwardian reigns little girls had it constantly drummed into them that it was their misfortune not to be little boys.

The suffragette movement was launched to allow women to do all the things they had been taught to admire in men. To be allowed to go to the university was the first thing, but later, as all the barriers in turn fell, women flew aeroplanes to Australia, swam the Channel, and joined the Army. The passiveness of many women to be turned into near-men is, of necessity, eagerly exploited by governments in wartime to fill the factories, work the trains and buses and expand the armed forces. In peacetime also governments play on the theme of equality to bind women more firmly into the machinery of the Welfare state.

How in these circumstances can the womanly woman, the woman aware of her biological and mental differences from men, enjoy the womanly interest of her babies, her linen cupboard, her sewing and the tremendous fun of cooking amusing and healthy meals? Have we forgotten that the basis of all cooking is butter and eggs and that everything said to the contrary is nonsense? If these are short the woman will give her share to the husband and the children. Our function in life is to give. So there remain the starchy things for us, and the strong brewed tea—and that unfeminine cigarette!

Why should men, therefore, bother so much about our kitchens? Of course, not one of them would dream of allowing his factory hands to waste their time with such out-of-date tools! While men thrive on the battle of politics and grow famous if not rich, our youth fades as the flower in the field, and we still have to pinch and to queue and to cook mock foods in dark kitchens.

I do not propose any remedy. Feminine women of my kind have no pretentions [*sic*] to politics. If I write this letter it is merely as a tribute to the *Sunday Times* and Mary Dunbar for daring to say something that most people like to hush up.

MADELEINE HENREY.
(Mrs Robert Henrey.)
London, W.1.[84]

The second reissue in 1952—the combined farms volume—went still further down the revisionist road than its predecessor. Entitled *A Farm in Normandy; incorporating, The Return to the Farm* it was published in October at 15*s*.[85] There's the usual veracity claim on the verso of the dedication page: 'The characters in this autobiography are real people, each bearing his or her own name.' This isn't quite true, as neither text was conceived as an autobiography and at least one character does not bear any name at all, just an occasional label: 'my husband.'

Most astonishingly, the original farm texts were laboriously edited to remove the focus from Bob. The nameless male narrator 'I' in *A Farm in Normandy* and 'Philip' in *The Return to the Farm* are changed to a feminine 'I' called Madeleine. 'My wife' becomes 'my husband' and so on.

It's hard to say so, but in the long run this methodical inversion process seems borderline hysterical. In her desire to assert herself as a famous woman writer, Mé like many shy people reacting to extreme circumstances was just going too far. People might think that she was hurt for some reason. Or even that it was all a tax ploy of Bob's invention. Both hypotheses seem unlikely when properly considered. The plain fact is that when writing this wild stuff in 1952 she was exhausted. In thirty months since *A Journey to Vienna*, she had drafted *Matilda and the Chickens, The Little Madeleine, Paloma*, a second big autobiographical volume *Madeleine Grown Up* and a novelised portrait of her mother's second marriage *An Exile in Soho* as well as revising the farm books—a published total of some 730K words—not to mention drafting her diary *Madeleine's Journal* to be delivered in October 1952 making a further 96K words and working on her French autobiography *La petite Madeleine* due for delivery in the second trimester of

1953 (156K words). She looks tired and discouraged in a photograph published by the *Tatler* on 4 February 1953, and Fifille in her arms looks as glum as she does.

Symptoms of emotional stress and mental fatigue were built into Mé's temperament, as she readily acknowledged in her writing. This time, things seem to have reached an explosive peak coinciding with the crisis concerning Bobby's future. Bob had to cope with the fallout. How he did so is all rather mysterious in the absence of personal documents. What happened has to be induced by reading between the lines of the published books. Bob had already saved Mé's life once by sending her away to the Pyrenees to cure her lungs. He seems to have helped her through this burnout in 1952 by taking a back seat in her life or even perhaps by clearing out for a time to allow her to find herself.

Extremely low blood pressure, high irritability... In his end-of-year log for 1952, Bob wrote: 'She writes *Madeleine Grown Up* at Carrington House but nearly dies.'[86]

* * *

WITH BOBBY FINALLY ENSCONCED at Downside, Mé grabbed a breather at Gstaad in February 1953, taking 'a good deal' of work with her, mainly women's feature articles it seems. She was missing her little boy's company, writing in her diary published in September 1953 as *Madeleine's Journal*: 'I feel suddenly very lonely and long to have my son with me.' In a moment of public introspection about her career as 'a woman who thought and acted for herself', she also confided to her diary the emotional unbalance that fame brought with it:

> I was aware of a quickening tempo. My mail became larger, and the green folders from the cutting agencies fatter and more frequent. In other ways my existence in the heart of London was lonely. Presumably I myself was responsible for this state of affairs. I was far too concerned with the fear of slipping back. I am always so little satisfied that I have no capacity to enjoy the process of going forward. […] I urge myself on towards success, however, with the seriousness that distinguishes clever girls in examinations. They do try so hard! I want very much to be the head girl. I have not come all the way from the heart of Montmartre to be satisfied with a second prize.[87]

Regarding women writers' relations with men, she was highly sensitive. When the *Times Literary Supplement* 'tried to be scathing' as she put it about Madeleine 'tottering on her high heels', she jumped to the conclusion that the anonymous reviewer was a man, when in fact it was the historian Helen Elizabeth FitzRandolph. Mé wrote (p. 242): 'The conflict comes when men find it difficult to accept the reactions of feminine women. [...] What is wonderful is the great eagerness of young women to write, but their letters [to me] often betray a feminine resentment against an increasingly scientific, warlike, inhuman world—a world in which men appear almost to take pleasure in doing without women.'[88]

Was this a veiled *pro domo sua* protestation? Probably not. Bob much preferred women's company to men's and certainly took no pleasure in doing without it. As a writer himself he knew all about the loneliness of a writing career and had every reason to cherish Mé's genius for portraying people and places. If she felt lonely, it wasn't because he was out at or for the *Star* all day—he almost always had been out all day anyway—or because he was having a Fleet Street fling. She knew perfectly well that what he relished wasn't flings but good copy, and in that field she had shown that she was hard to beat. But she was jealous of other women and Bobby was away at school. And she was knackered.

* * *

IN OCTOBER 1952, immediately after *Madeleine Grown Up*, Dent brought out *An Exile in Soho* written the previous year—the contract is dated 4 December 1951.[89] Advertised as 'The Third of the Madeleine Books', it's a strange sad volume, half novel and half autobiography. In a prologue set on Derby Day 1926 Étienne Leblanc comes home to Stacey Street, where he lives with his twenty-year-old daughter. He lies down and 'remembers' the next 150 pages in flashback from his childhood in Lyons to his widowhood in Soho. There's no reference at all to Madeleine. Suddenly chapter 11 begins: 'My mother and I were sewing.' The rest of the book is Madeleine's story of her mother's brief second marriage with Étienne, their separation, Étienne's pathetic departure to Ardèche, his wretched death as an invalid jobbing gardener. Finally, in a rather contrived epilogue, Madeleine is married, living in Knightsbridge, telling about Étienne's sister and daughter in Covent Garden and his little grandson, a real Londoner.

All in all, *An Exile in Soho* is a big muddle, clearly written from the heart but not clearly thought out. As such, it's a moving story of feminine predicaments told behind a wistful mesh of male failure. Étienne doesn't really exist either as a character or as a man. He does things, a lot of things, but he doesn't convince and achieves next to nothing, like his son Eddy who fools around in Soho before disappearing into the kitchens of a transatlantic liner, or his failed artist brother-in-law Rudolph. The story is really about Étienne's sisters, beautiful Jenny and unlucky Laura, his first wife Blanche, his daughter Kitty—and Mathilde-Matilda of course, touchingly unlovable and embittered. Among them Madeleine flits around, upstaged for once except during an adventitious grocery shop adventure with hard-as-nails Aunt Marguerite in Vernantes near Saumur.

Written during that fateful period when Mé appears to have been living alone in Mayfair at Carrington House, *An Exile in Soho* is an elegy, quite unlike the other Madeleine stories which bustle with ambition and *joie de vivre*.

In common with the three books published prior to this one in the same year 1952 it bears a dedicatory 'From the Authoress to the Reader' address, unsigned. More than one reader must have found this epistle mystifying: 'He was a genius at his art [...] but he lacked what drives a man to success. He also passionately loved women. His mind was constantly taken up with them but he failed to make them happy.' Is there a veiled allusion here? And what is the meaning of the last line: 'The final scene unfolds itself'? The ambiguity of this sentence is intriguing to say the least. As for the 'accuracy' claim, it's invalidated by the fact that Étienne's family name is altered throughout from Thibert to Leblanc, the French equivalent of Smith, obviously to preserve something of Mathilde-Matilda's privacy but pointlessly so, inasmuch as 'I' presents her transparently throughout as 'my mother'.

The *Times Literary Supplement* reviewer Helen Elizabeth FitzRandolph wrote: 'In spite of many precise statements the first part of the story is vague and colourless. In the second half for the first time the people become real.' Nonetheless, according to this writer: 'Although there is much about Soho the scene isn't really

England at all. The French village in which [Madeleine and her aunt] lived for a time is far more real than anything else described.'

Under the heading 'Madeleine's Stepfather', the *Daily Telegraph* critic wrote: 'Mrs Robert Henrey's *An Exile in Soho* lacks the strongly autobiographical element of her popular Madeleine books, and suffers from disjointedness as a result.' The account of her stepfather's early life, although based on stories he told her, was described with a detail which could only be considered as fiction. Verdict: 'It is easy light reading.'

The *Illustrated London News* reviewer, observing that money appeared 'the hard condition of romance' in all Mrs Robert Henrey's books, reacted tartly to *An Exile in Soho*:

> And there we get back to the little Madeleine. In those bad times, her mother thought that life with Étienne would be less hard. When it turned out still harder, she forsook him. That drab *ménage*, with Madeleine's irrepressible ambition thrusting to the sun like grass through asphalt, is as bleak, brilliant and original as anything in the whole record. And there are charming incidents as well. But one must own it is a desultory book; and these last strokes in the rare portrait of her mother are a trifle chilling.

The BBC Home Service broadcast a Saturday Night Theatre version of *An Exile in Soho* by Thea Holme, produced by Betty Davies, starring Geoffrey Mathews and Cecile Chevreau, other parts played by members of the BBC Drama Repertory Company, on 7 April 1962.

* * *

AFTER THE FLURRY of publications in 1951–52—a new book every four months—Dent put the brakes on in an attempt to save the Mrs Robert Henrey market from saturation. There had been signs from the trade that there was a risk of this happening. The reviewers in particular had ironised on the proliferation of her titles, several insinuating that her high output was beginning to affect her quality.

Mé put this deprecatory view down to the fact that the trade was dominated by men, and that men could not readily accept the rise of an authoress. She wrote in her sole title published in London in

1953, unfortunately entitled *Madeleine's Journal*::

> There is a feeling that the quality of a writer's work depends on the slowness with which each volume appears. This, of course, is nonsense. The giants of the nineteenth century tumbled books out of the presses. You need merely consider the output of George Sand. The idea that you must take a long time between each book is modern.[90]

Whatever ideas she had on the matter, however, she had to submit to Dent's marketing sense or go to another publisher, which she had no wish to do. With Bob out of the picture she relied, perhaps unwisely, on Dent's editor E. F. Bozman, novelist and tutelary of *Everyman's Encyclopedia*. Her future publication target seems to have been set at one title per year. A new genre was defined, the 'contemporary diary', so called to distinguish it from the autobiographies and any incidental volumes she might write. It would record Mrs Robert Henrey's life year by year in a form derived from the literary gossip columns of the 1930s.

Mé already jotted her daily life down almost every morning. The two film books had been successfully written this way. The fan mail showed that there was a following for the authoress herself as much as for her literary avatar. Keeping the figurine Madeleine separate from the live Mrs Robert Henrey made sound money sense. Unfortunately, Dent got their wires crossed and mixed things up from the start by entitling the first of the diaries *Madeleine's Journal*. Mé had signed for '*A Woman's Journal*' which was more in keeping with the feminine preoccupations she wished to foreground from now on, addressing herself mainly to women and more particularly to girls.

Her creed would never vary. Twenty years later she defined it in a four-page typewritten letter to the librarian of Texas Woman's University, Elizabeth Snapp:

> I am, as you know, feminine—not feminist. I believe that woman's lib is a lot of nonsense, at least from a writer's point of view. What is hard is for an aspiring young woman to realise how much she could tell about herself, even at the age of 18 or 19, if she discovered the gift of expression. Often (nearly always) she has diamonds in a mine she has not yet learned to exploit. I still believe that a young woman writer has the greatest chance of achieving success if she remains essentially feminine. Otherwise she would have little more to offer

than a man—without a man's physical and peculiar advantages. [...]

I would not mention this if I had not myself taken quite a time to discover it. But if I began by writing under a male pseudonym it was mostly through a desire to protect myself during a period of unsureness, of experiment, so that I could later, if I felt the need, repudiate what was immature, though on reflection, I was over sensitive and it is something I should not have done, even though there is a precedent in Colette (the authoress of *Gigi*) who also, but not entirely willingly, began by writing some of her most famous books under her husband's name.[91]

Though the final paragraph here is pretentious and utterly unfair to Bob, the fact is that Mé in 1953, having come to terms with her childhood, girlhood and early marriage in a spate of successful books, needed a new sense of purpose. Bobby's schooling had put an end to her role as a little boy's mother. Mathilde was happy at the farm. Bob was pursuing his own interests somewhere while continuing to work at the *Star*.

There had been a suggestion that they pack up at Carrington House and move permanently to Normandy, but the idea had horrified Mé. It was too early for her to leave the London scene, which she enjoyed and felt part of—she was only forty-seven. She decided that her vocation as an authoress consisted in helping other women to survive by sharing her experience with them, even by showing them the way. Hence the 'contemporary diary' notion. Simultaneously, references to her Protestant faith—though she never preached—became more frequent in her writings.

That *Madeleine's Journal* was intended as a new departure is clear from the 'Books by Mrs Robert Henrey' page among its prelims:

THE LITTLE MADELEINE (*her girlhood*)
AN EXILE IN SOHO (*her adolescence*)
MADELEINE GROWN UP (*her love story and marriage*)
A FARM IN NORMANDY *and* THE RETURN (*the birth of her child*)
MATILDA AND THE CHICKENS (*a winter on her farm*)
A JOURNEY TO VIENNA (*the making of a film*)
PALOMA (*her story of a friend*)
LONDON (*with watercolours by Phyllis Ginger*)

The immediately previous volumes had come out with a 'Books by' list of eighteen titles. This reduced list of nine no doubt represents the works Mé currently claimed under her 'Kill-Bill' policy. The fact that the recent reprint of *A Village in Piccadilly* isn't included is surprising until one remembers that Bob wrote most of it. Inversely, the exclusion of *A Film Star in Belgrave Square* makes him an unexpected candidate for co-authorship of this title. As for the presence of the farm books, Mé presumably judged that her recent rewrite justified listing them as all her own work. The parenthetical gloss in italics after each title appears for the first time, insisting on the person of the authoress: *her.*

THE *TATLER* IN FEBRUARY announced under a Pearl Freeman photograph of Mé clutching Fifille, her latest Pekingese: 'Mrs Robert Henrey, authoress of successful novels based in London and her farm in Normandy, is now working on *A Woman's Journal* to be published in the autumn.' It had in fact been delivered and signed for on 27 October 1952 but it came out extended from twenty-nine to thirty chapters to include the June coronation, in September 1953 as *Madeleine's Journal*.[92] The dedicatee was the Broadway producer Ethel Lerner Reiner whom Mé had just met briefly in Paris and was sucking up to in the hope she would put *The Little Madeleine* on the stage. (She didn't.)

Unusually, considering the success of *The Little Madeleine* and *Madeleine Grown Up* published simultaneously in New York by E.P. Dutton and propelled by good reviews from the *Chicago Tribune* and the *New York Times*'s Orville Prescott, *Madeleine's Journal* found no American publisher.

One can see why. The chapter incipits are disconcerting to say the least: 'There is not much news this week: nylons are in the shops for the first time...'; 'Here was another Monday and I was ironing a blouse while Mrs Terry dusted the room...'; 'Rain has been falling all night and yet spring is in the air...'; 'This morning I changed the sheets...'; 'The postman this morning brought me a postcard from Brittany...'; 'This summer will go down as Coronation summer...'. One is tempted to throw the book down in disgust: in its determination to be womanly, Mé's gift for telling the trivial appears to have lapsed into the banal. At times it looks positively self-parodical. Nonetheless, there are a few passages that don't insult her reader's intelligence, such as the prose poem describing a train journey from Southampton to London in a first-class compartment with Bobby and a nun.

Time and place in this book are haphazard. The narrative jumps to and fro as a function of the diarist's stream of consciousness. Each place, each person, each event recorded suggests another of the same or a different kind now, before or soon. The anchor is 1952–53 London, but the ship rears and dips as the tide of memory swirls around it. If the narrative could be plotted on a chart or a tree diagram, it would give a clinical psychologist food for thought about a creative mind's neuronal processes.

The picture that emerges isn't a social tapestry as in the earlier Mrs Robert Henrey books but a personal scrapbook held up for the admiration of the extended family of her readers worldwide. It would be damning—and probably unfair—to suggest that in speaking to the feminine mainstream this 'contemporary diary' and its successors were primarily intent on fuelling a myth. The amazing thing is that once one turns the first page one continues reading. This is entirely due to the vivacity of the narration. Literature, surprisingly, has its place here too.

Dent marshalled a bevy of women reviewers for the new genre and reaped in a goodly collection of reusable quotes for the on-publication advertisements. Anna Russell in *John O'London's*

Weekly: 'With Mrs Henrey small scenes, trifling events are vitalised with interest. People come to new life. She is like Eve when she opened her eyes on Creation.' The *Spectator*'s Margaret Crosland: 'Madeleine is the most striking proof that men may fulminate against women as much as they like, but the walls of the boudoir are thicker than the walls of Jericho.' *Queen* blatantly overstated her case: 'Art, fashions, politics, literature, and domestic matters are discussed, all with the friendly and discerning charm which has endeared her to such a wide public both in this country and in the United States.' Mé's bisexual friend Edith Shackleton contributed to *Lady*: 'That leading feminist—because she understands and delights in femininity—among our women writers, Mrs Robert Henrey, now tells more of her personal life in *Madeleine's Journal*. She includes many sensitively drawn vignettes of other women whose lives have interested her. [...] You will rejoice in *Madeleine's Journal*.'

Among other reviewers, the *Tatler*'s E. V. Knox liked this 'series of sketches—conversations for the most part—charming in their variety of detail, and captivating the reader because the characters are so obviously ready to open their hearts.' Vernon Fane's review in the *Sphere* did the job as usual, praising this 'further volume of diary entries, reminiscences, character sketches, dissertations on new hats and apricot tarts' evidencing the 'now-familiar imprint of the writer's highly personal style, her preoccupation with detail, her respect for the anecdotal form and her intense femininity'.

Despite this pæan, the book wasn't reprinted, perhaps because the potential reader didn't recognise herself in the sophisticated jacket illustration, a highly sophisticated Madeleine in furs, earrings, long green gloves and a conical red hat pointing haughtily at something or someone.

Dent's own Non-Fiction Book Club issued the surplus sheets in a club edition in 1954.

* * *

IN THE SPRING OF 1953, before writing the Coronation chapter for *Madeleine's Journal*, Mé had spent a month in Paris drafting a new book to be entitled unsurprisingly *A Month in Paris*. The idea was basically to revisit the scenes of her childhood, linking back to the published autobiographies to feminise their narratives and incidentally push their sales.

As it turned out, she spent most of the month swanning around theatres, bars, parties, race courses, fashion houses, shops, polo pitches, the Plaza-Athénée, the Aga Khan with his Begum, a 'Mr X' (*sic*) with a Cadillac, a number of women friends mostly rich. There's also a copious sprinkling of ordinary people for social flavour—lavatory attendants, cab drivers, cooks and such. From them all the authoress extracts stories galore, constantly adding pith to her own personality cult initiated in *Madeleine's Journal.*

A simple chapter recounting her impromptu appearance at the wedding of Thérèse, daughter of her surrogate sister Rolande, makes up for things a little. There's also an intriguing account of a children's birthday party at the luxurious home of an unnamed 'widow of considerable taste' just off the Champs Elysées. Why Madeleine didn't drop her name when she dropped everyone else's is a mystery until one discovers that *A Month in Paris* came out just as the widow's fashion house went bust. She was Elsa Schiaparelli.

Perhaps the fairest summary one could give here of this book is provided by the blurb:

> The present 'diary' is her maturest work, gay and sparkling, inform-
> ative and sensible, never trivial, never dull. The passing scene and
> situation, happenings seemingly small but always the stuff of life,
> are caught and held by Mrs Henrey's keen eyes and skilful use of the
> language of her adoption. [...] It is not too much to say that within the
> covers of this book the English reader will see more of the real Paris
> in a month than she, or he, would otherwise see in years.

Despite this guff, there are moments of disarming frankness in the narrative that make up for its originator's blatant pursuit of copy. Apropos her memory she writes: 'I have the impression that little pieces of my girlhood remain caught up like shreds of a torn dress in all the streets of Paris. [...] My university was the street. And now it would appear that I was going back to the street for a refresher course!'

Again, when describing the way she writes every morning from seven to midday: 'I arrange the pillows comfortably at my back, take up my pad and fountain pen, and allow my memory to empty itself gently on the smooth paper. The words flow contentedly, never asking to be rearranged, dominating me—not I them. My pleasure is to be led, not to lead. I am passive, and in this essentially feminine, savouring the joys of no responsibility.'[93]

When Mrs Robert Henrey writes as well as that, one can forgive her almost everything. *Almost* everything, because she persistently—and infuriatingly—translates the French '*tu*' and '*toi*' as 'thou' and 'thee', as when she reproduces chat between two gallery attendants at the Louvre: 'I saw thy daughter looking for thee. Didst thou see her?—Now that thou tellest me that she has passed her examination, I am right glad.'[94] Such a lack of feeling for the praxis of the English language is *impardonnable*.

The contract with Dent was dated 17 August 1953 and the book came out in April 1954.[95] It was preceded in January by a half-column puff on the *Tatler* books page under a black and white photograph of Mé in her Carrington House pictures corner, one of a series taken by Maurice Ambler for Dent. The jacket and frontispiece reproduced a pastel portrait of the authoress done in 1952 by Honor Earl, Lord Maugham's daughter (and Somerset Maugham's niece), who had drawn Bobby for a charity show in 1948. The book's dedication was 'Affectionately for Violette Béchet de Balan Neilson', apparently one of the three Maroger sisters from Clichy, Ariane Vardon''s aunt.

There were more advertisements than reviews of *A Month in Paris*, and what reviews it did receive cribbed from the blurb. The *Daily Telegraph* reckoned that the author's 'feverish zest' could not save *A Month in Paris* from being 'little more than instalments taken from a glossy weekly's Paris letter'. The *Observer* reviewer (possibly a disguised C. E. Vulliamy) wrote: 'A great many people read that excellent piece of autobiography *The Little Madeleine* by Mrs Robert Henrey. It was a fine, in many ways an astonishing, book. But the frilly, chirruping, scented style of Mrs Henrey's following volumes cannot be applauded.' Elizabeth Bowen, who had returned temporarily to the *Tatler*, gave it a parenthetic mention when reviewing a different book. It wasn't reprinted.

* * *

NEITHER WAS *SHOCKING LIFE* by Elsa Schiaparelli, ghosted in the third person by Bob in 1953 from copy supplied by Mé, initially for a feature series in the *Star*.[96] Published by Dent in October 1954, it's clever and funny, but it came too late to save Schiap, whose *haute couture* business collapsed in April.

Denoel in Paris brought out a translation by Henry Muller the same year entitled *Shocking: Les Souvenirs d'Elsa Schiaparelli.* It was reprinted in 2022 to coincide with a Schiaparelli exhibition at the Musée des Arts Décoratifs on Rue de Rivoli. An editorial foreword to the reprint explains that the text is republished unchanged, despite a number of 'insulting comments' made by the author, because the book is a 'rich and abundant testimony to a bygone era'. Interestingly, though Denoel claim copyright on the Muller translation, the authorship rights seem somehow to have entered the Schiaparelli S. A. portfolio in 2013, judging from the copyright notices.

* * *

In 1954—a bumper year if ever there was one: six titles published—Dutton in New York published an omnibus volume that wasn't issued in London until 1960, *Madeleine—Young Wife: The Autobiography of a French Girl.*[97] This bore a message from the authoress to the reader signed Madeleine Henrey stating that 'the action' taking place from 1937 to 1953 was 'a true saga' without mentioning that most of the book had already been published. It contained rewritten versions of *A Farm in Normandy, A Village in Picadilly* and *The Return to the Farm,* with a new epilogue. This final section headed 'The Days of Peace' was apparently written during the period coinciding with Bobby's tribulations at his prep school and immediately preceding the partnership crisis in early 1952.

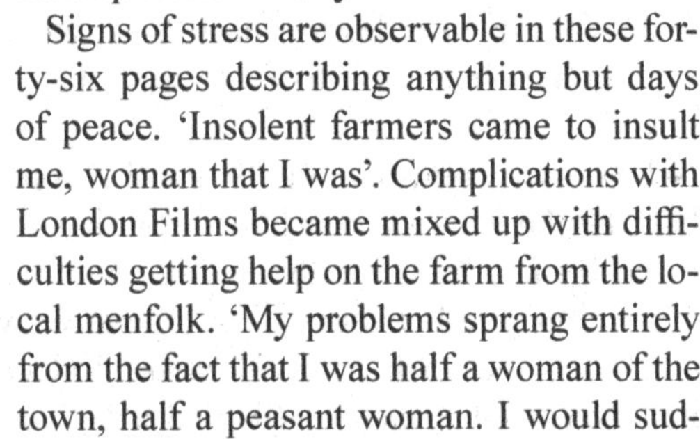

Signs of stress are observable in these forty-six pages describing anything but days of peace. 'Insolent farmers came to insult me, woman that I was'. Complications with London Films became mixed up with difficulties getting help on the farm from the local menfolk. 'My problems sprang entirely from the fact that I was half a woman of the town, half a peasant woman. I would suddenly be obliged to exchange a rough dress for a tailor-made, and fly to London on business'. There was also a feeling of insecurity:

165

'Having been poor in my girlhood I was haunted by the fear of being poor again, poor in old age when I had no longer the vivacious ways and pretty face that so successfully lifted me out of poverty when I was a girl of twenty'. And there was always the driving ambition that led her to boast to herself as much as to her readers: 'This [*The Little Madeleine*] was the first time I had written a book deliriously as if inspired by some force other than my own, and it brought me the calm, certain realization that I had it within my power to become a woman of letters'.

The strange thing is that while all this is going on, 'my husband' is off stage. 'If my husband happened to be at the farm, all was well, but in fact he was not often there'. She alone rules the roost: 'My authority on the farm was virtually absolute. [...] My husband never interfered with the running of the farm'. She alone buys Berlequet and writes: 'My farm was one of the richest on the plateau'.[98] When 'Robert' does show up for once he catches chicken pox and is only saved from almost certain death by Dr Lehérissey, a specialist, penicillin and, of course, 'I'.

* * *

ABOUT THE TIME IN 1953 when Mé delivered her copy for *Madeleine—Young Wife* to Dutton for publication in 1954 she also handed in *La petite Madeleine* to the Paris publisher La Table Ronde, who brought it out in May 1954.[99] The English and French texts match, though there are no scene breaks in the French. It would of course be interesting to know which was the source. Mé told Elizabeth Snapp in 1974 that the French holograph of *The Little Madeleine* was 'destroyed in Paris' without saying why, how, when or by whom. So there's no way of checking one way or the other.

The French publishers rightly put the word *'poétique'* in bold to describe the book in their blurb, pointing out that the French girl in the book is 'such as the author—now an Englishwoman—is able to imagine her today'. The operative word is *imagine*. The cover calls the book a novel, *roman*. Indeed the blurb goes further and calls it a *romance* ('ballad'), saying: *'Il y avait longtemps que l'on n'avait pas écrit quelque chose d'aussi simple et beau sur Paris, sur le Paris des enfants tristes.'* ('It's been a long time

166

since something so simple and beautiful was written about Paris, *le Paris des enfants tristes.'*) How interesting to note that Madeleine's Paris qualified by the English reviewers as 'lively', 'gay', 'truculent' comes across in French as 'the Paris of sad children'!

* * *

ACCORDING TO THE AUTHORESS, the next book in her 'contemporary diary' series, *Milou's Daughter*, came about in 1954 when Raoul Bosio, mayor Jean Médecin's right hand man in Nice, asked her personally at a dinner party in Paris to come and write about his town. It's more likely that she was recruited into a programme of promotional trips laid on by the Médecin regime for influential media people. Nice was invaded by all kinds in the summer, but the winter season, which had been the main money-spinner from Queen Victoria's day up to Mussolini, was moribund. The aim was to attract tourists back during the winter. The little open air aerodrome on the sea front was about to be extended. The Carnaval with its Battle of Flowers was being revived. The Opera House had been revamped. Consequently, a best-selling Franco-British authoress represented a good catch for Nice in 1954. Her blonde vivacity would go down well in the Californian ambiance of the Côte d'Azur and her book would help to repopulate the Promenade des Anglais off-season.

The many thousands of readers of *The Little Madeleine* had made the acquaintance of the swaggering meridional ex-miner Émile Gal, alias Milou. In order to fit Nice into her writing schedule, Mé hit on the idea of pretending to go south in his footsteps, accomplishing 'the strangest pilgrimage' in memory of her adoptive father and her childhood.

Her dedication in French reads translated: 'For Jean Médecin, Member of the French Parliament and Mayor of Nice, who helped me to recapture the sunshine of my girlhood.' Perhaps he did, though to him it must have seemed a perfectly normal sort of business arrangement. When she sent him her book in 1955, he signed a typed reply on Assemblée Nationale letterhead saying her '*impressions si vivantes de Nice et de la Riviera*' made an attractive volume that reminded him of the '*heures charmantes*' she had spent '*parmi nous*'. All his family thanked her for the book

167

and sent their *'messages de meilleure sympathie'*. In French, that's called an *accusé de réception*. True, Mrs Robert Henrey's visit to the Riviera had by then been eclipsed *'parmi nous'* by that of a certain Grace Kelly making Alfred Hitchcock's *To Catch A Thief* with Cary Grant.

Dent spent a lot of money promoting *Milou's Daughter*—a sure sign that the two previous diaries had not sold at all well. Readers expecting more Milou were disappointed, however. The number of pages devoted to him amounts to exactly twelve. All the rest is made up of contemporary tourist visits—a far cry from the crisp historical topography of the London books—and gossip sessions, brilliantly recorded and highly readable as usual, but so what? The reader learns nothing, except that Madeleine lunched with the Médecin family, watched Chauviré in *Giselle* from the Médecins' box at the Opéra, visited the Médecins' country estate, watched the fireworks from the Médecins' front window and the *corso* from the Médecins' grandstand, befriended Huguette Lumière in her dressing room after a performance of *Les Pêcheurs de perles*, went to a play at the Palais de la Méditerranée, dropped in at the Municipal Casino, hobnobbed with the Aga Khan and the Begum for the third time in three successive books, popped in behind the scenes of the *bal masqué*, talked to just about everybody in Nice, and so on. There's little of real literary value, except perhaps a dream flashback to a Madeleine aged twenty just after her marriage returning from a two-month stay at Mentone for her lungs—with no mention of Bob who paid for it all.

Most regrettably, the authoress once more lays on a display of grotesque 'translations' of *tutoiement* forms: 'The deputy mayor said to me: "Go thou and find Mme Henrey... Thou shalt take her to the Hotel Splendid"' (p. 3), 'Hey, there, intrepid policeman! Gettest thou out of the way!' (p. 37), 'Madame! Madame! Whither dost thou go?' (p. 167), etc. For the first of these travesties, she actually wonders 'what answer would be suitable to this biblical speech', as if the English of King James could possibly correspond to the normal speech of the deputy mayor of Nice in 1954.

The contract was dated 26 April 1954 and the book came out on 3 May 1955.[100] The reviews were dreadful. Even loyal Elizabeth Bowen found the book hard to defend in the *Tatler*: 'The author can convey many sensations. And she is, and we are, happy in her style, which has the diaphanousness of spun sugar without being ever what one calls "sugary". She builds us a rainbow bridge between France and England.' Guy Ramsey in the *Daily Telegraph* pleaded mitigating circumstances:

Mrs Robert Henrey is a sundial of a writer—she chronicles only the happy hours: even her occasional pathos has a sweetness like that of an April day. [...] It is 'tuppence coloured' writing, but the Riviera is a tuppence coloured sort of place, almost specifically created to serve such a craftsman. But it would not be fair to disregard the extraordinary skill, within its narrow compass, of this author's work. She is selective, perceptive. inexhaustibly (though sometimes exhaustingly) emotional. To read *Milou's Daughter* from cover to cover is like dining on Sole Véronique, Poulet Bonne Femme and peaches in cream to the accompaniment of Château Yquem.

The *Times* reviewer pressed for a severe sentence:

The slender scaffolding of this sentimental journey is a search for traces of her father Milou, a Grand'Combe coal miner who had served with a cavalry regiment in Nice. Research into the past, however, is the smallest item on a programme favouring the distractions and diversions of the moment. Stylistically, Mrs Henrey might well curb some extravagances; her continuous, breathless present tense is awkward and enervating in the English language; and her effortless rare pronouncements of real insight risk being choked by an excess of trivial talk.

In the *Times Literary Supplement* Helen Elizabeth FitzRandolph doffed the black cap:

Unfortunately, Nice brings out all that is of least value in her writing, which flows on absorbed in trivialities like the columns of the gossip writer or the fashion magazines. Every conversation is expanded, every emotion exploited, and the superficial nature of her interests and her judgements can no longer be hidden.

In short Mrs Robert Henrey's writing career had taken a turn for the worse, arguably because of the prolonged absence of 'my husband'. Expunged from the farm books, ridiculed in 'The Days of Peace', relegated to the distant past in the 'contemporary diaries',

Bob had been away for too long. When he emerged from whatever limbo he had been occupying since the success of *The Little Madeleine*, he noted in his log of the year 1954: 'She goes to Nice to write *Milou's Daughter*. Her articles in the *Star* placarded on all the London buses but my situation there gets worse and I leave at Christmas very depressed. In a fierce effort to rebuild our fortune spent on diamonds, pearls and Berlequet, I sell the silver and she writes *Bloomsbury Fair*.' The bank balance stood at just £9,000.

* * *

AT EASTER 1955 the Henrey family were back together again in Normandy while *Bloomsbury Fair* was being typeset by Dent's Aldine Press at Letchworth. The contract had been signed in London on 10 March. Mé noted cryptically (and royally): 'My husband and I at that time were in the full flood of our activities.'[101] In fact Bob was out of a job and mainly trying to recover from depression.

A small stainless steel plaque engraved in New Bond Street was let into the fireplace of the low room at Villers. It reflected on winter evenings the flames of the four-foot elm logs which Bob religiously carried in and kept alight or smouldering from one day to the next. The inscription on the plaque read:

1555–1955
We thank thee dear God, for having spared this house
through four centuries.
The Robert Henrey family
Easter 1955

Normandie herbagère, éclatante et mouillée
Nous voulons venir vivre un jour, doux et vieillis
Parmi tes prés, au fond d'une maison rayée.
Lucie Delarue-Mardrus

Dent got *Bloomsbury Fair* 'recommended' (not 'chosen' which would have been much better) by the Book Society when it was published on 10 November 1955 for the Christmas season.[102]

There's the customary 'true story' epigraph from the author-

170

ess to the reader. The volume is dedicated to Mary Oliver, the friend remembered in *A Daughter for a Fortnight* who sent Mé a tiny rubber plant in Mayfair that grew and grew. 'My husband' is mentioned twice rather disparagingly on page 134 but plays no further part in the tale. 'My mother' appears fifteen times, Bobby's films are mentioned twice. All the rest is 'I' and 'I's' women friends—including Paloma who makes a brief appearance to serve as a bridge between Mayfair and Bloomsbury, the narrative's two poles.

Why this title *Bloomsbury Fair* was chosen isn't explained. In fact the book's *raison d'être* isn't at all obvious, except that it's another book by Mrs Robert Henrey about places and people. It isn't an autobiography, though 'I' is Madeleine. It isn't a topography, though London is its subject. It isn't a biography, though it retraces the history of three famous families. The title obviously puns on the 'pen and pencil sketches of English society' that Thackeray gathered together in his *Vanity Fair*. Constituting a wordplay on Bloomsbury and Mayfair, it alludes above all to the humble origins in Bloomsbury of the Barbirollis, Debrys and Joelins—penniless immigrants raised by talent and hard work to fame and riches like someone else the reader knows. This someone isn't foregrounded for once, or less so than usual. It's left to the reader to understand the fable and induce the moral.

From the genetic viewpoint, 'I' isn't the conjunct Mé plus Bob of the pre–1952 books but a distinctly feminine 'I' at the centre of a solo narrative in which Bob's witty prose style isn't at all evident. However, there's a structure here that strongly suggests editing by him. 'I's' Londoners are cleverly caught in a spider web woven between pre–1914 Bloomsbury and mid-century Mayfair, a continuous criss-cross narrative thread starting from and returning to Katie and Millie's hat and dress shop 'Madame Rita' in Grosvenor Square.

Saying things simply, Bob was back in *Bloomsbury Fair*, and literature—writing as subject, composition as theme—was back with him. The Quality Book Club run by Dent issued a special edition for its members in the year of its trade publication. Nonetheless, in common with all the rest of the Henrey titles in which Bob played a prominent role as author or coauthor, *Bloomsbury Fair* was excluded from the official Mrs Robert Henrey canon listed in *Who's Who,* though Dent's listed it among 'Her other books' in subsequent publications.

After its three predecessors, which didn't make much sense as anything but celebrity journalism, the London reviewers of *Bloomsbury Fair* were prudently non-committal. Vernon Fane in the *Sphere* didn't venture beyond this: 'As always, Mrs Henrey brings to the description that fresh wonder and appreciation that is her particular gift to contemporary letters.' There was enthusiasm in the counties, however. An anonymous contributor to the *Tewkesbury Register* got space between the Beckford Whist Drive and the sudden death of Major A. H. Gibbs to state: 'Few people are immune to the glamour of London, and *Bloomsbury Fair* contains all the colours of the moving kaleidoscope of life in the capital.' An 'AJB' in the *Bradford Observer* observed: 'It is indeed a joy to welcome "a true story of real people" which so thoroughly redeems the reputation of Bloomsbury—too long supposed to be the haunt exclusively of the long-legged crank or the long-haired fanatic.' C. E. Vulliamy, who had championed *The Little Madeleine* when it came out, kicked into touch in the *Observer*: 'There is much in this diverting book which can be regarded as literary artistry of a very high order.'

* * *

1955 SAW THE PUBLICATION OF *PALOMA* by Dutton in New York and the French translation of *Madeleine Grown Up* by La Table Ronde in Paris.

Like its predecessor from the same French publisher *Madeleine jeune fille* sticks close to the supposed source, this time respecting the original scene breaks.[103] According to the blurb, the 'translation' was the work of the authoress herself intent on offering the authentic text to her French readers. The dedicatee was Ariane Vardon (Sorbonne student grand-daughter of Simone Maroger from Clichy), who figures in *A Month in Paris*. The title *Madeleine jeune fille* was cribbed from Claude Farrère's huge best-seller *Mademoiselle Dax jeune fille*, which Robert supposedly gave to Madeleine at the Savoy in 1927 just after it had been reissued for the umpteenth time since its first appearance in 1907. Madeleine in French didn't fare as well as Dax: after her first impression La

Table Ronde never called on her services again.

* * *

A YEAR AFTER QUITTING his features editor job on the *Star*, Bob was hired on New Year's Eve by James Wedgwood Drawbell, managing editor of *Woman's Own*. The ebullient Scot, his elder by two years, had met the Henreys during a promotional cruise to southern Italy in the 1930s, when he was editor-in-chief of the *Sunday Chronicle*. In March 1950, he had pulled off a colossal scoop at *Woman's Own*: the pre-publication memoirs of Marion Crawford, former governess of the 'little princesses' Margaret and Elizabeth. It scandalised the Royal Family and Household, particularly when Crawford subsequently lent her name to a ghosted 'Crawfie's Column' in *Woman's Own*. In 1955, when Bob joined the paper to take the place of the fiction editress, 'Crawfie' had just been exposed as a fraud: *Woman's Own* had published her pre-written account of Trooping the Colour and Royal Ascot when the two events had in fact been called off under the state of emergency declared on 1 June.

Bob found himself the sole man working in the Fiction Room with four sub-editors and three secretaries, clever young women with whom he felt perfectly in tune. In those days, *Woman's Own* specialized in abridged serial versions of novels and in short stories for women with florid illustrations chosen by Drawbell in person. Two novels and two or more short stories were featured every week. Each issue ran to eighty-odd, sometimes one hundred-odd pages, over a third in colour, and sold over one million copies every Wednesday at fivepence, later sixpence or sevenpence.

Neither Drawbell nor Bob had the slightest illusion about the function of *Woman's Own*, which was to give the readers what they wanted. But what *did* they want? Perhaps they could be encouraged to want better writing than usual without asking too much of them as readers. Nobody had ever found Charles Dickens, H. G. Wells or Arnold Bennett hard to read in their day. Good modern stories tended to be more convoluted, but they could be edited to make them simple, and splashes of illustrations could make them look appealing to everyone.

Well-known writers were attracted by the large sums offered—

enough to buy a nice semi-detached house—knowing full well that their work would be pruned like a rose bush and surrounded by much humbler plants. Bob recorded in his log that with Judith Burnley as his associate editress he got the quality of new fiction at *Woman's Own* to 'great heights', buying work from 'all the world's best writers'—including William Saroyan, Truman Capote, Victoria Sackville-West.

Burnley joined the *Woman's Own* fiction room at twenty-six from another Newnes publication, the boys' weekly *Eagle*. She remembered in 2021 that the office in Tower House looked down Southampton Street towards the Strand from a window under the clock. 'JWD' was dictatorial and scared everyone, but 'RH' was a mixture of male and female who loved women and despised men. This led to friction with the male executives who ran the magazine. He found them inferior, they found him peculiar. He dressed in a classic Prince of Wales suit over silk shirts made for him at home, Old Etonian tie, brogues, silk stockings with no socks— and an anklet. Most unusually in London in those days, his custom-made shirts were short-sleeved, no doubt copying a fashion he had picked up in the Canadian newsrooms.

Mé dropped in to see 'the girls' at the office, describing them and their like in *The Dream Makers*: 'They are almost all in their early twenties, extremely pretty and above the average in intelligence. Theirs is the eternal problem of equating brains and high wages with love, for all the world knows that most men are suspicious of career girls, resenting their efficiency and the money they earn with such apparent ease.'[104] Their main problem in London was how to pay their rent, although some of them were beginning to think that a husband might be a better option than a career.

Boiling the Pot

OVER THE DECADE coinciding with Bob's *Woman's Own* years Mrs Robert Henrey produced nine books from Carrington House and/or the farm in Normandy at the rate of one per year with a contractless gap in 1958. Two of the nine are outstanding, the rest distinctly less so. Though it would be easy to reckon that the better titles were probably edited by Bob and the others not, it wouldn't be too far off the mark to suppose so. The first three were bought by the London Library, but a consecutive series of six between 1959 and 1964 weren't, for the simple reason that the library, judging from reviews and members' requests, deemed they weren't worth buying. They weren't donated by the authoress either.

It would be easy to give them short shrift, were it not for the fact that they *belong* in every respect to the period they describe, mirroring the tastes of the mid-century reading public as well as a phase in the career of a professional writing team. Their coverage of the social scene remains interesting in its very triviality owing to the wide variety of people and places depicted by a lively pen intent on leaving a trace while earning an honest living. If the *Woman's Own* ethos predominates in most of them, at least four being the result of direct commissions, Mé's wish to connect with the average woman reader was undoubtedly as sincere as Bob's tended to be detached.

The foundation of her success was the 'homely relationship' sold by the feminine press to its readers in the 1950s, when the monthly circulation of the thirty-odd British women's magazines totalled over forty-three million copies.[105] This prodigious audience, not unlike the 2020s world of social and entertainment media, coexisted with a more demanding universe reflected in the quality press and the book trade. By trying to hedge her bets in both fields, Mrs Robert Henrey ultimately estranged the critics and lost those of her readers who believed in higher things than the world around them.

* * *

THIS FEMININE WORLD contracted with Dent on 4 January 1956 and published in September the same year price*d* 18*s*. is a ragbag of visits, mainly to Paris fashion houses and a London hospital.[106]

The dust cover and frontispiece reproduce a portrait of the authoress painted specially for the book by Eduardo Malta, to whom Bob and Mé were introduced by the book's dedicatees, Mary and Alured Denne, the latter being 'a senior executive of one of our great oil companies'. The haughty elegance of Malta's portrait is positively scary, a Mrs Robert Henrey disguised as a Duchess of Windsor. The family today don't like this pretentious pose, although Bob seems to have thought at the time that it faithfully depicted the Mé he currently had to compose with.

The opening pages of the book describe the sittings at Malta's studio in Ryder Street, arty talk with Eduardo and his Dolce, and

176

a drive with them to Hampton Court with 'my husband' at the wheel. After this painting episode enter the Aga Khan and the Begum yet again followed by a Thackerayan procession of snobs and chatterboxes clustered around 'I'.

Faithful Vernon Fane in the *Sphere* put in a few kind words about this old-fashioned medley after giving three brisk sentences in his column to Wallis Simpson's sensational *The Heart Has Its Reasons*, which came out from Michael Joseph the same week. Fane chose his words carefully:

> Mrs Robert Henrey is a small phenomenon in her own right, if it is only because she makes very attractive bricks with the minimum of straw. Her books of memoirs may cover her French childhood or her London existence of the moment, may dwell on her Normandy farm or her London milliner, but there is absolutely nothing sensational about them, nothing, one might think on dissecting them, even of acute interest. The miracle is that she makes all her doings and all her to-ings and fro-ings very interesting indeed, and not only to female readers. *This Feminine World* follows the pattern which Mrs Henrey has designed with care and success.

Puckish Siriol Hugh-Jones (aka Siriol Hart) was distinctly less indulgent under the heading 'Venus Absorbed' in the *Times Literary Supplement*:

> Most bizarre and most characteristic are her chapters on Madame Volterra the racehorse owner. This extraordinary concoction of chit-chat about horses, scent, clothes, bedroom furnishing, love and death may indeed present a faithful picture of Madame Volterra, though one rather hopes not; but the after-effect is as though one had eaten oneself silly on six-layer cream cake and crystallized violets.

* * *

THE 1957 SPECIAL OFFER from the House of Henrey was contracted on 23 January and published by Dent that September at 18*s*.[107] The reader has to wait ninety-seven pages to discover the motive behind *A Daughter for a Fortnight*: 'Can there be any greater satisfaction for a woman than to see herself young and beautiful again on the threshold of life as she sees herself in the entrancing mirror of a young daughter?'

The girl thrown upon the authoress for a fortnight by James Wedgwood Drawbell at the behest of Paris editor Hélène Gordon Lazareff had won a competition organised by Lazareff's *Elle*, the prize being a trip to Britain. She was called Marie-Paule Mollard, came from a poor family in Paris, had just passed her *baccalauréat*, clapped her hands when pleased, and exclaimed frequently 'I am so happy!' The authoress thought (p. 98) 'how fortunate' she was to have 'such virginal intellectual soil to deal with'.

A mother-daughter fixation had frequently found expression in the corpus till now, most recently with young Ariane Vardon in *A Month in Paris*. Its origin was undoubtedly Mé's long cohabitation and connivance with Mathilde in Clichy and Soho. The poor seamstress had passed on to her daughter quite a lot of her philosophy, including her mistrust of the male sex. Mé, both as a woman and in her posture as an authoress, was on the whole disappointed by men and found women more stimulating. In this Bob, luckily enough, agreed with her wholeheartedly.

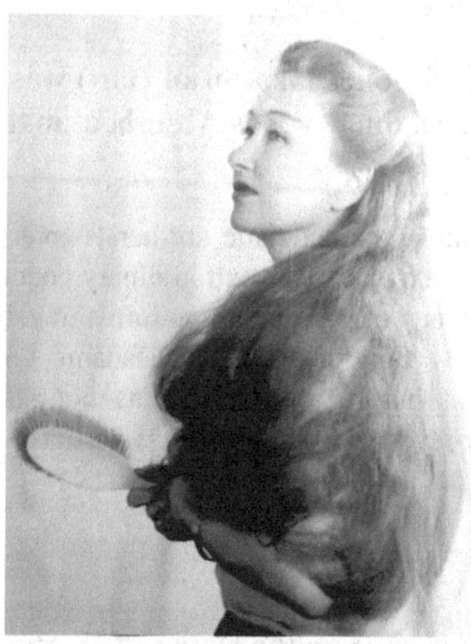

For the authoress's latest work in 1957 Vernon Fane did his stuff in the *Sphere* once again, treading on eggs as the French say:

Mrs Robert Henrey is adept at the autobiographical form and it is no surprise that *A Daughter for a Fortnight* should tell us quite as much about herself as about the subject of the title. By this I do not mean that Mrs Henrey is an impossibly egotistical writer: simply that she is of that genus of writers whose personality deeply pervades every page of her books. [...] In the present book Mrs Henrey writes about a young French girl to whom she undertook to introduce London and, later, Edinburgh, and whom she later visited in Paris. The recital is light-hearted, affectionate and not too name-studded, and the changing background of the Normandy farm, the newspaper office and the elegant drawing room really diverting.

At the *Tatler* Elizabeth Bowen was about to leave the books pages definitively. She was to be replaced by Siriol Hugh-Jones, a brilliant thirty-year-old Oxford graduate with quite different views on life and literature, formerly features editor at *Vogue* in her early twenties and now a freelance columnist and reviewer with a baby daughter and a famous husband, the TV journalist Derek Hart.

Bowen's final bow to the Henreys read: '*A Daughter for a Fortnight* is decidedly a tribute to French girlhood, of the non-bonjour-tristesse type. The chronicle lags a little, though not much, after the exit of Marie-Paule; however, we are consoled by a trip to Paris and an inside view of the feminine magazine world.' That's a world that Hugh-Jones ex-*Vogue* knew inside out, but for her first *Tatler* review the Henreys would have to wait.

* * *

SIX MONTHS AFTER the Marie-Paule contract Dent accepted a new London book on 23 July 1957: *The Virgin of Aldermanbury: Rebirth of the City of London*, a splendid topographical parenthesis in the diary series which was published in June 1958 at 20s.[108]

The book was dedicated to Bob's cousin Edmund de Rothschild, head of the London House of Rothschild, part of whose archives Bob and Mé had sorted by candlelight under the Carrington House dining table at the height of the 1940 Blitz. That was for *Letters from Paris 1870–1875*. The morning after the calamitous raid that set the City on fire on 30 December 1940, Bob had lunched alone with Edmund's uncle Anthony at New Court in St Swithin's Lane when all around was rubble and burning debris.

In this *Rebirth of the City* 'I' (mainly Bob) walks around from place to place, discovering new ones, recalling historical facts, reviving memories of relatives and friends à la Proust, meeting new people. The theme is at once nostalgic, actual and forward-looking, staunchly positive in its mix of monarchy, religion, nation and pride. Bob's influence on this narrative of survival is everywhere apparent. Gossip for gossip's sake is left out of the account for the first time in several years.

The Virgin of Aldermanbury is first-rate literature, but it didn't belong to its age, as the bright new wave of young critics weren't long in pointing out. Siriol Hugh-Jones in the *Tatler* sounded the diapason of the approaching sixties:

> I have also read—this is quite a week for women—*The Virgin of Aldermanbury* by the indefatigable Mrs Robert Henrey in her own strongly idiosyncratic style and in that sunshine-and-showers, tears-and-laughter, women-are-so-wise tone of voice that is so characteristic and feminine and that you can either like very much or leave quite alone. This book is about the rebuilding of the City of London, and Mrs Henrey darts about between tenses and buildings and facts and colourful local characters and charming little boys on tricycles. When she comes to the architecture of Fountain House, she observes: 'One wonders, as one does at Stonehenge, if giants have not been at play.' Fans will faithfully wonder right away; sourer, less gaily fanciful readers may wonder instead what makes Mrs Henrey sugar the pill quite so thickly.

* * *

THE SIX BOOKS ignored by the London Library between 1959 and 1964 are a varied lot.

The first, *Mistress of Myself*, came out in October 1959 (contract dated 28 January the same year).[109] It was heralded by Dent in these terms: 'Mrs Henrey's finest book since *The Little Madeleine* (still a world best seller) tears wide open the heart of a sensitive, deeply wondering woman. While she trips through a gay social life she shares the secrets of her reflections with her readers.' Ouch!

The jacket design 'drawn specially for Mrs Robert Henrey by Anne Thompson' according to the blurb shows a summer scene dominated by a slim barefoot feminine figure in red striped trousers, red shirt and bell-shaped white sun hat standing sideways on the Normandy sands, while a front view of the farmhouse in winter, its chimney smoking, floats top left in a bubble against a background of sea and sky.[110] It seems Dent forgot to include the epigraph borrowed from Kipling: 'Daughter am I in my mother's house, but mistress in my own.'

Despite its possibly off-putting title, cover and sales pitch, *Mistress of Myself* is far from negligible—a constructed chronicle with some fine prose passages, marred here and there by lapses into soppiness. It was written when Mé had just turned fifty and was taking stock of her life.

Bobby was due to enter Lincoln College, Oxford, in the Michaelmas term. He had left Downside and was spending his in-between year reading Spanish and French literature and the classics in Normandy with his grandmother. The farm really was the one place he could call home. Bob was busy at *Woman's Own*. Mé was doing nothing, dissatisfied with everything, starting with her hair.

There's a photograph dating from 1957 showing it falling down to her waist, not having been cut since 1942. Bob loved her hair, but she was fed up with it.

> 'If you must cut it off,' he said, 'do it while I am not here. Do it as soon as I have gone back to the office. I could not be here and know that you were doing it.'
>
> On a sudden impulse he got up and buried his face in my hair, breathing its wild, untamed smell, taking a sad leave of it.
>
> 'Goodbye, beloved chignon!'
>
> He went away quickly, and I heard the door click.[111]

Off went the chignon into a paper bag, six ounces that she sold to a human hair merchant in Great Marlborough Street for only ten shillings because it was old town hair, the best being mountain hair from girls under twenty-five.

She was fed up with her flat, too. She sold half the furniture and had the rest boxed and crated while the place was repainted. Once it was done up a decision had to be made about the lease. Assign it with a premium, renew it or rescind it? Bob had proposed some years earlier that they relocate to Normandy, and they had re-thatched the cottage roof and installed a bathroom accordingly.

The decision was up to her, she wrote. 'My husband would agree to my decision; he had interests in both countries, and I never doubted my capacity to get my own way.'[112] But the flat had grown to be part of her. How could she voluntarily banish herself, for more than a few weeks at a time, from 'that distracting stretch of asphalt that runs from the Green Park to Piccadilly Circus'? So the lease was renewed for a further seven years and Mé went off to Normandy for the summer to sleep alone in the big double bed, listening to the night owl and feeling mistress of herself.

When in November Bob began clamouring for her return, when Bobby was writing a paper on Montesquieu for his tutor at Oxford, when Mathilde was on cortisone and feeling better, Mé finally took the bus from Deauville to Le Havre, talked old times with her friend Mme Le Moing the customs officer, got on the ferry and the train, caught sight of her husband from a great distance hurrying towards her at Waterloo, and felt how good it was to be home. Stretching out before her was 'a whole winter of delicious content'—and she had the manuscript draft of *Mistress of Myself* in her bag.

The anonymous admirer in Gloucestershire procured one and a half columns in the *Tewkesbury Register* to enthuse about this latetest collection of everyday sketches under the heading 'How All Her Dreams Came True For Madeleine'.

Siriol Hugh-Jones in the *Tatler* reacted rather differently:

> For devotees, *Mistress of Myself* offers the same dainty fare as ever: the baking of bread, the cut of clothes, the babies, the knitting, the laughter and tears, and this time most of it takes place in Normandy [...] We discover that Mrs Henrey has 'an Oriental streak' in her (she worships ancestors), and that she used to invite Elinor Glyn to tea. ('We shared in our extreme youth a passion for the waltz.') Many will be glad to know that the loss of her wild untamed chignon has in no way dimmed Mrs Henrey's passionate sensibility.

The *Times Literary Supplement*'s reviewer (Helen Elizabeth FitzRandolph) couldn't quite manage to feel feminine about *Mistress of Myself*:

> Amid generalisations about men and women, she says that men do not take women writers seriously. If she were to pause awhile and re-read the books of some of the women whose writing has been taken seriously, it might deepen her own. As it is, the anecdotes that begin so brightly end with flatness and triviality.

* * *

THE NEXT BOOK TO COME OUT in the UK, *Madeleine Young Wife*, had relegated Bob to a literary limbo when it came out in New York in 1954. Dent published it in London in November 1960 at 21*s*. (the first at more than a pound), reprinting from Dutton's edition, American spelling and all. The American wrapper suggesting a New England homestead was replaced by a new jacket by Sax displaying an imaginary Madeleine in front of an imaginary Norman farmhouse, with the real Mé holding baby Bobby in a full page photograph on the back.

Siriol Hugh-Jones dispatched the book in the *Tatler*:

> 'This great saga', as the jacket mildly puts it, takes in the war and the writer's return to Normandy. Those strong enough not to quail before Mrs Henrey's simple-sweetness and hyper-femininity will welcome another ramble around the orchards. 'It is in the country that, as women, we live with intensity.' Very true, no doubt, but it's that low, vibrant throb that unnerves me. Mrs Henrey describes herself as 'a packet of sensitivity', which seems fair enough.

A second impression was nonetheless called for immediately, which only goes to show that the 'packet of sensibility' readership wasn't wholly exhausted in the British Isles, whatever the bright young London reviewers had to say. Mrs Robert Henrey was even roped in by *Books and Bookmen* to review feminine autobiographies in the late fifties and early sixties.

* * *

CONTRACTED WITH DENT IN 1961 on 2 February and 10 October respectively, *The Dream Makers* and *Spring in a Soho Street* came out one after the other in September 1961 and May 1962. They marked a return to the 'contemporary diary' vein which had produced mixed results in 1956 and 1957. Like their two predecessors, *This Feminine World* and *A Daughter for a Fortnight*, the new titles were sponsored for serialisation by *Woman's Own*. Though they document parts of an unusual woman's world with a lively pen, their inspiration was definitely commercial rather than literary, stuff for the supposed tastes of faithful readers.

The Dream Makers takes the English housewife on a luxury tour of London, Paris, Milan, Verona, Florence and Rome to discover how the inspirers of women's dreams operate: the French fashion artist Hervé Mille of *Marie Claire* visiting *Woman's Own*, Mlle Chanel, Anny Blatt, a brace of Commendatores—Mondadori and Zammaretti—and even the Pope, not forgetting the Aga Khan and the Begum.[113]

Young Bernard McElwaine, who evidently stopped reading before the bits about the Pope, wrote in the *Sunday Mirror*: 'If you like name-dropping chit-chat about Paris high society, hair styles and fashion, this is an easy-reading, completely forgettable book.'

Even the *Sphere* reviewer, who took care not to sign, remarked:

There is no writer exactly like Mrs Robert Henrey, whether among men, women or children, and she purveys exactly her own brand of tireless femininity in her discursive, pleasant and not particularly significant memoirs. [...] Taxi drivers, restaurateurs or famous dress-makers appear to chatter away to Mrs Henrey like so many loquacious starlings and the funny thing is that the reader is convinced that this really is what happens.

About the second title from 1961, *Spring in a Soho Street*, almost everything pertinent was expressed by Siriol Hugh-Jones in her *Tatler* review:

Spring In A Soho Street is Mrs Robert Henrey tripping on her gay, gallant, almost unendurably feminine way once more and telling us yet more heart-warming stories about the courage, humour, sentiment, loyalty and homespun philosophy of the Soho traders, the sort of thing that makes me understand why some men go deadly pale when you mention lady writers and dash back to their bound editions of the works of Sir Walter Scott.

It's a series of interviews disguised as social visits cleverly linked together in the form of word pictures to make a continuous narrative. Dent advertised it under the heading 'Romance in Soho' as an answer to the question 'What is the real Soho like, this tiny republic with a Montmartre flavour?'[114]

Lost for words, the *Illustrated London News* reviewer just stated: 'She made my mouth water for parmesan and Chianti.' Dent plugged it in many advertisements, but there were few reviews of note apart from Siriol Hugh-Jones's quoted above and Alan Dent's 'Adrift in Soho' in the *Sunday Telegraph* objecting that the book was 'after all, *about* Soho as well as about Mrs Henrey'. He added: 'She is full of wayward charm, which turns rather too often into wayward gush.' The *Times* reviewer, expecting topography and getting chit-chat, found it 'inconsequential' and 'rambling'. It was 'too spontaneous and diffuse', and the reviewer complained: 'No passing thought seems to be allowed to escape.'

When the first instalment of this haphazard narrative appeared in *Woman's Own* as 'Springtime in Soho' on 5 May 1962, it was announced in sensational terms: 'Mrs Robert Henrey, in this pre-publication of her latest book, shares with you the secrets of that magic village in the heart of London, which holds in its golden mile all the gaiety, romance and sorrow of a great city.'

Thereafter the story was heavily doctored, not by Bob's fiction room but by the non-fiction staff bossed by Drawbell. It starts on page ten of the magazine amid a lurid four-colour spread of Bohemian eating places, Princess Margaret, a dance cellar, Breton onion sellers, Chez Auguste, Peter Cook in his satirical night-club, an Espresso bar ('Their interiors are gay, original and truly Continental—many a secretary has her lunchtime coffee, sandwich or salad at one of these gaily decorated counters'), a jazz club, a romantic young couple dashing across Soho Square.

Cut up into short sections with bold headings every four column inches or so, it opens with text from the book's page 63, backtracks to page 15, jumps to page 5, thence to page 26 where there's we meet May and her sister Jessie: 'They enjoyed the sort of girlhood every girl dreams about. They were dancers in Paris when Paris was at its most fabulously gay...'. All the rest of the instalment is about May and Jessie. For 'NEXT WEEK' the reader is promised: 'Mrs Henrey goes behind the scenes of a Soho shop where famous stage and screen stars buy their dancing shoes.'

* * *

'SO WHAT?' the disappointed reader exclaims today when confronted with much of Mrs Robert Henrey's output during Bob's *Woman's Own* decade. Why this deliberate lapse from literature?

185

What excuse can there be for this leap from the successful pursuit of fine writing into the abyss of a glossy but essentially mediocre entertainment humdrum? The answer must be money. Reflected in the large numbers of takeovers and mergers recorded by the *Financial Times* in the fifties and sixties, book and magazine publishing had shrugged off its mantle of social improvement and joined the mass market. The motive now was to give the people what the sales figures showed to be what they wanted.

Mé appears to have believed in the mass market to begin with. It wasn't until 1975 that she realised she had been wrong, writing to her American correspondent Elizabeth Snapp:

> *Woman's Own* was, and still is, a 2 million circulation weekly magazine for women published in London. They serialised quite a number of my lesser books but though they paid me well, I rather fancy serialisation does an authoress more harm than good. It is apt (at least in England) to antagonise the critics.[115]

Bob's log records explicitly that he and Drawbell used *Woman's Own* to make money while they could. Drawbell had no qualms about serialising his own stories in the magazine. He bought the serial rights of *The Dream Makers* for £1,500 and paid £2,000 for *Spring in a Soho Street*—high rates, indeed. In comparison, when the BBC Home Service did their theatre version of the Henreys' farm books on 7 and 9 March 1964 they paid £180.

According to Judith Burnley, the rates paid for magazine serials were inflated by the argument that they attracted readers anxious to learn the end of the story for less than the price of the book. The bottom ultimately fell out of this argument when the TV series *The Forsyte Saga* sold books by the million despite the fact that everyone already knew how the story ended.

* * *

THE HENREYS' FORTUNE, which had sunk low by 1957, gradually increased despite the expense of keeping Bobby at Downside, Mathilde at Villers and their travelling to and fro France. In 1957 they kept their boat afloat by selling the small diamonds and getting out of Wall Street, ending the year with £25,000. A year later they had £30,000 and Bobby went to Oxford. In 1959 they sold the solitaire and pearls at Sotheby's for £4,400 and their bottom line reached £38,000. The following year Mé used the equivalent of £360 she received as French war damage to buy her first 2CV second-hand from Hélène Vincent at Villers. Bobby reached twenty-one. Despite the slump in oils they made a lot of money out of Revlon shares and, after bringing in electric power at the farm, doing away with the water tank and putting in a giant refrigerator to keep Mathilde going when nobody else was around, ended up with £39,500. The liquidation of Bobby's Rothschild Trust enabled him to leave Oxford in May 1961 with enough money to live on independently until he found a suitable occupation. His parents' end of year balance stood at £44,500.

These figures from Bob's log are given to show that, while he and Mé had enough, they by no means hit the jackpot with their books at the height of their career. The public image of luxurious living given by Mrs Robert Henrey in her flashier volumes wasn't false, but it masked a great deal of hard work and a thrifty private lifestyle. A humble farmhouse, a poky flat were not all that much to show for a successful life in letters. Daphne du Maurier was much better off. Mé made most of her clothes from her old ones, cutting, sewing and knitting as her mother had taught her. Bob still liked dressing up in town, but his Savile Row days were over. At Villers both went about like ordinary villagers, not nearly as smart as the notables though with an elegant bookish aura that set them apart from even Dr Lehérissey and Maître Vincent.

While shy and sharp-tongued Mathilde wasn't particularly considered in Villers, Bobby was accepted as a true Villérois farm boy, shopping on his bike, making hay, harvesting, pressing cider, distilling applejack, speaking French with a Norman accent— everyone knew and loved him, and most had never heard of *The Fallen Idol* or didn't care. The only wealth that counted over there (though things were changing) was land, and Bobby had plenty of that by local standards.

Incidentally, Bobby swapped the Church of England for the Church of Rome while at Downside. His father didn't mind all that much, but Mé faithful to her girlhood reformed-church beliefs was upset at first it seems, though she soon felt she could cope with her son's Papism as long as he knelt to say his prayers before getting into bed every night. Later on, in the wake of Vatican II,

Bob fixed with the bishop of Bayeux that he and Mé should be allowed to commune at Holy Mass. They sat in the front row in the parish church at Villers, being deaf, and Bob followed the Catholic Ordinary in his Anglican Book of Common Prayer, while Protestant Mé thought about Jesus.

* * *

In any writer's career, lesser works identified as potboilers can justify their presence in an œuvre provided they don't damage the reputation of the rest. In Mrs Robert Henrey's case, it was some time before reviewers, librarians, and discerning non-professional readers realised that she could still write good books after a series of lapses. *Her April Days* contracted on 18 October 1962 and published in April 1963 was one of her better works of middlebrow literature, but the London Library didn't buy it and the reviewers didn't read it. Nor did the ordinary reading public apparently, as its first impression has sunk without a trace in the world's second-hand book market.

Fortunately, it was revived by Dent in 1976.[116] It's a fine book, carefully written and edited, recounting Mathilde's final months and death in Normandy. The narrative is centred on the activity of her daughter Madeleine in London and Normandy, along with reminiscences of their particularly close mother-daughter relationship spanning fifty-five years.

Some of Mé's best writing is elegiac, and this time the theme was specially ripe for her saddest prose. Astonishingly, after his diminished or inexistent role in her books since 1952, 'my husband' is a major figure in this one. With his character and upbringing, Bob necessarily proved stalwart in the time of Mé's grief. What is quite unexpected is the open expression of her love for him, her need for his presence, her surrender to his strength.

Poor Mathilde had become increasingly crippled by rheumatoid arthritis. She had moved into a ground-floor room next to the kitchen in the farmhouse. Nobody lived in the cottage, but Georgette Déliquaire came every day with the milk and did Mathilde's shopping with her own. Bobby no longer came to stay at what had been his real home. He had graduated from Oxford and found a job as an articled clerk at £500 per year with the venerable City accounting firm of Cooper Bros in Gutter Lane. He lived in a rented room in Kensington and was seeing Lisette, whom he had met at Oxford but not yet mentioned to anyone to avoid interference.

The postman brought Mathilde the *Daily Express* and *Daily Mail*, letters from Mé and Bobby, her pension and parcels. Only one old village widow called on her from time to time to natter. This solitude suited her. She had her radio and TV, her cats and chickens, Fifille the Pekingese, and did what gardening her poor hands permitted. Mé was with her often for one or two months at a time. They drove around the countryside in the 2CV to Mathilde's delight.

The old seamstress had a bad fall in May 1962 while Mé was in London. Alerted by Georgette via Patsy Poirot, Mé got a seat when all the flights were full—Bob telephoned the director of Air France—and nursed her mother during her last hours with the help of Georgette and a visiting carer.

Early on 29 May Bob called Bobby to say Grand'mère had just died in her room at the farm. He was flying over but preferred Bobby didn't come, it might be too harrowing. Why didn't the two of them have dinner that evening at Wheeler's?

Next day, in the midst of the great Wall Street slide that took the Dow to 550 and a nationwide electricity strike that turned off all the traffic lights in Paris creating chaos, Bob managed to get a train to Lisieux and was picked up by the Poirots who deposited him at the farm. Mé recorded:

> I took him to see Matilda. This was the last night she would spend under our roof. When I kissed her I broke down and sobbed. Yet even as my husband and I, hand in hand, went upstairs I began to experience again that wonderful comfort of being two, of having somebody to share my unhappiness, and, with my husband beside me, I fell asleep and to my shame never woke till morning.[117]

* * *

THERE'S SOME FINE WRITING in *Her April Day*s. Here 'I' is watching Truffaut's *Jules et Jim* with 'my husband' in a London cinema just before learning of Mathilde's fatal fall:

189

As I watched *Jules et Jim* the scenes in the sixth-floor room, the half-remembered conversations between my mother and Mme Réni, the colour of their clothes, the sound of their voices, even the smell of the wine and the fried potatoes, all became mixed up with the happenings on the screen, and I found myself crying gently for no reason at all. But what I know for certain is that the story of the film became less and less important to me as the scenes of my girlhood and the pictures of Matilda, as she then was, became more vivid and more real…

From time to time I would wake up from this reverie and look cautiously at my husband, but he was intent on the film. Then I would try to concentrate once again on what was going on. There is a scene when Jeanne Moreau is married to Oscar and we see them in the chalet with the mountain behind. [...] Afterwards she goes indoors to give instructions to her maid—and the maid's name is Matilda!

'Mathilde! Mathilde!' she cried, and I was startled to hear this name on Jeanne Moreau's lips, the sound filling the theatre, making public what as yet I had kept a secret in my mind. I am not even sure that today I can disentangle the plot of this picture from all that I superimposed upon it.[118]

Again, when 'I' arrives at the farm where Mathilde is dying:

The gate was open and I drove straight into the orchard. My house was brilliantly lit—this house that when I first set eyes on it obscurely housed farmer Goguet and his family. I have a curious mind that plays tricks on me. As I bounced and jolted down the grass road with the twisted apple trees on both sides of me, these lines of Victor Hugo suddenly came rushing upon me:

> *Il est nuit. La cabane est pauvre mais bien close,*
> *Le logis est plein d'ombre, et l'on sent quelque chose*
> *Qui rayonne à travers ce crépuscule obscur—*
> *Des filets de pêcheur sont accrochés au mur.*

Hugo, of course, was talking about a fisherman's cabin in Brittany. But I know now why at this poignant moment my brain brought back these lines from the past. As a girl I was made to learn them by heart and, because children invariably put their own interpretations on the work of grown-ups, I had substituted Milou, my father, for Victor Hugo's fisherman, and when

I saw my father standing joyously on the threshold, not with a fisherman's net as in the poem but with a sackful of broken wood, as I remember him so often, when he came back from a day's work on a building site. I could just see my mother looking up critically from her sewing, her narrow lips pursed as Milou put the sack down roughly on her newly waxed floor.

I switched off the engine of my car and hurried into the house.[119]

Alas, the reviewers failed to notice this book's return to grace. Siriol Hugh-Jones in the *Tatler* didn't get beyond the blurb. All she could bring herself to write was: 'Another instalment in Mrs Robert Henrey's memoirs, which have been going on for some time now—this one is mostly about the last months and death of her mother.' The anonymous reviewer in the *Sphere* produced but three sentences, of which the third reads: '*Her April Days* is, as one has come to expect and indeed enjoy, extremely discursive for it is one of Mrs Henrey's especial qualities that she can let her pen roam at will and can explore all kinds of fascinating byways before coming back to the subject.' This reviewer can't have read it either, because this book is one of the least discursive in the corpus.

Margaret Wilson in the *Staffordshire Newsletter* did read it, praised it, and raised an interesting point. She wrote that, not having read the books which preceded, she found *Her April Days* at first rather heavy going. 'The author assumes that her readers know all about Madeleine's childhood and bringing-up, about her marriage and farm in Normandy. These provide the necessary background for *Her April Days*, and it is slow work to deduce them from the book itself.'

Wilson's point was an important one. All sagas present a coherence problem on their appearance, particularly when their components are published piecemeal regardless of the chronological order of events, as in this case. That each new book by Mrs Robert Henrey should be read as part of a larger ensemble with something serious to say about survival and about the world in a continuum was an idea that had not begun to gain currency in the 1960s. Indeed, such a notion was almost impossible to associate with stuff like *The Dream Makers* or *This Feminine World*—unless one was a follower.

* * *

WHEN BOB RETURNED to *Woman's Own* after Mathilde's funeral, an office cabal—apparently inspired by Judith using Maureen to foment trouble—declared war on his protégée Jane in order to isolate him. Drawbell had left and been replaced by George Rogers, known as 'Rodge', an ex-sailor who according to Judith tended to navigate the corridors of Tower House in the rolling gait of his former profession. Bob had foreseen trouble and had obtained a contract for himself and Judith from 'JWD' so that they should remain protected after his departure. Judith, though proving 'a splendid and very clever associate editress', had been intriguing for his job more or less from the start. Nonetheless, *Woman's Own* was obliged by contract to serialise Mrs Robert Henrey's *Her April Days* and the crisis blew over.

Jane came to Villers for a week during Bob's summer holiday. Mé wrote that she felt for her as she would have felt for a daughter. She was a tall, thin, not very pretty working-class girl who had left her home in Salford to work in London, and London was sometimes more than she could take. At the office, her Lancashire accent and unsophisticated bewilderment let her in for a great deal of mockery. Bob's solicitude for her well-being was such that Judith, amazed that he should lavish such kindness on her—even menial things such as going to her flat to clean the cooker—exclaimed: 'She enslaved him!'[120]

On his return from Normandy, he signed up Edna O'Brien, whose brilliant first novel *The Country Girls* had just been banned by the Irish censorship board and condemned as 'filth' by the Minister of Justice. At this point Judith came back from her holiday in New York and, according to Bob's log, incited Renée and Elizabeth to resign. Then Maureen resigned. On 5 March 1963, Rodge called in Jane, who was wearing a new suit and had gone to the hairdressers' for a sensational hair-do, and sacked her. She went off for a cruise on the *Empress of Britain*, returning later to

192

'wait for something to happen'. The something turned out to be a job at *Reader's Digest*. Incredibly, Rodge then gave Bob a £1,950 contract to 'teach Judith the job'.

While this nonsense was being played out at Tower House, Bobby was in the Congo, sent by Cooper Bros with a colleague to audit a client's books. Mé was in Normandy, where she suddenly received a card from the Lord Chamberlain stating he was 'commanded by Her Majesty to invite Mr and Mrs Robert Henrey to an Afternoon Party in the Garden of Buckingham Palace on Wednesday, the 17th July 1963, from 4 to 6 o'clock P.M. (Weather Permitting.)—Morning Dress, or Uniform, or Lounge Suit.' The invitation was addressed to Mrs Robert Henrey at Carrington House. Mé was astonished, abashed, scared, thrilled. What on earth would she wear? She would need a hat.

* * *

THE ROYAL GARDEN PARTY was duly recorded in a new chronicle entitled *Wednesday at Four* contracted with Dent on 7 February 1964 and published the same year in September. Sub-titled on the jacket 'A Year In My Life', it also recounts her daily round at Villers and three *Woman's Own* assignments: a Mediterranean cruise with Bob on the post-war *Empress of Britain*, a trip to Moscow and Leningrad, a visit to Manchester's Coronation Street iconified by the popular ITV series.[121]

Although *Wednesday at Four* belongs to the 'contemporary diary' genre, it's structured and well-written. There's a fine chapter[122] (pp. 110–15) describing a meal with the Déliquaire family and many amusing scenes with little nine-year-old Brigitte Déliquaire in a surrogate grandmother relationship. The stream of consciousness produces some nice touches, such as this one (pp. 101–102):

> I felt increasingly that my mother's personality had merged into mine, and that might well explain my indifference to solitude. With her, of course, it had been a passion; with me, it was a question of waiting. I suffered my loneliness and had learned by experience what use I could make of it. Besides, I was never alone. Many of my evenings were passed in communion with her and I could now tell myself that we were at peace.'[123]

Many things have changed at the farm since Mathilde's death. Dr Lehérissey has died, as has the giant woodcutter Raiteault (misspelt 'Rettol' in *Matilda and the Chickens*). The authoress no longer writes in bed, since there's nobody to bring her breakfast upstairs, but on a corner of the kitchen table. Fifille is still there, but goes to a neighbour when her mistress is away. There are only five hens who escaped when the rest were herded up to be sold. Georgette and Brigitte look after the survivors in her absence. The cats have been dispersed. The garden is growing wild. 'I' spends a lot of time on the sands, and bathes almost daily till the season ends.

When she returns to London from Moscow, Patsy telephones on 11 December—Mathilde's birthday—to say the farm has been broken into and burgled. 'My husband' is sent to sort things out. He discovers that a vagrant farm labourer has slept in Mé's bed with his boots on, stolen some of her clothes recovered in sacks in the cider press, soiled the carpets, broken objects. He is on the run, but the gendarmerie are on to him. Georgette is scared he might come back. Jacques has his shotgun ready.

The book year ends with a *Woman's Own* visit to Salford that in reality took place early in 1965. 'I' takes advantage of this trip to drop in on Jane's parents, whose obscure address she happens to remember, just as she happens to remember so many places and people that can provide her with copy. Perhaps Bob asked her to pop in, though he may have been with her. Jane almost certainly didn't and definitely wasn't.

One would have liked to read the witty and perceptive Siriol Hugh-Jones on *Wednesday at Four*. Would she have devastated it or, more likely, found much to esteem? Alas, the *Tatler* had recorded her death the previous year. She was thirty-nine. Her last article had appeared on 4 March 1964. Apparently the blood for her final transfusion was given by a bookmaker. 'Will this shorten my odds on survival?' she asked.

Hugh-Jones's successor Oliver Warner was non-committal about *Wednesday at Four*, merely echoing 'her enthusiasm for the architectural beauties' of Leningrad. The other reviews were fairly numerous and mostly favourable. The *Tewkesbury Register* fan produced an interesting observation: 'People, places, history and anecdotes are the staple material that have enabled Mrs Robert

Henrey to become a literary celebrity. In *Wednesday at Four* she pursues the same vein, but carefully separates the gold from the dross.' One is left to understand that this sifting has not always taken place.

The younger generation of women critics were unsympathetic. Fiona MacCarthy in the *Guardian* was particularly caustic:

> I am afraid I lose patience with Mrs Robert Henrey, in her new book *Wednesday at Four*, when she tells us how she burst out crying at the sight of our small, slim Queen in Buckingham Palace gardens. [...] What can one say but big deal?
>
> One goes on saying it right through the book, right through a year in Mrs Robert Henrey's life. [...] She moves on to Moscow, because, she says, she wants to tell young women in Britain about their sisters in Russia. [...] She manages to make Russia sound cosy, and last time I saw Moscow, cosy is just not what it was.

Sylva Norman's ironic review in the *Times Literary Supplement* spun a droll metaphor while contriving to say something valid about life and literature:

> If Mrs Henrey were to spend a year chained like Andromeda to a rock she would still produce a full-length book about the ships and bathers, the family-life of sea birds, the clothes and conversations of the sightseers. She would manage to write it if her hands were tied. [...] The open secret of Mrs Henrey's popularity is this delight in the surface aspects of living. Familiar events on the paths of the modest multitudes are mirrored back, recognizable yet with fresher colours.

The *TLS* itself apparently decided at this point that Mrs Robert Henrey wasn't worth reviewing any more: none of her titles appeared in its pages after *Wednesday at Four*.

No Repentance

JUDITH BURNLEY, in her second novel *Unrepentant Women* (1983), has left a vivid portrait of 'RH' as she knew him at *Woman's Own* in the early 1960s. She calls him Adrian and his wife Adriana. The couple met when Adriana was a manicurist at the Savoy, and he's utterly at her feet. 'Got to be home for lunch, or Adriana won't be best pleased,' he tells a girl in the office. He's an upper-class eccentric with an Etonian accent ('gels' for girls, 'well-orf' for rich), a distinguished look (tall and slim, a 'neat white head', a 'soberly checked suit'). He despises men: 'If I had your brothers in my department instead of you bright gels, the level of intelligence would drop by twenty per cent overnight.' There's something sad about his situation: 'Here was a man with an impressive male physique, who admired women so much he had wanted desperately all his life to be one.'

His colleague Sarah in the novel is convinced that he wants to be a woman so he can make love with another woman. 'What about husbands who want to become their wives?' he asks her. She imagines him as a boy child 'besotted with his mother, a busy young person much given to charitable work', wandering into her room while she's out, trying on her clothes. 'He stares in the mirror. If he screws up his eyes, he resembles his mother. He is said to be just like her. Everyone remarks upon it. [...] He looks again. And this time he unscrews his eyes. He *is* his mother.'[124]

Becoming his wife, *being* his mother. This is surely a key to the dual identity of the authoress Mrs Robert Henrey: all those 'I's that can't possibly be Mé and the many more that can't be Bob, except insofar as he dresses her French in his English, seeing her as him and him as her. The act of translation *per se* implies impersonation at the least, at the most (and best) fusion of the self with the other. When something as deep as love intervenes in the impersonation process, the result is the erasure of difference.

Adrian in Burnley's novel scoffs at his magazine's male executives and their crude pub jokes about feminism turning History into Herstory. Sarah isn't at all convinced that the single life is a woman's epiphany, and Mé wasn't either. On several occasions Mé reacted to affirm her independence—to be one of Burnley's 'unrepentant women'—and each time she came back to 'my husband', as Sarah does too up to the day she realises that she is watching her Adam die.

* * *

Bob had never wanted to be an executive. He was a writer, and writers on the whole consider themselves superior to their editorial masters. They have the same fear of an office desk as a robin has of a gilded cage. When down in the dumps after his experience at the *Star*, he would have preferred to move to Normandy right there and then instead of going to *Woman's Own*, but Mé wasn't ready.

Not that he was averse to life in the Fiction Room. The girls confided their woes to him, and he revelled in their stories. Jane, for instance, had a flat-mate called Ann, madly in love with an American economist who wrote for the *Sunday Times*. When she was jilted, Ann tried to commit suicide and was replaced at the flat by Patricia, with whom Jane went to a marriage bureau. They got introduced to a Canadian bigamist called Griff and he, after promising marriage to one of them, was arrested by the police who discovered that he had a wife in New York. And so on. Bob jotted it all down in his log. With Judith he had tea most afternoons at the Waldorf searching for new ideas. Together they continued buying the work of writers with world reputations. The names of Arthur Miller, Lawrence Durell, Françoise Sagan appeared on the contents pages of *Woman's Own*.

A double takeover at Tower House and further changes of administration finally sapped his morale. The new men wanted to see new faces around them. He had worked in plenty of editorial offices in various parts of the world and knew them all to be hotbeds of intrigue, but this time he conceded defeat. He 'swanned around' (in Judith's words) pending his anticipated retirement,

197

walking miles every day between the West End and the City, attending press showings of new films, calling at Dent's old-fashioned offices in Bedford Street and the premises of his bookbinder friend Ernest Zaehnsdorf in Covent Garden, meeting people at the Savoy—Juliette Gréco was one. The lease on the Carrington House flat had only six months to run and this time he was determined to move to Normandy.

Mé had been over there since February and was thoroughly enjoying herself, invited to parties, sunning herself on the sands, gardening, running the farm—Bob called it 'administering his dominions overseas.'[125] Leaving London would be a wrench for both of them, but keeping up a place in town without being there, or only being there from time to time, was a luxury hardly anybody could afford anymore.

Bobby, who was by now living with two other young men in a shared flat in Hampstead, had passed his final professional examinations and was planning to resign from Cooper Bros and find a more satisfying position abroad.

His parents' joint fortune had reached a sum that should enable them to live comfortably for the rest of their lives, whatever pension rights came into play from National Insurance, Sécurité Sociale, and the current owners of *Woman's Own* (International Publishing Company).

A complication which worried Bob considerably was how to retain control over their savings from abroad. By applying to the Bank of England for permission to leave the country they could virtually free their entire capital, which could either remain at their disposal (in any currency they chose) in England, or go in part or in whole to any other country in the world. In addition, they would be exempt from British income tax except on money they continued to earn in England, such as royalties, or on dividends of purely English companies. This perspective was tantamount to offering themselves a new and perhaps more exciting life.

But at what cost—leaving London! Had they lost some of their adventurousness, at a time when Bobby was preparing to go off into the unknown as both his parents had done more or less at his age?

* * *

WHILE MÉ WAS ENJOYING the hot sun on her back in the Normandy summer of 1964 Bob was trying to find a solution to these problems and also to shrug off the changed atmosphere at the office. He was due to join her for a week's holiday in August, and as usual she sent him a list of British eatables to bring over. After attending a magazine screening at the Plaza, he went to the bank to cash a cheque and sign some papers, and on his return to the flat picked up a wicker basket in which to put Mé's shopping. He was worried about a reader's report he had promised to deliver to a publisher. He did this first, and with his mind still occupied with it, he went to a chemist's to buy a number of things, and then turned into a self-service shop.

Instead of picking up a steel mesh basket on the way in, he used his own wicker basket already containing the packages he had bought at the chemist's. Having added the things set out in Mé's letter, he walked to the cash desk where he has was annoyed to have to queue up. When it was his turn to pay, he pushed his wicker basket in front of the girl, paid, and hurried out into the sunshine.

At this moment a woman barred his way and asked: 'Did you pay for the tea?'

She snatched the basket from him and, diving into it, produced the tea that had slipped between the other goods and the packages bought at the chemist's.

Bob laughed: 'How stupid! I'll go and tell the girl.'

'No,' said the woman. 'You must follow me.'

The shop manager asked him what had happened. Bob said he was entirely to blame, he had been too absorbed to notice that the girl hadn't rung up the tea. In that case, said the manager, he would have to call the police. At the station, the duty sergeant told him to plead guilty and be done with it, there would just be a small fine. The detective disagreed. If he was innocent, Bob should fight the case. There was still everything to be said for British justice. Too many innocent people pleaded guilty because they were put off by the expense of engaging a solicitor and a barrister.

Bob had been in newspapers all his life and knew that if a cub reporter got a whiff of the case, it might destroy several existences. Never having had much opinion of his own, he was concerned above all about Mé's and Bobby's. *Wednesday at Four* was due to be published the following week, Bobby was about to change jobs. The slightest skit in the papers could do incalculable harm. After a sleepless night he appeared in Bow Street magistrate's court and pleaded: 'Guilty—but only by my lack of attention. I had no idea that the tea had not passed through the cashier's hands.'

The magistrate having heard the charge read out, declared that in view of what the accused had said to the police and repeated in court he could no longer try the case. The plea must be altered to 'Not Guilty' and the case would have to go before another magistrate.

That evening the Bow Street detective called to say that the store, wishing to brief its usual solicitor who was on holiday, had obtained a postponement till 10 September. The detective himself was also going on a fortnight's holiday. This meant Bob had to postpone his own holiday without alarming Mé with what was happening. He did call in Bobby, who was still working in London. Over boiled fish fillets and frozen peas at Carrington House, he owned up to his son. In return, Bobby let on about about Lisette. It was the first time they had established a grown-up bond between them, and both were delighted. Bob suggested they attend a book launch party together the following evening in the River Room at the Savoy, and that Bobby bring Lisette along.[126] It proved a delightful occasion and afterwards Bob invited them to supper at the recently rebuilt (and terribly British) Stone's Chop House in Panton Street, now gone alas.

Later that night he wrote Mé a long letter to tell her the surprising news about Bobby and to describe Lisette, who quite obviously would one day become their daughter-in-law. He said she was charming and that her parents lived in Gloucestershire. She was in London working at Macmillan's, the publishers.

Typically, Mé thought Bob might be exaggerating in his conviction that their son was about to become engaged. Had Bobby not lived with her in Normandy, preparing for his finals, from February till early summer, and said nothing? Was it possible that this great secret had been locked so tightly in his heart that she, his mother, had not guessed a word of it? Of course, she knew nothing of the private drama taking place in London nor how it had led to a new confidence between father and son.

The weather in Normandy continued unusually fine. Mé was

full of plans for the future and a little vexed that Bob should continue to talk about leaving London the following spring, though she realised it made sense. Bob meanwhile was beginning to feel much better. There wasn't the least squeak in the press. He stirred from the numbness that had come over his mind. He remembered lunching a short time before with a partner of a distinguished solicitors' firm in the City. He contacted this man, got severely scolded for not acting sooner, and a young barrister was briefed for the 10 September hearing.

On the critical morning, Bob had arranged to meet the barrister at 9 A.M. at his chambers in the Temple. The solicitors also sent a representative. The three of them, after a short conference, walked slowly and amicably down the Strand, conversing not on the law but on literature. Though the case lasted rather longer than Bob had expected, there was, after the first few minutes, little doubt in anybody's mind how it would end.

Before the clocks of the City churches chimed eleven, the case was dismissed and a police officer was congratulating him as he led him down a short flight of steps. There he unlocked a door with iron bars. Through this door Bob walked out into what was once more his ordinary world. In the front hall the barrister and the solicitor's clerk were waiting for him with smiling faces. Everything was back to normal.

Next morning Bob telephoned to tell Mé that he and Bobby would be coming over by the afternoon plane, the last of the summer. Bobby's girl friend—she could not yet be called his fiancée—had accompanied them to a film preview the night before and afterwards they had all gone to Wheeler's for oysters and Chablis. Mé asked whether they were celebrating something in her absence. Bob was uncommunicative. He just said he would be bringing over most of the things she had asked for, except perhaps the tea. Did it matter if there was no tea? 'Oh, really!' Mé objected. 'Surely it's not asking too much of you!'

She disapproved of Bobby's decision to leave Cooper Bros and go to South America on his own for a few months. Unlike her, Bob thought it was an excellent idea. Secretly thinking no doubt that the separation from Lisette before they married would somehow be in the family tradition, like FitzRoy and Peli, like himself and Mé, he declared that it would be good for Bobby's Spanish.

The experience, however it turned out, would greatly enhance his chances of professional success. In short he was proud of his son's adventurous spirit. She objected that the couple weren't even engaged yet. Bob, who had seen them together, said the inherent toughness of both their characters shouldn't be underestimated.

He eventually spoke to Mé about what had happened to postpone his holiday. He asked her to stop the car on the way to the village because he had something to tell her—nothing to do with the office or their leaving London in March, something worse. She immediately imagined visits to doctors and dire diagnostics.

I ran the car into the side of the lane, put on the handbrake and cut off the engine. There was a horrible silence. The trees were full of birds, but they were silent. A squirrel ran across in front of the car, disappeared for a moment in the hedgerow and then could be seen scurrying up the pale grey trunk of a tall ash. I turned to my husband. 'Go on!' I said almost harshly.

'1 was taken to court for forgetting to pay for your tea. It was dreadful!' Suddenly he collapsed and covered his face with his hands.

'Good heavens!' I cried. 'Is that all? I thought you were going to tell me that you had cancer!'[127]

She put it all down to being too sure of themselves. He ran their affairs in England, she ran the business in France. From the point of view of an efficient money-making partnership, it had proved ideal. But she wondered if they had paid enough attention to loneliness. Bob said the risk was calculated. No one was worth his salt if he didn't try to 'build up'. Every plan entailed a risk. In his case he got over-tired. In retrospect the whole affair was chastening. Something ought to happen every now and again to humble one, like a good thrashing in a Punch and Judy show.

A week later they all three closed up the house for the winter and returned to London by the new Norwegian car ferry from Le Havre. Mé recorded that her son's departure for South America as much as his possible engagement were brutal reminders that at least as far as he was concerned her usefulness had come to an end. She and her husband would increasingly be alone 'in the dim, questionable future'.

Bobby organised his departure, brought Lisette to a film premiere with his parents. Mé still found it difficult to equate his enthusiasm for his South American adventure with his desire to marry the slim, almost shy girl who came back to the flat after the film for bacon and eggs. There was still no talk of an engagement, though it seemed obvious there would be. The two young people drove down together for a weekend with her parents—near Tewkesbury of all places!—and then only a few days later he was gone. On 22 January 1965 their engagement was announced in the *Times*.

To help Mé come to terms with their own departure from London, Bob gave her a mink cape and suggested they put some of their furniture in store in case they ever decided to take a *pied à terre* in town after all. All of his antique stuff had already been sold, but Mé had to deal with what was left, and in the end everything was either scrapped or given away, except the books, pictures and other heirlooms that were crated for shipment to Le Havre.

On 24 March 1965 they settled everything and left for Villers in a chauffeur-driven limousine from Harrods with Didi, the latest Pekingese, seventeen pieces of luggage of various shapes and sizes and a coffee pot that Bob refused to leave behind at the last minute. Jane, now living near Palace Gate and working for an American film company, adopted Mary Oliver's rubber plant that by now quite filled the living room window at Carrington House.

* * *

ALL THIS CAME OUT in a new and splendid book, *Winter Wild*, written carefully in Normandy during 1965, contracted with Dent on 30 March 1966 and published in November the same year.[128]

Winter Wild marked a return to thoughtful, well-written autobiography, i.e. literature, after a number of misguided sorties into the world of the mass circulation women's magazines. The 'contemporary diaries' series definitely harmed the Mrs Robert Henrey signature—adverse reviews, reduced public library accessions, lower bookshop sales. Responsibility for this fell mainly on Mé's shoulders. Bob was in disgrace at her court and she was sure of herself, convinced that she had the admiring eye of the postwar British housewife. She did have it for a time. What she didn't realise in the late fifties and early sixties was that the postwar British housewife was on the road to extinction, now that she was flying to Cyprus and driving to Spain for her holidays. When Mé pushed Bob into *Woman's Own,* intrigued by the sudden success that fiction in women's magazines was enjoying in London, it was already too late. The young women in the fiction office were quite alien to the myth sustained by the radio serial 'Mrs Dale's Diary', the supposed yardstick for feminine values in Britain until the BBC woke up and scrapped it in 1969. What these career girls read and wrote about was sex and the city. *Woman's Own*'s florid romances were a rearguard action fought by the male management of the paper believing that they held the key to British women's hearts. The girls in Tower House were to prove them wrong. They played the system in the early sixties but were already streaks ahead of it.

Mé to her credit realised this, and *Winter Wild* was her response, written in full-time renewed partnership with Bob at Villers during the latter part of 1965. This book is the first in which the word 'sex' is used in its modern sense—until then it had just meant male or female, or been used in the term 'sex appeal'—though *Wednesday at Four* had sneezed *en passant* at 'our literature of brutality and sex' (p. 33), and the disreputable Compton Cinema in *Spring in a Soho Street* had billed (p. 27) 'a compelling action story charged with sex and suspense.'

The three-letter word cropped up in Mrs Robert Henrey's own prose in *Winter Wild* as an antonym to interest in political ideas:

> The girls with whom my husband worked had practically no interest in politics, so that in the evening when we discussed the day's happenings, that subject seldom came up. Even the young generation of women writers—girls suddenly writing a thoughtful novel that got talked about and whom my husband met and admired—were much more concerned in the problems of youth and sex, the immorality and deception that came the way of girls catapulted into great cities, than in what was discussed by politicians in the corridors of Westminster. A contract for a film, a journey to New York to receive a prize, the planning of the next novel, how their literary success would affect their chances of marriage or, if they were already married, their relationship with the husband, were much more vital subjects.[129]

Politics had always been taken for granted in the Henreys' books.

Both were liberal conservatives, irritated by taxation, firm in their attachment to the accumulation of capital by hard work, opposed to the factory culture of trade unions and social benefits. In Mé's case, considering her impoverished childhood, this involved a fair amount of Protestant stoicism. Bob was attracted postwar by the socialist ideas of Pierre Brossolette and the firm regime of General de Gaulle, but he put their joint savings in dollars and kept a close eye on Wall Street.

Winter Wild reflects a change in their views, a change consonant with the changes in British society propelled by the grammar schools and the redbrick universities, with new creative talents and disruptive audiences transforming the cinema, book, theatre and art worlds. The Labour victory in the 1964 General Election produced this sentence: 'It was only the uncertainty of what the new administration would do financially that affected us, and in this matter it became quickly clear that the new men might well prove less inconsequent than their Conservative predecessors.'[130] Implicit criticism, but criticism all the same, at a time when the Beatles' *A Hard Day's Night* was knocking the stuffing out of Harold Macmillan's 'You've never had it so good.'

'I' in *Winter Wild* spends a lot of time talking to the young *au pair* nannies in the Green Park, she exercising her Pekingese, they pushing their prams. No fewer than fifty-seven pages are devoted to a cumulative portrait of a young Corsican children's nurse called Annie. Truculent and ambitious, Annie corresponds to a modern version of the little Madeleine, a cross-generational *alter ego*. She adopts 'I', calls at Carrington House, gives her views on everything, explains the changing world to her friend in a trenchant and condescending tone that makes 'I' feel old.

The title of course refers to the disarray caused in the authoress by the prospect of being uprooted from her beloved London, her life told in so many books. It was probably borrowed from an anniversary song by Robert Burns dating from 1788, 'The Day Returns':

> *The day returns, my bosom burns,*
> *The blissful day we twa did meet!*
> *Tho' winter wild in tempest toil'd,*
> *Ne'er summer sun was half sae sweet.*

'We twa' are indeed given plenty of space in *Winter Wild*, which consecrates the Henrey couple's reunion. There's a walk together through the West End streets on a crisp November night after a party:

> As we turned into Shepherd Street from Whitehorse Street, sounds of laughter and raised voices came from public houses whose coal fires could be glimpsed from outside. Christmas decorations hung across the windows of White's, the grocery store. Inside Sheam's, by a single table lamp, Sylvia counted her till (at this time of night!) and, seeing us, waved. The Free Vintner, immaculate and slim, with a flower in his buttonhole, stood at the door of his sherry bar. A street musician played 'Marlene' on a penny whistle out of tune, the collar of his grubby raincoat turned up to give the passer-by the illusion that he was miserable and cold. A window opened and a coin bounced in the middle of the road.
>
> 'It's nice to get home,' said my husband, pulling out his latch-key.[131]

This whole walk is fine writing by any chalk, particularly evocative in the context of what the reader knows of their lives. 'My husband' gets several nice paragraphs to himself, including this one (p. 92):

> My husband treated his native city much as a bee treats the flowers in an old English garden. He daily criss-crossed the centre of the town, looking in at a publisher's, then at an exhibition, at Sotheby's, at Christie's, at the London Library, in a store, at Coutts' in the Strand, in a newspaper office, never bored, never tired. It was this incorrigible urge to make the most of every moment of the day, not for the benefit of a career but for his own satisfaction, that prevented him from ever wishing to acquire executive responsibility that might have impinged on his liberty. To some extent he paid for it by becoming a rolling stone, though he had an uncanny way of acquiring enough moss to make its conservation a matter of importance.[132]

And, 'I' being 'I', there are many self-portraits in scenes such as the comedy sequence describing her 'gigantic wash' (pp. 162–65) or this astonishing stream of associated ideas:

> My fingers ran thoughtfully through some skeins of coloured silk which I had chosen to embroider a linen tablecloth. There was to be

the usual garland of flowers in the middle, and much as I tried to alter it my only hope of originality would consist in the choice of tints. I rather despised myself for resorting to embroidery of such a useless kind, but it rested my eyes from making buttonholes and my fingers from knitting. Christmas carols arrived softly into the room from the transistor at my side. They reminded me of my very first Christmas tree presided over in that most poignant of years 1916 (Verdun and the opening of the battle of the Somme) by M. Maroger, our pastor at Clichy, wearing his blue uniform of captain in the French army. He was on leave from the trenches and had entered the room carrying his helmet under his arm, a tall, broad-shouldered figure of such unusual good looks that we stared at him in wonderment. The tree was lit by innumerable coloured candles, waving, spluttering and occasionally setting fire to a fir twig above or below which emitted when smouldering a smell so romantic that one could easily believe oneself to be in an enchanted forest, in which fairy princes rode on white horses and witches gathered sticks. It must have been a cold Christmas because I recall that on leaving the party we wound rags about our shoes so as not to slip on the icy road. Horses had fallen between the shafts of vans and drays and the night air was filled with drunken oaths as the drivers cracked their whips in an effort to get their miserable animals on their feet.

I became suddenly aware that warm tears were trickling down my cheeks. Was this self-pity? Regret? I still felt resentment against the draymen with their long unkempt moustaches who cursed and lashed at the animals, and on these occasions I found myself evoking the help of Jean Valjean, whose exploits in *Les Misérables* had so coloured that period of my girlhood. The pastor so beautiful in his uniform was dead; so were both my parents now. The half-million slain in France and Belgium were almost forgotten. What had the little girl I saw so clearly in retrospect done with the opportunities given her?[133]

From the viewpoint of clever narrative structure, a passage about sudden death starts with a dinner on a Mediterranean cruise, veers to a stole worn by Lady Lindsay at a dinner party at the Priory in Regent's Park, where it was fingered and admired by George Eliot, thence to a long quote from a letter of Blanche Lindsay describing tea with the Leweses, via a bridge back to 'the black moiré stole which I wore on the cruise as a two-piece (and which I still wear)', thence again to another Lindsay letter about George Eliot after

Lewes's death, back to 'the moiré two-piece, which gave me the impression of wearing the mantle of the famous' and to the first-class lounge on the cruise where 'I danced a few turns with one of the ship's officers' and ends up with a thud on the dance floor and 'a heavily-built man lying, legs slightly apart, a trickle of moisture running off the end of a trouser leg'.[134]

In short, *Winter Wild* is a mature, controlled, unfeverish volume of autobiography. Someone at Dent's—Bozman had left—must surely have seen that it was in a different league from the series of 'contemporary diaries' that they had been marketing for the past ten years on the mistaken assumption that most women found them delightful. 'Delightful to at least ninety-five women in every hundred' was the claim quoted from the *Scotsman* on the back flap. This just wasn't true, or wasn't true any more.

Looking at the recent review record, not to mention the sales figures, surely somebody must have wondered whether the damage hadn't been done permanently. Whoever composed the *Winter Wild* blurb in 1966 must have crossed his or her fingers when writing: 'The "Madeleine" books will one day be seen in perspective. Meanwhile this one has nearly all the elements that go to bring hope and despair to a woman.' Bob, who had never lost faith in his joint enterprise with Mé, told his son: 'Your mother's a genius.' She was indeed, but she had fallen foul of two reefs that can wreck a writer: pride and complacency. Could she recover her critical standing on the Normandy sands?

Dent advertised *Winter Wild* in the Christmas columns of both the *Sunday Times* and the *Times Literary Supplement* but, amazingly and quite unfairly, it didn't receive a single review anywhere. Even the *Tewkesbury Register* ignored it, perhaps because Lisette wasn't around in Gloucestershire any more to nudge elbows.

She and Bobby married at Kemerton on 23 April 1965 as soon as he came back from South America. They went off immediately to New York where he had found a job at Lybrand Ross Bros and Montgomery on Lower Broadway. His parents didn't attend the wedding, alleging that a trip back to England would affect their newly-acquired non-resident tax status. Thus the bizarre family wedding history (from Rothschild to FitzRoy to Lindsay to Henrey) lived on. Only Bob's sister Blanche was present to attest to the bridegroom's illustrious lineage. A blue cedar was nonetheless planted at the farm to celebrate the event. It's still there.

* * *

BY THE TIME Mrs Robert Henrey's next book came out, Bob had recorded in his log that their 'darling Didi' had been operated on and died, that the devaluation of the pound had made them better off by £9,000, that Bobby and Lisette had been to stay at the farm as had Blanche and her friend Mme Nielsen, that Judith had left *Woman's Own* and gone to Pan Books, that Patsy had bought the Bellay farm, that he Bob had had dizzy spells, that there were plans to build a motorway smack through their farmhouse, that this project had made Mé (who had been unwell since the death of Didi) nervous and poorly, that the May Revolution had broken out, that he and Mé had driven to the Sorbonne and Nanterre University to see what was happening, that the first part of a book about it all had been approved by Dent, that Dr Salmond had died and Denos his farmer while cutting wood before going to the funeral had lost an eye, that Martin Dent had agreed to Madeleine's 'great idea' of re-writing the war books, and that their cash in hand stood at £85,000.

The new book was *She Who Pays*—a strange title for a strange piece of social topography not unlike the earlier volumes about the farm and the Blitz, nothing to do with paying the piper and calling the tune but, as the blurb points out, a reminder that in times of trouble 'the woman pays'. The contract was dated 9 September 1968 and the book came out the following May extended by a few pages, the last being dated Villers-sur-Mer, 1 February 1969.[135] The epigraph bears a sentence ascribed to an 'English proverb' (Apperson dates it 1639): 'He that pryeth into every cloud may be stricken with a thunderbolt.'[136]

In a rather silly reaction to the reviewers' indifference towards the depreciated Mrs Robert Henrey signature, the blurb attempts to present *She Who Pays* as the work of an authoress of importance dealing with important current events. The story of Madeleine from her childhood in France to the present day is presented as 'a series of autobiographical volumes whose sales in hardback alone total over half a million copies'. Her 'modest farmhouse' is said to be 'known to women readers all over the world, from South

209

Africa to Japan'. Fair enough. However, the farm's threatened destruction by motorway and revolution is blown up to ridiculous proportions:

While the menace of the autoroute remained poised over Madeleine's head, the whole of France was torn asunder by what will become known as the 'revolution' of May. Nanterre, the Sorbonne, the Odeon theatre, the battles in the Latin Quarter of Paris, Madeleine found herself in the middle of them all. To men writers, Madeleine leaves the political and social implications. This is a woman's story told by this most essentially feminine writer, of how events of such puzzling importance struck her farmer's wife, little girls at school, young married women whose husbands went off gaily to the barricades.

Nothing could be farther from reality. The motorway never got off the drawing board. The whole of France wasn't 'torn asunder' by the so-called revolution, just copiously buggered up. Madeleine wasn't 'in the middle' of the student battles—Mé and Bob drove to Nanterre and Paris in late June when all the fighting was over. As for the husbands of Villers-sur-Mer going off 'gaily to the barricades...' What husbands? What barricades? Mé's dramas are often exaggerated, but this one as promoted by the blurb is just too dramatic for words.

In truth, *She Who Pays* is an elegy on the demise of a dream, the little Eden discovered in 1937. By 1968 the mechanisation and monetisation of farm life, together with taxation, property development, tourism and the rest had transformed Villers-sur-Mer into a different place with different people. In particular its dialect-speaking, hard-drinking peasant farmers and their long-suffering wives had died. Their sons had left the land, got jobs, bought cars, built new houses, moved to the cities, begun taking holidays. Most were subservient either to the State or to business concerns. Their farmhouses had caved in or been dolled up as *résidences secondaires*. Their orchards had been built on. Only the dream remained unchanged.

Bob was haunted by the freedom of his childhood, the vicarage, Gunnersbury, and by the memory of his mother whom he resembled. In a way he wanted to *be* his mother—studious, self-giving, collected—in a small safe space surrounded by beauty and simplicity. He was to Mé as Effie had been to Burr, a loving companion and inspirer, part of the other's soul to the point of identification. *She Who Pays* is his *Paradise Lost*, the work of a free spirit devoted to literature and womanhood—his two anchors in life, wife and mother. Its complex structure bears his hallmark as an editor, and stylistic analysis shows that much of the English narrative is his. Mé's contributions, as in the days of their collaboration on the *Evening News*, are factual. Brilliantly observed and recorded, they relate as always to appearances and conversations, chance meetings, unexpected events, dramas, deaths.

Despite her attempt to renew the readership by providing copy in *She Who Pays* about younger women—schoolgirl Brigitte, the Pradeau débutantes, Nanterre undergraduates in miniskirts, topless girls on the sands—there was only one review. It came from the *Grantham Journal*'s 'Family Bookshelf' column in the 'FOR MOTHER' category, with the comment: 'Compulsively readable, this is a woman's story told by this essentially feminine writer.'

How unfair! This sad little book, certainly 'compulsively readable' but much better than that, deserved a more discerning review. It's a tale about a sensitive soul's beginning to feel left behind, a journey in quest of truth in a world of change.

PART FOUR

Posterity in View

Wrapping Up

BOB MUST HAVE CONNIVED in innumerable changes that were made to *A Village in Piccadilly*, *The Incredible City* and *The Siege of London* by Robert Henrey to befit them for *London Under Fire 1940–45* by Mrs Robert Henrey. The originals' total of 229K words comes down to 82K for the reissue, 'my husband' virtually disappears (seventeen occurrences), and the first person singular pronoun occurs over 650 times, not always with reference to the authoress but mostly so, and of course never to Bob who was the original narrator.[137]

Contracted on 26 December 1968 and published in September 1969, advertised as 'an omnibus of small wartime classics' for 'a host of new readers', *London Under Fire 1940–45* opens on the original *A Village in Piccadilly* epigraph by Richard Church minus the dedication. The text starts on page thirteen with the first two sentences from *A Village in Piccadilly* (in quotation marks!) immediately followed by five additional pages of Madeleine talking about herself—though as usual there may be some writing by Bob in the royal 'I' subsuming the two of them. A passage in this interpolation is recognizably by her alone, writing in her un-English English and laying on the drama.

Following these embarrassing (and disparaging) pages, the 1942 text picks up as far as the original narrator's recruitment for a secret mission. Being unable to claim that she had simultaneously been a mother in Mayfair and a spy in Lisbon, the authoress cuts thirty pages from *A Village in Piccadilly* and dives into *The Incredible City* in the third person describing a ship sailing home from Gibraltar, turning the original 'we' into 'they' and so on. After a great deal of editing and many interpolations about herself, Bobby (and even Paloma), the story skips Bob's splendid description of Midnight Communion at Westminster Abbey,[138] skates through to the Rainbow Club and Adele Astaire, cuts the last chapter and tackles 1944 with no further ado, thereafter reducing the 86K words of *The Siege of London* to 30K by omitting most of the story of Pierre Brossolette and the French resistance refugees.

Whatever Bob thought of this slapdash rehash of his books, which received no reviews in spite of Dent's numerous ads (*Sunday Times* twice, *Daily Telegraph*, *Times Literary Supplement*, *Sunday Telegraph*, *Listener...*), he kept his reflections to himself, merely recording in his log entry for 1969 that Mé bought a portable TV enabling them to move from the 'Big Room' into her study at night, and that Dent began sending out first *She Who Pays* and then *London Under Fire 1940–45* to 150 U. K. girls' schools and colleges, later extending the scheme to cover South Africa, Canada, Australia and the United States.

It's not clear who initiated this donation scheme, whether Dent as a marketing exercise or Bob intent on preserving the Mrs Robert Henrey presence in print. It may well have been the latter, as surviving correspondence from the 1970s shows Bob paying Dent to send copies of the Madeleine books to selected libraries.

It would appear that like every other London publisher Dent was feeling the pinch as early as 1969 due to rising fixed costs and falling sales revenue. Inflation and television were taking their toll on the book trade in general, more particularly on Dent's fundamental back list of the Everyman's Library series and the twelve-volume *Everyman's Encyclopaedia*. In the 1970s Dent's successively closed their print works at Letchworth, moved their historic Aldine House offices from Bedford Street to Albemarle Street to Welbeck Street, shut down their stock department and bindery at Letchworth, and eventually sold out on 31 December 1987 to George Weidenfeld & Nicolson.

Bob knew more about the book trade than Mé did. She shrieked when he accepted royalties of ten percent and finally five percent in the late 1970s and early 1980s. Hitherto their contracts had been for fifteen percent on the first 10,000 copies and twenty percent thereafter, with ninety percent of all subsidiaries. But Bob loved Dent's and was ready to fall over backwards to keep the old boat afloat, because he felt—justifiably—that they were in it together. It just wasn't in his nature to pinch pennies, anyway. And books were his life, quintessentially those of Mrs Robert Henrey.

He was delighted when, on his mother's birthday (15 May) in 1970, Mé decided to take up again an unfinished script about her year as a girl of seventeen at the Galeries Lafayette in Regent Street. Thus *Julia* was born. 'She wrote fast and happily', he recorded in his log, 'making a wonderful book which Dent accepted with great alacrity towards the end of the summer.' At the same time, the publisher 'greatly widened' the girls' school and university donation project, which Bob found 'most exciting'.

Dent advertised *Julia,* subtitled absurdly *Reminiscences of a Year in Madeleine's Life as a London Shop-Girl*, as an extension of the autobiographical Madeleine sequence, blurbing 'the Little Madeleine becomes the Little Julia' despite the fact that Madeleine doesn't appear in it at all and that the story is told in the third person.[139]

Dent's blurbist added: 'This episode in Madeleine's life, lived with febrile intensity, falls between *The Little Madeleine* and *Madeleine Grown Up*, and has so far remained a troubled, difficult secret.' Balderdash! In fact, *Julia* is more akin to the novel *Philippa* than to any of the Madeleine stories. The narrative is carried forward by dialogues and streams of consciousness, often changing focus or overlapping within the same scene. The two protagonists, Julia and her older workmate Edith, are two sides of one character, the absent and unmentioned Madeleine. One is naive and fair, mother-oppressed, the other cynical and dark, world-harassed. Sex, abortion and venereal disease penetrate Julia's consciousness via Edith. It's all quite cleverly and consciously done, the intention clearly being to steer back from 'true' autobiography to the truth of the novel, Bob's preferred form.

Novelist Elizabeth Bowen, who had once advised the Henreys to keep novel and autobiography distinct, would probably have liked *Julia* even more than she had admired *Philippa*. Alas, no reviewer was around any more to enthuse as Bowen had done. No books page gave *Julia* even a passing mention, though the *Wishaw Press and Advertiser* did list it on 6 August 1971 under 'Non Fiction' among the latest additions at Wishaw Library.

* * *

THE NEXT VOLUME was *A Girl at Twenty*, subtitled *Six Months in the Life of the Young Madeleine*. The contract date is 16 June 1973, and the book came out in May 1974, after Dent's Aldine House had relocated to Albemarle Street but before the Aldine Press at Letchworth was shut down.[140]

An epigraph quotes three lines from Feste's song in *Twelfth Night*, act 2, sc. 3:

> *In delay there lies no plenty;*
> *Then come kiss me, sweet and twenty,*
> *Youth's a stuff will not endure.*

In key with this Shakespearian nostalgia, the blurb does its utmost to turn the clock back to the earliest Madeleine books:

Dancing at the Kit-Kat Club, lunch at the Café Royal, a beautiful new dress for the Italian Club's New Year Ball—for a girl at twenty life should be cloudless and clear. It is a measure of Mrs Robert Henrey's great skill as a writer that she presents not just the sketch of herself as a frivolous girl but a rounded portrait, often happy and thoughtless, sometimes searching for more, and just a little sad. Above all she records for history how it felt to be a young woman at this moment of a troubled and fast-changing century.

A Girl at Twenty is a wonderful addition to the established canon of 'Madeleine' books, and it will be welcomed by Mrs Henrey's admirers all over the world.

There was a good deal of sense in this blurb. By making Madeleine young again, Mrs Robert Henrey was indeed hoping to rejuvenate her image and extend her readership to a younger audience.

Because *A Girl at Twenty* slotted neatly into the rest of the famous sequence, which it resembled closely in its structure and style, it was actually graced with a review—the first in five years. Elizabeth Harvey in the *Birmingham Post* wrote, perhaps with more apropos to the life of an ageing authoress than she imagined: 'The author in her usual comfortably discursive and often amusing style describes her life in 1926 working in a little barber's shop near Piccadilly Circus, enjoying new experiences and realising how nice it was not to have a past.'

* * *

THE HENREYS' LIFE IN THE SEVENTIES is recorded mainly in Bob's log, the typed summary he drew up year by year from his papers and diaries before he destroyed them in the farm's huge fireplace or on an orchard bonfire. Only two further Henrey titles appeared as the ageing writers and their ailing publisher J. M. Dent & Sons declined together. Exiled since 1965 from the great city that had provided them with their spiritual and professional nourishment, they didn't really find the inspiration in Normandy that Bob had dreamed about. Mé tried to provide him with copy about their rural existence that their readership might go along with, but the world had changed and ecology was not yet a value in the market-place.

On the family front Bobby and Lisette led a much-travelled existence between New York, Gloucestershire, Normandy and Singapore, bringing first their daughter Dominique then their son Edward to stay with their grandparents. Dominique as a baby spent some time at the farm in 1971 while her parents toured France. When they all came over from Singapore in 1973, they left behind Tiggy, their cat from Greenwich Village, who only understood English and stood aloof from her French counterparts at the farm.

One of these—the little black cat—had a caesarian. Jane came for ten days that autumn. Edward was baptised at Villers in 1974 and there was a small party on the lawn.

Blanche Henrey came several times. Her life-work, the three-volume *British Botanical and Horticultural Literature before 1800*, was recognised as a major contribution to botanical bibliography when it came out in 1975. Edmund de Rothschild and Elizabeth came to tea on the lawn on 7 June 1975. Bob corresponded with Lord Crawford about Peli that autumn, but Crawford died before Christmas. From Kitty Henrey there were regular letters. She made a will in 1976 leaving money to Madeleine before entering a nursing home in Gloucester Road. Both she and Blanche remained unmarried. In 1976–77, by when Bobby and Lisette had settled in Greenwich, Connecticut, Dominique spent a whole year in Villers, returning for part of the summer in 1978.

On the literature front there were big reprints of *The Little Madeleine* and *Wednesday at Four* in 1971 to supply a publicity drive, and complimentary copies of these two went out with *Julia* to over 200 schools and colleges. Then Dent's closed their stock department and joined the Book Centre at Southport, which threw everything into deep confusion. Their editorial committee hesitated for several weeks before accepting *Green Leaves* in 1975.

Mé started *The Golden Visit* on 24 August 1978 and sent the first 103 pages to London on 10 October. Five days later Malcolm Gerratt wrote to say they liked it. Dent's moved from Albemarle Street to Welbeck Street in November. For the Henreys' golden wedding anniversary—fifty years of marriage since 1 December 1928 at St George's, Hanover Square—Martin Dent sent a telegram and signed the contract for *The Golden Visit.*

On the health front Mé had a brooch from Van Cleef for her birthday in 1971, but began to feel ill and depressed. She was radiographed and nothing was found amiss. After grieving for the loss of her gold heart, she found it in the garden. Bob had a cardiogram in 1975 following a fierce bout of sciatica. He made a new handwritten French will in 1976 leaving the land at Villers to Bobby, the house and home orchard to Mé. His possessions in England were safely covered, he thought, by an earlier witnessed deed leaving everything to Mé and naming Coutts as his executors. The same year Harold Wilson resigned as P.M. and Mé had a bad fall on her right arm in the yard. There were deaths aplenty: Dr Durville in 1971, Schiap in 1973, Lord Crawford in 1975, Yvonne de Rothschild, Mme de Carpentier and Maître Vincent in 1977.

On the money front Wall Street and the dollar slumped together in 1971, costing them some £8,000. Rothschild's refused to deal for them and they moved to Coutts in the Strand. In January 1973, fearing a slump and a French capital gains tax which never happened, Bob sold their Exxons at $93 and could have bought them back for $60 when there was a small world depression, but failed to do so, keeping the money on seven days at Coutts. They bought a new blue 2CV on 17 February 1974. Giscard became President and they paid heavy French income tax (£2,500) because of high interest rates.

At the end of 1976 they had $260,000 on deposit, which at £1.70 equalled £150,000, two bars of gold and £10,000 in French francs. The following year, having closed their account with N. M. Rothschild and sent all their money to Coutts on seven days and sixty days call, they unwisely remained in US $ while the £ improved from £1.70 to $1.93. Bob bought 500 Exxon shares for Mé but sold his gold bar at a low price to pay heavy income tax. Mé kept her lingot.

Finally, on the farm front there were big disappointments. They had placed great faith in Jacques Déliquaire and his wife Georgette. Jacques they had known and liked since he was a boy. Georgette had become for Mé an everyday friend, bringing milk and gossip, helping out. Their lively little Brigitte, who was heading to become a schoolmistress, was a virtual grand-daughter for a time until Dominique came along. Berlequet had been bought partly to give them a comfortable home close to the Henreys' orchards, where they farmed their cows, hay and apples under a generous lease. They suddenly decided to quit the land and build a new house in the village. Georgette just brought the milk one day and said that was the last, they had sold their cows. Jacques got a job driving trucks for a Camembert factory but craftily held on to his lease on a small piece of Bobby's land in order to keep his official status as an *agriculteur*, which carried a number of advantages.

Upset, Mé put Berlequet on the market, refused a £30,000 offer and finally sold it for £10,000 to a young couple because they reminded her of herself and Bob when young. Then the young couple divorced and sold up making a handsome profit. A satisfactory farmer was found for the Ferme Henrey land at £1,000 per year. The summer of 1976 was the hottest on record and there was a serious drought. Town water was laid on to the house from the top of the orchard. Dominique had her eighth birthday on the farm in January 1977 and was much loved.

Elizabeth Snapp, librarian of Texas Woman's University, organised a campus reception in Denton on 9 October 1977 for the publication of *...magnificently mistress of her trade*. This was a nicely printed booklet on hand-made paper reproducing a signed four-page typewritten letter on embossed blue letterhead ('FROM MRS. ROBERT HENREY') that Mé had sent Snapp specially on 27 May 1974. The booklet also contained an explanatory note and a press photograph of the authoress at her white writing table (in reality Bob's desk) in the Carrington House flat. The publication went on display in the Special Collections Room of the University Library with a number of inscribed volumes and several watercolours redrawn by Phyllis Ginger from her jacket designs for Mrs Robert

Henrey's books, all donated by Bob and still at Denton.

The following year 1978 ended triumphantly with £132,000 at $1.96 plus £12,000 in French francs in the bank. Important negotiations with the Bodleian and the Library of Congress had got the chronological sequence catalogued to Bob's satisfaction. The portraits by de Glehn and G. F. Watts were hung on indefinite loan at John Rylands Library in Manchester. (The former went AWOL during a Rylands refurbishment, the latter was returned to Bobby in Connecticut after being lent to the Met in New York.) Nobody wanted the Malta portrait which stayed in the vault at Coutts. Bob found safe homes for his beloved souvenirs of Peli—her *Book of Robins* went to Wellesley, her *String of Beads* and her original *Green Leaves* went to John Rylands where they appear to be in place still.

* * *

BOB WROTE A LONG INVENTORIAL MEMO to Bobby dated 23 May 1980, his literary testament, referring to Mé by another of his nicknames 'GM' ('Grand'mère'). Part of the memo concerned their joint literary output, which he attributed entirely to her:

> Because GM's books have been the consuming interest of the major part of my life, I must talk to you about them because otherwise you will know nothing about me. In the folder in my room called Private Accounts you will find all the exact sales figures and other information. GM has never been a so called best-seller. Though her books have sold about three quarters of a million copies in hard-back their chief particularity lies in the fact that the major five titles have never once been out of print since they were first published. For an author to have as many titles constantly in print in hard-back for so long is to say the least of it highly exceptional.
>
> There are no ways of assessing lasting worth. She may be quickly forgotten. She may not. I would be foolish to hazard a guess.

He had done his utmost to avoid oblivion. Throughout the 1970s he had heartily encouraged Dent's complimentary copies scheme, chivvied the editors of *Who's Who* and other biographical dictionaries, cajoled the librarians to whom he personally sent copies at his expense, some on hand-made paper, many bound by

221

Zaehnsdorf, all signed by himself in red ink imitating Mé's signature. According to Bobby, his mother found this bibliographical parcel post ridiculous and expensive.

In his memo to their son Bob wrote:

GM's autobiographical sequence is now classified in most great libraries not in the order the volumes happened first to be published but in the correct chronological sequence, thus:-

1. The Little Madeleine
2. An Exile in Soho
3. Julia
4. A Girl at Twenty
5. Madeleine Grown Up
6. Green Leaves
7. Madeleine Young Wife
8. London Under Fire
9. Her April Days
10. Wednesday at Four
11. She Who Pays
12. The Golden Visit

These represent only about one quarter of her books.

There are also her two famous books on London, both of which have been continuously in print since they were first published, *London* for thirty years, *The Virgin of Aldermanbury* for over twenty years.

If, however, anybody needed to judge GM's work as a whole it would be impossible not to take into account books which are now out of print but which are vital to the œuvre. Certain important university and national libraries began to realise this too late. By the time they busied themselves making complete collections, some of the out-of-print titles had become scarce and hard to obtain.

I also, rather late in the day, tried to put my hands on a complete set which I could bequeath to you. In order to give them a certain permanence I had them bound by Zaehnsdorf either in full red morocco or in blue buckram with gold edgings. This was not easy. [...]

At the moment of writing this memorandum to you, I have succeeded in putting together in my room at Villers nineteen titles in full red morocco, five titles in blue buckram.

The collection at Villers today is slightly more numerous than that. The titles in fine bindings have extra leaves on which Bob pasted photographs, letters and typewritten information about the books' history. The family have a further small collection on their shelves in Connecticut. The copies brought together for the present book—other than those loaned by the London Library— came from the second-hand market via AbeBooks. Many of these were ex-public library or had been privately owned, but a few had been part of Bob's memorial dispatches in the 1970s. It's frankly heart-breaking to open a second-hand volume gifted personally by Madeleine Henrey in 1974 to a wealthy American women's college and to find its flyleaf rubber-stamped in red: 'DISCARD.'

* * *

Bob's memo to Bobby consciously tolled the knell of Mrs Robert Henrey's literary adventure:

> GM's output is over a span of forty years. To have kept so many titles in print for so long is much due to the fact that Dent was a major firm with its own printing works and a solid financial structure. But today books are no longer printed as they used to be so that Dent's works ceased to be an asset, and no English publisher today keeps any book continually in print. Storage charges are too high, and the public has ceased to read classics, old or modern. They go for what is diffused on TV—and a new book is liquidated some six weeks after its appearance.
>
> Presumably therefore this unusual record is about to end. Forty years in print is a long time. Dent has new editors, new ideas. One day even *The Little Madeleine* will go out of print.

Indeed. One after the other, Mrs Robert Henrey's books went out of print at Dent's, who decided not to reprint them and reverted their rights to the author. A director wrote in 1983: 'It is sad, after all these years, to see these books disappear from our list but at least they have enjoyed a very long life—and, who knows, perhaps they may one day be revived to bring pleasure to a new generation.'[141] The flagship *The Little Madeleine* finally sank on 19 May 1986.

* * *

In April 1977 Mé sent Martin Dent a collection of letters from her to Bob dating from their reconciliation years 1959–62. Translated from French into English and annotated, they included a letter or two from Bobby. Put together under the title 'To Dearest Him' the collection's epigraph quoted Gerard Manley Hopkins: '... letters sent | To dearest him that lives alas! away.' This was Mé's way of showing her gush of love for the man who was literally her *alter ego*, to whom she owed her books and so much else. Dent's editors, beset with troubles of their own (though of a distinctly less emotional nature), judged that 'To Dearest Him' belonged properly to the private sphere, and sent it back. Bob gave the original typescript to Texas Woman's University along with other material he sent them during his memorial bonanza. The carbon copy went to Boston University Library, who seem to have lost it.

Binding Together

AN IMPORTANT BOOK sits on the shelves in Bob's room at Villers. Its title is *Towards Androgyny: Aspects of Male and Female in Literature*. Written by a Columbia University professor of English literature, Carolyn G. Heilbrun, whose previous publications included books on the Garnett family and Christopher Isherwood, it was published in London in 1973 by Victor Gollancz incorporating published material from various journals dating back as far as 1964.

'Androgyny', Heilbrun writes, 'suggests a spirit of reconciliation between the sexes; it suggests, further, a full range of experience open to individuals who may, as women, be aggressive, as men, tender; it suggests a spectrum upon which human beings choose their places without regard to propriety or custom.' As an illustration of the possibilities of an androgynous world, Heilbrun offers a study of the Bloomsbury group and of some of their works seen in the light of androgyny.

Bob could have written Heilbrun's lively essay, had he been a professor of English literature rather than a professional writer. Its subject certainly corresponded both to his views on gender in literature and to his personal attitudes. The shelves in his room at Villers contain a great many books by women writers among the usual male classics, and his portrait as Adrian in Judith Burnley's *Unrepentant Women* shows him to have been a nonchalant blend of 'masculine' and 'feminine' characteristics with a preference for the womanly. Mé shared this preference from the opposite stance, a manly one committed to the pursuit of responsibility and prestige—Bob's negative. Together they formed Madeleine, an astonishingly post-modern example of androgyny merging two histories, cultures, genders, principles.

Their joint devotion to literature and womanhood found expression in *Green Leaves*, which Dent accepted with some hesitation in 1975. The contract is dated 19 September 1975 and the book came out the following June.[142] In many ways it recalls Bob's first book *A Century Between* and its successor *Letters from Paris 1870–1875*. Based on documents quoted in extenso or at length, it is a tribute to the women in his line—Hannah, Peli, Effie, and of course Madeleine, his and Mé's joint creation, who tells the story as 'I' even when I was he.

The title *Green Leaves* is the same as that of a collection of memoirs by Lady Lindsay, the originals of which Bob presented to John Rylands Library in 1977 as part of his memorial campaign. In the same curatorial spirit the book's prelims contain a summary of the official Mrs Robert Henrey titles (the autobiographical sequence and 'Her other books') and a full-page Madeleine Henrey chronology (from the birth of Mé to the death of Mathilde) cross-referenced both to the titles in the sequence and to significant dates in her life.

Purporting to be the story of Madeleine and her mother-in-law Effie, *Green Leaves* makes its honey from many sources, not the least being Bob's *A Century Between* and Peli's original booklets with the same title. The true purpose of the book is clearly to bind together Madeleine's life story and Bob's. Family lore told in writing or in conversation by one or other of the Rothschild-Fitz-Roy-Lindsay-Henrey ilk is interwoven with Madeleine's own memories of Clichy, Stacey Street, Milou, Mathilde... and Robert, named as such for the first time since *Winter Wild* in 1966. (He's called 'my husband' in all but five of Mrs Robert Henrey's books. In one of them, *A Daughter for a Fortnight*, he's just 'the Robert in my married name'.) A narrative device used several times—a journey by train or tram interrupted by branching digressions then resumed—symbolises this bringing together of strands of memory into a continuum—Bob's world view and, aided by Mé's eye for detail and her prodigious memory, his main aim in literature.

If not the last, *Green Leaves* was one of the last books printed and bound at Letchworth by the Aldine Press.

That Dent didn't really believe in it, a fine book nonetheless, is shown by the sole advertisement that has been traced. Its single sentence states: 'A new addition to Mrs Henrey's well-known autobiographical sequence.' How succinct can you get? There were no reviews. The London Library didn't buy it. It did come out, however, in a large-print Christmas edition from the Firecrest Publishing imprint run by the Chivers family in Bath.

* * *

THE BLURB of Mrs Robert Henrey's final book, *The Golden Visit*, was undoubtedly written by Mé and touched up by Bob, who left a gallicism or two in there for flavour:

> A little girl of eight is the heroine of this new and perhaps final volume in Madeleine Henrey's world famous autobiographical sequence.
>
> The Little Madeleine has grown old. She has reached the age of seventy-two. The farm in Normandy which she bought as a young married woman just before the Second World War is menaced from all sides by steel and concrete—ugly apartment buildings, hastily built secondary residences which annihilate the small family farms of the former French peasant, cider-apple trees, hand-milked dairy herds and shady lanes where once grew the primrose, the violet and the wood strawberry.
>
> What a sad thing to become old! To see so much of what one loved disappear! But into the Little Madeleine's narrowing world comes suddenly from America her little grand-daughter, Dominique, to stay with her—oh joy!— for a whole year!

This story of 'a little bundle of femininity, aged eight, finding beauty in a modern world, turning tragedy into comedy, deceptions into eager tomorrows' (as the blurb wrote) clearly worked wonders on two ageing writers, egoistic by definition, like a redis-covered movie of their own childhood.

Contracted on 4 December 1978, *The Golden Visit* was pub-lished on 30 September 1979 at £5.95 (subsequently increased to £9.50).[143] The ultimate net price seems steep considering the title's moderate page count and its contractual royalty of only five per cent. Granted that book prices were inflating rapidly and that J. M. Dent & Sons were in financial trouble, this price suggests that the expected sales were low.

Despite what the blurb says, Dominique isn't the heroine of

this Norman tragicomedy any more than Perdita is the heroine of Shakespeare's *A Winter's Tale*. Dominique is the main accessory to the central, overpowering march of fate called Madeleine—antagonist rather than protagonist. Dominique doesn't come into the story until page 132, once all the sinister stuff has been defined. Death is afoot in the orchards. Madeleine is losing control for the first time, faced not really with age but with youth, the upsurge of progress. She tries to project herself into the little one when she arrives from New York, exults, but in her heart of hearts knows the party's nearly over. The king ('my husband') is ailing, he's hardly worth mentioning any more. When Dominique asks: 'When you are dead, Grand'mère, we shall have your farm, won't we?' Madeleine can but answer: 'I hope so.'

The prologue up to Dominique's arrival from abroad is remarkably Shakespearian, with a wonderful first chapter in which Madeleine distraught is confronted with Yvonne, a ghost from the past on the path to her farm. Again, the sixth chapter is haunted by memories of Elsa Schiaparelli. Discovering in one Saturday morning's *Figaro* that Schiap is to be buried that afternoon near Frucourt in the Somme, 'I' drives impetuously in her 2CV to be there on time—over 200 km of icy roads in bitter weather. The narrative mixes the anguish of the journey with flashback scenes.

Then comes the ceremony crux. In the tiny candlelit church, where the service had begun, somebody was playing a harmonium which had been installed beside a makeshift stove. 'As the hot air climbed up from the stove into the ancient beams and rafters it set a-quivering a great, unbroken sheet of cobwebs that hung above our heads in one solid, ethereal mass, dark, alive, breathing, ghostlike.'[144] Schiap would have loved it. There were a few villagers in box pews and a handful of family mourners in the choir stalls. Could it be that they were so few to bid her farewell?

After the service:

I smiled at Gogo wrapped up in her huge fox furs.

'Do you remember me?' I asked.

'No,' she said.

'When I came to Gstaad to be with your mother?' I whispered, yearningly.

'No,' she repeated.

There was not a glimmer of recognition on her pale face. I had wept for Schiap. I was weeping for myself now, to discover how little I had counted in all that had gone before. How desperately unimportant I was! How utterly lonely and unknown![145]

Marisa was there too, Gogo's daughter, future Marisa Berenson, fashion model and actress. Her sister, who had married the actor Anthony Perkins, was expecting a baby. Did Marisa remember that sixth birthday party in the Rue de Berri? Schiap had invited Mé along to share the fun. Did Marisa remember? It seemed not.

Thereafter, *The Golden Visit* chronicles the deeds and words of the declining Villers social set, Madeleine's court, completely upstaged by the charm and energy of the American princess supported by her little brother the crown prince and their calmly competent parents. The animals—cats, kittens, hens, chicks and those stupid turkeys—play an important part in the farm pageant, thrusting forward, disappearing, dying. It's all so gay and so sad. The final sentence chills: 'So many other problems loomed ahead now that another winter was on the way.'

There were no reviews. An anonymous local librarian in the *Buckinghamshire Examiner* in April 1980 reduced this lovely book to a handful of facts, harking on its value as testimony without a word for its value as literature.

* * *

THE EMPHASIS OFTEN LAID BY CRITICS on the factuality of the Mrs Robert Henrey corpus was caused mainly by Mé's insistence in her epigraphs and addresses on the strict veracity of her narratives. Of course she intended them to be true, but her Cartesian view of truth meant that she tended to swear to the facts as if she was testifying in a court of law. *'Mais c'est la vérité, mon petit!'* she often told her son when he queried her versions of events.

Bob as a newspaperman and as a reader of Proust, raised on the King James Bible and the Book of Common Prayer, knew that a story must be shaped in literature to fit the truth it expressed. It was undoubtedly he who was responsible for a sublime metaphor in *The Golden Visit*. 'I' hesitates at the door of a posh book party, feeling inadequate, until she remembers that she's wearing a Schiaparelli dress:

229

Oh, how this lovely dress showed to advantage what was good about my body! The girls who fitted me, kneeling round me, pinching here, adding there, had reached the perfection of magicians in fairy tales. I felt about this dress what I felt about truth in literature, that when normally so unsure of myself as I write, I have drawn the character of a living person, described some trivial but entirely true action, I have hoisted myself, because of the veracity of my facts, above the criticisms of the cruellest critics. A critic may say: 'This character is hateful. That action is base', but he can never write: 'She is a liar! She writes nonsense!' for though her prose may be imperfect, it is invested with the halo of truth.[146]

And on the threshold of the party, where she will find herself among beautiful women and famous writers, Bob lovingly puts these words on the printed page: 'I shall be equal!' I told myself. 'Equal to the best of them!'

* * *

BOB'S FULL DIARY FOR 1982 has survived. It shows him preoccupied with currency and interest rates, health problems (his flu, her aches and pains), contacts with librarians and Zaehnsdorf adding full red morocco or blue buckram copies of Mrs Robert Henrey's books with extra prelims pages to the libraries' special collections, phone calls and letters to and from Dent's, coping with the bad weather that froze the car and TV aerial, getting to 8 A.M. Sunday mass, doing the shopping, picking up the mail, finding a new farmer for the grass and apples, repairing the donkey boiler, writing to Phyllis Ginger about a new book jacket, caring for Mé in bed disheartened for days on end, getting her to write to Earl Crawford, writing to Crawford himself about the special collections at Boston University etc., paying the income tax, TV colour licence, insurance premiums, Mé's entry in *Who's Who* (£42.50), requesting four copies of *Who's Who of Women*, ordering Spring books from Hatchards in Piccadilly...

During the bad weather at the start of the year, his flu 'very painful' and Mé 'in agony' after slipping on the ice, they both expected to die in the night of 14 January. They were rescued by Andrée Pradeau's farmer Christian Ruel—'an angel'—who brought them food in his tractor and drove them to Deauville for X-rays. 'Thank God all is well.' He was exhausted and full of flu, but very happy after 'a lovely supper in the kitchen'. During the days that followed, Mé showed little sign of improvement. His flu allowed him little sleep at night. 'I get up and roam.' He wrote to Bobby about their difficult situation, but their son was still in Chile. Then the sun came out, the snow melted, and the crisis passed.

In a last-ditch attempt to stay in print, Bob had persuaded Dent to reissue *The Little Madeleine* and a two-in-one volume of *Green Leaves* and *London Under Fire 1940–45* as by Madeleine Henrey, dropping the Mrs Robert. Feeling frail at the age of eighty, he thought this was a way of clearing up the copyrights, in order to leave Mé free for whatever deals might come along when he was no longer around.

Writing from Letchworth on 16 September 1981, Dent's director and company secretary V. F. Chamberlain had summarised to a theoretical 'Mrs Madeleine Henrey', i.e. Bob, the 'various arrangements' that they (meaning Bob and Dent) had 'agreed over the telephone and in writing over the past week or so'. These involved the print runs (1,000 copies of *The Little Madeleine*, 1,500 copies of the two-in-one volume), the royalties (five per cent), the paper quality ('as good as *Madeleine Grown Up*') and the reversion of rights (automatic six months after the end of an edition in the absence of any new agreement on terms). Bob had duly signed and returned the duplicate letter to clinch the contract, despite Mé's expression of horror at the low royalty rate. Another letter shows that the deal had been made possible by Bob's promising to buy 'several hundred' copies of each work at a fifty per cent discount on the published price.

On 13 October 1981, 'following a telephone conversation last week with Mr Henrey', John Sundell stuck his oar in from Dent's new London office, writing to Mrs Madeleine Henrey: 'First of all, let me say how delighted we all are that—with your generous cooperation— a way has been found for us to put in hand reprints of *The Little Madeleine* and (in a combined volume) *Green Leaves* and *London Under Fire*.' However, Sundell went on, the previous letter from Mr Chamberlain had mentioned a royalty of five per cent on the published price. Mr Henrey had been kind enough to agree on her behalf that if they should (in their mutual interest) accept any orders at discount of 45% or more, the royalty payable on these should, as was normal practice, be based on the price actually received.

'There, I have done,' Sundell concluded. 'I'm sorry to be so long-winded over what is, in essence, an absolutely simple and straightforward affair. But I am sure you appreciate that, clear as the understanding between us now is in these matters, it still needs placing on record so that what we have decided can be faithfully carried out by others.' Please endorse and return the enclosed copy. Bob endorsed and returned. Then he died.

* * *

THE *LITTLE MADELEINE* REISSUE was presumably set to come out unchanged—except for the printer, copyright and author credits—in this its eighth (and last) impression, but it has not been seen and may well have been scrapped.

On the other hand, the *Green Leaves; and, London Under Fire 1940–45* combined volume was in effect a new title.[147] The blurb presented the title in these terms: 'Here for the first time in a single volume are two major books in Madeleine Henrey's long-acclaimed autobiographical sequence.' If the buyers expected a bargain, getting two books for the price of one, they were cheated, because all twenty-six half-tone illustrations to the 1969 impression of *London Under Fire 1940–45* were tacitly omitted, obviously to keep costs down.

Flu-stricken Phyllis Ginger hand-delivered her watercolour drawing for the jacket to Dent's editorial office in Welbeck Street, where almost everyone was flu-stricken too, on 23 February. It showed a demure and remarkably young-looking Madeleine standing with her Pekingese in her arms among the rose bushes in front of the Normandy farmhouse, presumably drawn from an old photograph as Didi the last Peke died in 1966.

For this two-in-one edition the rejuvenated authoress, credited as Madeleine Henrey for the first and next-to-last time, added a Foreword to *Green Leaves* and an Introduction to *London Under Fire 1940–45*. The long, rambling, dispirited Introduction dated March 1982 is quite as confused as the Foreword. It concludes

232

mysteriously: 'We may be moving towards a time when truth takes upon itself (as in *Madeleine Grown Up*) almost by accident, some of the forms of the traditional English novel.' Could this mean that she had changed her mind? Could the ultimate reality be literature, and not plain facts after all?

This was the last piece of writing published by the Robert Henrey partnership. Bob never held the final volume in his hands, and Mé never submitted a further text to a publisher.

Last Words

ON MONDAY 22 MARCH 1982 Bob recorded in his diary in red ink: 'Get up at 6 A.M. after horrible heart attack.' The same day he noted telephone calls to Cambridge University Library checking that they had received Zaehnsdorf's parcel of red morocco *Paloma* and *Bloomsbury Fair*, and to London University Library ensuring they had received a blue buckram *Her April Days*. There are two other notes at the top of the page: 'Cold lamb' and 'Mé clears coal from cottage bathroom.'

The handwriting then changes to Mé's in the space for Tuesday 23 March, recording in French that the doctor came at two P.M. and obtained an emergency appointment at the Polyclinique in Deauville. They set off at 5 P.M. in the 2CV, Bob insisting on driving. The specialist decided to keep him in for observation, and Mé helped him to undress before driving back alone to the farm, full of foreboding. Next morning, she phoned and was told he had spent a good night, but when she arrived at four he scolded her for not coming sooner. He seemed much better, and the electrocardiometer was working normally as far as she could judge. She had parked the 2CV badly, and manœuvring out of the car park gave her *'des palpitations terribles'*.

She telephoned the clinic next day but stayed at home to recover. That night she slept badly, with *'des douleurs cardiaques atroces'* around two in the morning. When she called the clinic later that morning, a nurse told her he had not been well during the night. An hour later, at ten, the specialist phoned to say he had just died. It was Friday 26 March. She wrote in Bob's diary that Friday had always been a lucky day in her youth, but from now on it would be *'un jour néfaste'*.

Jean Vincent, Maître Vincent's son and successor, drove her

to Deauville. Bob was still warm, but in peace. *'C'est effrayant.'* They went to Trouville to choose a coffin. *'C'est affreux.'* Alone at the farm she drank some coffee. *'Je suis anéantie.'* She had already called Bobby in America, waking him up. Kitty and Blanche were upset when she phoned them in England. Bobby arrived in time for the encoffinment, the *mise en bière*. His mother found him very stoical. The small private ceremony impressed her deeply. Bob's handsome face was already changed, and his bright blue eyes were no more.

The church service was perfect. Bobby read passages from the Bible which Mé for once didn't register in her memory. Not many people were present, but those who were had all been fond of him. Gaston Duprez, son of the patriarch who had prevailed on Victor to sell Bob the farm back in 1937, struck her as extremely frail. The weather was dreadful, windy and pouring with freezing rain.

The grave at Auberville, next to Mathilde's, wasn't ready, so the coffin was placed in 'a kind of cupboard' in the church for the night. Bobby spent several days writing letters and went to see Jean Vincent about the will, which Bob had proudly written the English way (though in French), not taking into account the peculiarities of French successoral law. *'Heureusement, il n'en saura rien.'* He wouldn't know, so it didn't matter.

Mé and Bobby went back to Auberville together for the burial. It was a fine calm April evening, the graveyard was full of primroses. They had brought some flowers from the garden. They felt comforted that his last resting place was so lovely.

She spent a sad but wonderful week with her son. They drove to the station early the following Friday morning for his train to Paris. He parked the 2CV in a convenient spot but left the gearstick in reverse, so that she shot backwards when she turned on the ignition. She was scared to death, but felt His presence at her side, watching and caring. *'Il est là!'* Not Bob, Jesus.

* * *

GREEN LEAVES; AND, LONDON UNDER FIRE 1940–45 came out on 12 August 1982 price £7.95 net U.K. As Dent's bindery had closed down, the contractual provision of four copies on special paper presented difficulties, as no record of the specifications was available. Dent's production department got in touch with several people who had worked at the bindery for many years and remembered looking after the Henreys' books, but they couldn't supply precise information. A woman editor wrote in July asking Mé to send a previous copy so that the new ones might be matched with the rest. They would take great care of it and return it with the new copies. Mé didn't answer until 17 November, by which time Biddles had sent the four contractual copies off the cuff and ended the matter.

As early as 9 December 1982 V. F. Chamberlain, Dent's chairman, wrote to say that *Green Leaves; and, London Under Fire 1940–45* was down to fewer than 100 copies in stock, partly due to the dispatch of 145 copies at the author's expense (Bob's special curatorial arrangement). The cost of books plus postage and packing came to £703.68, depleting the balance of outstanding royalties to £263.82, which had been remitted to Coutts. In order for the book to stay in print, the author should request a reprint as per contract.

How Dent's managed to sell over 1,400 copies between 12 August and 9 December with no advertisements and no reviews is fairly amazing, but Mé answered Chamberlain on 28 December giving 'authorisation' (her term) to reprint. At this point Chamberlain wrote back on 26 January 1983 saying that he had now had the opportunity of discussing the situation with the Editorial Committee and regretted to inform her that it was felt that the level of demand did not justify their keeping this title in their list and that they must inform her therefore that they had decided against reprinting. It was acknowledged that under the terms of their agreement the rights in both titles would revert to her, but before making a final decision he would appreciate her views on the subject, particularly if she felt that there was any way that they might be able to help her keep these titles in print. Kindest regards. Yours truly.

Mé evidently had no views on the subject, as John Sundell chipped in again on 27 June 1983 giving formal notification of the reversion of rights on both *Green Leaves* and *London Under Fire 1940–45*, at the same time notifying that they were almost out of stock of *London* (the book illustrated by Phyllis Ginger) and did not wish to reprint. They were accordingly willing to return to her all the rights in this title also, and (subject only to their being allowed to sell the balance of their stock) now did so.

Silence followed until the axe fell on *The Little Madeleine* in 1986, wielded by John Sundell on 23 April: 'As this book went out of print on 19th November last year (and since we have no plans to reissue it), all our rights in it will return to you on 19th May.' He did hope she was keeping well.

And that was it, apart from a modest photographic reprint of *Milou's Daughter* licensed to Chivers Press in Bath for their New Portway Reprints series (at the request of the London and Home Counties Branch of the Library Association of Great Britain) in February 1987.

J. M. Dent & Sons was sold on 31 December 1987 to George Weidenfeld & Nicolson (Holdings) by J. M. Dent & Sons (Holdings), who changed their name to Quartermans (Holdings) and went into receivership the following spring. This hindered the transfer of information which Weidenfeld needed in order to pay out the royalties and sub rights earnings owed to Dent's authors for 1987.[148] These quite naturally didn't turn out to be huge.

It has to be said that the few royalty statements that have survived paint a pretty dismal picture of the end of Mrs Robert Henrey's career. Her earnings after income tax at thirty percent in December 1982 came to a total of £545.14. Ten years later, by which date both Weidenfeld and Dent had been absorbed by the Orion Publishing Group, nowadays Hachette U.K., *The Virgin of Aldermanbury* for instance earned a royalty of £1.43 before tax. The entire œuvre is currently out of print but still in copyright, the rights having as per contract reverted to the authoress as the stocks became exhausted.

* * *

Though she published nothing after Bob's death, Mé didn't—couldn't—stop writing. Her journal for 1982 continues in his navy-blue leather diary up to 31 October, when it stops short on the eve of All Saints' Day, as if the commemoration of the death of her companion of the past fifty-five years was just too painful to envisage. Thereafter she took up again her habit of writing in bed, surrounded by her cats and her adopted long-haired Dachshund

Tessa, covering the pages of a series of school exercise books in her fluid round Protestant-school hand using whatever ink her fountain pen happened to contain. When the pen clogged up, she moved her writing activity to the little room off the kitchen where Mathilde had spent her final years, dipping the Waterman into bottles of Quink from Harrods.

The exercise books came from the paper shop in Villers, mostly the Magellan brand with square feints used by generations of French schoolchildren. Thirteen of these journals, consecutive from 27 September 1983 to 29 September 1991, have been preserved. Each is numbered in her hand—'Number One' to 'Number Thirteen'—with its start and end dates, containing her day-by-day chronicles of things seen and done, ready to be translated and written up into a book if only 'my husband' were still with her.

They tell of her shopping, her gardening, her animals, her visits to and from old friends—the Villers set were remarkably faithful—and new friends like her young Vietnamese neighbours or a British journalist by the name of John Whale. (He dropped in regularly to read Evensong with her at the farm and wrote her obituary for the *Guardian*.[149]) Her transistor radio accompanied her as she gardened, and she never missed an episode of *The Archers* or a BBC play, preferably by Shakespeare. Most of the programmes on TV displeased her, except old films. She read constantly, returning to her old favourites but also giving time to new books, women's books in particular, sent to her by Hatchards. She had no enemies but the fox and her 2CV, both of which played all kinds of tricks on her.

Though she was dependent on her little car, she feared driving, particularly in summer when there was such a lot of traffic in and around Villers, and the town council kept changing the one-way streets and parking zones.

Bobby was relieved when his mother eventually stopped driving at the age of ninety-five and entrusted her shopping to friends. Even though at an early age he had felt separate from his parents' life, an odd man out from the day he was sent to school, he remained a dutiful son throughout her widowhood, writing, telephoning every Sunday afternoon, stopping over for weekends whenever his business trips allowed four or five times a year, coming with Lisette and the children for their summer holiday, doing her tax returns, taking her to the doctor, watching over her investments, listening to her woes.

The farm and Grand'mère were really where his soul was rooted. He hoped that his children would feel the same magic, and they did to some extent, although his mother's strong character repelled them all. She loved them without the slightest doubt but, unsure of herself as Mathilde had been, she couldn't help complaining, carping, criticizing. When Dominique as a teenager shut herself away in an outhouse and pretended to be Anne Frank, Mé discovered her diary and found in it an image of herself that didn't match hers. This caused an emotional breach.

Yet the girl's accidental death at nearly nineteen in Chichicastenango, on a Christmas holiday in Guatemala with her parents and brother, left her feeling 'amputated'. On 1 January 1989, she wrote in 'Number Twelve': 'I can't write any more, I can't stop crying, and all over the house I find a host of little things she always left behind from one holiday to the next, expecting to find them here again when she came back.'

* * *

It comes as no surprise to find Bobby, in his Connecticut *persona* of Robert Henrey, prolonging the family connection with the book world. From his great-grandmother Lady Lindsay, via his grand-parents the vicar and the vicar's erudite wife Effie, to his multi-volume parents whose eccentric lifestyle was dedicated to the printed word, he had books in his blood. As a partner at Lybrand, Ross Bros & Montgomery he put pen to paper on financial matters in a number of professional publications (some of which owing to his parents' bibliographical interventionism are catalogued at the Bodleian as by Madeleine Henrey).

Following his retirement he wrote a number of private memoirs including several celebrations of Dominique and a splendid series of 'Conversations With My Mother' about their mother-son relationship after his father's death. In his role as a Roman Catholic deacon, he contributed several papers to books on inter-religious hospitality. Above all, encouraged by Lisette, he finally came to terms in writing with his odd childhood and its sequels crystallised around the movie *The Fallen Idol*. In 2013 he published at

Polperro Heritage Press his major work *Through Grown-up Eyes: Living with Childhood Fame* including twenty-four pages of photographic plates, four vignettes by Diana Stanley from *Matilda and the Chickens*, and three reproductions of film posters.

Perhaps it will seem fitting that a few words from Robert's story should conclude the present work that it partly set afoot in the first place:

My mother lived into her ninety-eighth year, and her wish that she never be confined to a nursing home was granted. Early one morning in mid-April 2004 the telephone rang in Greenwich while Lisette and I were still asleep. My mother had fallen on the way back from the chicken coop, inside the house fortunately, and outwardly was only bruised. A neighbour who luckily had dropped by that morning had found her. The disagreeable truth was that my mother could not get up from the chair into which she had been lifted. There was no choice but to call an ambulance. They took her to the local hospital, and at first she did well. She was alert enough to worry about her dog and her chickens.

The early morning call was from the hospital. The nurse I spoke to was reassuring and I told her I would be on my way. Within forty-eight hours Lisette and I were at her bedside. She immediately recognised me and told me she was glad I had come because she was now well enough to be taken home. 'I'm tired of this place,' she said, 'get me out of here!' That was quintessentially my mother. Then, within minutes, she fell silent, and never spoke again. She was moved to a room of her own and the nurses helped set up a cot for me so I could sleep beside her. I could tell from the intermittent rhythm of her breathing that she was near death: so could the doctor who suggested we do nothing except keep her comfortable with a hydrating intravenous drip. He thought she might have had a series of strokes but, wisely, recommended against doing any kind of test or scan. 'We don't really need to know, do we?'

At dawn, at the end of the third night I had spent beside her, I noticed she had stopped breathing. She had been granted her wish.[150]

NOTES

1. *Little Madeleine*, p. 1.

2. Register of births Paris 10ᵉ, no. 3243, 13 August 1906. Her mother's address is given as 1 Rue Achille Martinet (a small Louis-Philippe rental property at the rear of 184-186 Rue Marcadet in Clignancourt). The Sacré-Cœur may just about have been visible from the topmost storeys in those days.

3. The Assistance Publique *prévention de l'abandon* scheme is described by Antoine Rivière in *Genre et Histoire 16* (2015). <https://journals.openedition.org/genrehistoire/2292>.

4. Register of marriages Paris 18ᵉ, no. 2259, 8 September 1908. Her address is given as 4 Rue Puget (adjoining the Moulin Rouge on Boulevard de Clichy), his as 87 Rue Lamarck (in Clignancourt). Witnesses' addresses are given as 172, 178 and 186 Rue Marcadet (just around the corner from 1 Rue Achille Martinet). The register states that the marriage 'recognises and legitimises' Mathilde Bernard (*sic*),

5. Robert Émile born 26 December 1909 to Mathilde and Émile Gal died at the Bretonneau Hospital in Paris on 14 December 1912 (register of deaths Paris 18ᵉ, n° 5038). The certificate gives the Gals' address as 29 Rue Kloch, Clichy.

6. Rolande born on 27 April 1907 (Paris 10ᵉ no. 1715), possibly fathered by Milou, was adopted at the age of four by Louis Soilly when he married Marie-Thérèse in Paris 16ᵉ (no. 455) on 22 April 1911. Mé doubtless fudged the details of Rolande's birth in *Little Madeleine* (p. 5), as she fudged the truth about her own birth (p. 1), to save face for her mother.

7. Her name registered when witnessing Émile's death declaration on 9 April 1920 (Clichy, no. 267) was Louise Adèle Jouard, widow Maurer, aged sixty-three. The Gals' address at this time was 3 Rue Souchal. Mme Maurer lived at no. 4.

8. *Little Madeleine*, p. 209.

9. Stacey Street, a dilapidated cul-de-sac leading from New Compton Street to St Giles's, was wiped out by bombing during the Blitz. It's now the Phoenix Garden.

10. Marriage by licence, St Giles Register Office, 6 June 1922. His birth is given as 15 November 1878, their common address as 14 Stacey Street. His

death was registered at Aubenas on 2 November 1948.

11.   *Exile*, p. 235. He was the future antiquarian bookseller Jean Le Bodo,

12.   *Exile*, p. 264.

13.   *Little Madeleine*, p. 346 vs. *Madeleine Grown Up*, p. [iv]. Mé told her son in 1997 that the fateful interview with Monsieur Adolphe was obtained via the manager of Simpson's restaurant in the Strand, to whom she was referred by the nice old gentleman in Paris, a certain Comte Charles d'Adhémar.

14.   *Mademoiselle Dax jeune fille*, first published by Ollendorff in 1907, was frequently reprinted. According to the BnF catalogue, an illustrated edition came out from Éditions d'Art de l'Intermédiaire du Livre in 1926. This is presumably the edition referred to in *Madeleine Grown Up*, pp. 63 and 222.

15.   *Madeleine Young Wife*, p. 97.

16.   The Naval Disarmament Conference known as the Coolidge Conference was held in Geneva from 20 June to 4 August 1927.

17.   *Green Leaves*, p. 12.

18.   Beauchamp Mansion, 1 Beauchamp Place, Knightsbridge, SW3 (Flat 3).

19.   *April*, p. 83.

20.   *Green Leaves*, p. 132.

21.   *Green Leaves*, p. 171.

22.   *Century*, p. 295.

23.   *A Century Between* ran to 320 pp. Demy 8vo (c. 117K words) with a four-page double-column index, a black and white frontispiece and nineteen single-sided black and white plates, and came bound in blue cloth boards with a woodcut-like vignette of the temple at Gunnersbury printed in black on the front board. The same vignette appeared on the title page. More online.

24.   *Century*, p. 319. Captain Edward FitzRoy was Speaker of the House of Commons from 1928 to his death in 1943. In *Foolish,* pp. 119-120, 'Madeleine' is a guest 'by marriage' at his pre-Coronation reception.

25.   *Farm*, p. 13.

26.   *Farm*, p. 25.

27.   *Farm*, p. 47.

28.   *Farm*, p. 98.

29.   *Farm*, p. 265.

30.   For example by the *Edmonton Journal* (Alberta, Canada), 25 September 1940, p. 4.

31.   Anthony Powell, *To Keep the Ball Rolling*. The Memoirs of Anthony Powell. Foreword by Ferdinand Mount. University of Chicago Press, 1983. pp. 117–18.

32.   'Madeleine' occurs around 200 times in *Farm*, as against the 900-odd occurrences of the narrator's 'I'.

33.   *Green Leaves*, p. 188.

34.   The book ran to 288 pp. Demy 8vo (c. 85K words) bound in black cloth boards with gilt lettering on the spine, a black and white photographic frontispiece of the Italian poplars showing the farmhouse in the background, and twelve separate photographic plates of life on the farm captioned by phrases from the text. The end papers by D. L. Ghilchik, a London artist on the editorial

staff of the *Daily Sketch*, show green line drawings mapping the Vallée d'Auge (front) and the immediate farm neighbourhood (back) illustrated and captioned by hand as in children's history books, probably with Bobby in mind as a future reader.The woodcut-like title-page illustration was taken from the endpapers. More online.

35. *Letters*, p. 3.

36. *Letters*, p. 1. 'C. de B.' may have been the professional news correspondent Alexandre Guyard de Saint-Chéron (<https://www.jstor.org/stable/286156>).

37. *Letters from Paris 1870–1875* ran to 228 pp. Demy 8vo (c. 83K words) bound in black cloth boards with gilt lettering on the spine, nine double-column index pages, a frontispiece and sixteen single-sided plates or in-text vignettes of contemporary life in Paris. The unsigned end papers show commented family trees of the Bourbon dynasty (front) and the house of Orleans (back). No jacket has been seen. More online.

38. *A Village in Piccadilly* was reprinted twice in 1943 and once in 1944 and 1946. A sixth impression was issued in 1952 with an added foreword. The later impressions carried a five-line epigraph from an elegy 'The Twentieth Day' published in *Twentieth Century Psalter* (Dent, December 1943) by the book's dedicatee, the poet and novelist Richard Church. It ran to 163 pp. Demy 8vo in 1952 (c. 67K words). Sixteen black and white photographic plates were originally grouped together after page fifty-two. In later impressions they were tipped in at irregular intervals through the book, double-sided, with captions referring to specific text pages. According to a reviewer, the first impression had 'gay, nursery-style street maps', presumably as end papers, but this printing has not been seen. The jacket for the sixth impression was a scrapbook-style street map of the West End containing black on green title panels, with five black and white snapshots cropped from the inside plates and pasted between the streets, with an extra photograph top right apparently showing Bob and Mé doing their shopping at 5 Shepherd Market, Mr Hayward's greengrocery. More online.

39. *Piccadilly*, p. 162.

40. *Gibraltar*, p. 131.

41. *Gibraltar*, p. 1. Next sentence references pp. 10, 81, 34 respectively.

42. *A Journey to Gibraltar* ran to 169 pp. Demy 8vo (c. 66K words). There's a frontispiece reproducing a poster for a bullfight at La Linea de la Concepción in July 1942. Twenty-one further illustrations drawn from picture postcards and several foreign weeklies brought back from the tour are grouped on fourteen single-sided plates distributed at irregular intervals through the book. The front and back end papers show identical sepia spreads signed 'R. C. K.' mapping the journey to Portugal and Spain (left) and the Straight of Gibraltar (right). More online.

43. Charles d'Ydevalle is identified in *Siege*, p. 136. His book *Spanish Interlude* was published by Macmillan in 1944.

44. *Incredible*, p. 149.

45. *Incredible*, p. 194.

46. *Incredible*, p. 94.

47. *The Incredible City* ran to 195 pp. Demy 8vo (c. 76K words) with twenty-four chapters and twenty-seven scene breaks. Eighteen double-sided black and white plates are grouped at the end of the book. The orange end papers represent Mayfair with 'Our Flat' (front) and the three West End parks (back). The jacket reproducing the scrapbook map design of *A Village in Piccadilly*'s jacket contains cropped photographs drawn from the new set of plates. More online.

48. *The Siege of London* ran to 200 pp. Demy 8vo (c. 85K words) bound as usual in black cloth boards with oblique gilt titling on the spine. It included sixteen black and white double-sided plates between pp. 90 and 92. The photographs, ten of which were also fitted into the street map on the jacket, are credited partly to Eduard Mandinian, partly to an American soldier named Neil Kaplan, partly to others named or unnamed. There are twenty-five chapters with seventeen scene breaks. More online.

49. *Incredible*, p. 81, *Siege*, p. 71, *Through Grown-up Eyes*, p. 25.

50. *The Foolish Decade* ran to 156 pp. (c. 60K words) with twenty-one chapters, twenty-seven scene breaks, and eighteen black and white illustrations in a single sixteen-page signature between pp. 90 and 91. The photographs are credited to Eduard Mandinian and others. The first picture (commissioned from Mandinian) shows Mé with Bobby on the bombed site of Stacey Street. There's also a caricature of Mé on the Golden Arrow by Fernando Autori, whom the Henreys met with Chaliapin in their newspaper days. More online.

51. *Green Leaves*, pp. 193-95.

52. *King*, p. 28.

53. *The King of Brentford* ran to 176 pp. Demy 8vo (c. 71K words), seventeen chapters with twenty-six scene breaks. Eighteen black and white illustrations are placed between pp. 48 and 49 representing sites captioned with short quotations from the text. The front and back end papers show an identical freehand map in green of Brentford from the Great West Road to Kew Gardens and the Thames from Strand on the Green to Twickenham by D. L. Ghilchik (the artist of *A Farm in Normandy*), who also drew the jacket in the manner of a Georgian print representing Pope's villa at Twickenham seen across the river from the vicarage shore. More online.

54. *King*, p. 66.

55. *Through Grown-up Eyes*, p. 35.

56. *The Return to the Farm* ran to 173 pp. (prelims included) Demy 8vo (c. 67K words) and was bound in orange cloth with gilt italic titling on the spine. A sixteen-page signature containing twenty uncredited black and white photographs was placed between pp. 48 and 49. The images captioned with quotes from the text like those in *A Farm in Normandy* represent local scenes and people, apart from the last one showing a page from *Ouest-France* dated 5 September 1945 reporting the Goguet trial. The green end paper map (front and back) was drawn and illustrated in the same style as before by D. L. Ghilchik. The jacket bore a mosaic of four black and white photographs of the farm with a red title panel top right. The text is divided into nine chapters with thirty-six

scene breaks. This high ratio of breaks is a reflection of the degree of fragmentation of the book's timeline and perspective linked to Mé's daily writing stints. More online.

57. *Delphine and Other Stories* ran to 215 pp. Sm. 8vo (c. 70K words) in the smaller hardback format commonly used for fiction, with no page breaks between stories for postwar paper economy. The gap between the *Delphine* contract dated 24 June 1946 and the book's publication seems unusually long, considering Bob's rule of signing on acceptance of the completed manuscript. *Delphine* should thus have come out in late 1946 or in the first months of 1947. One reason for the year-long gap may be a marketing decision inspired by Mé to give publication priority to the farm sequel rather than to this new fiction venture. Another reason may be a bottleneck at the busy Windmill Press due to further material being added to the *Delphine* collection at the last minute. 'Cold Fear' at the end of the volume is a fictionalised account of the burglary at Carrington House. This incident definitely occurred during the summer of 1946 while Mé was alone and Bob away in Normandy with Bobby. If the rest of the *Delphine* manuscript was in hand at the Windmill Press by the time 'Cold Fear' was written, as seems likely, the need to accommodate the extra story may well have thrown the schedule out of sync and caused a switch in publication dates, the farm volume by the same publisher being ready at a different press (Sherratt's St Ann's Press in Altrincham). More online.

58. *An Attic in Jermyn Street* ran to 319 pp. (prelims included) Sm. 8vo (c. 111K words), with twenty-seven chapters and forty-two scene breaks. More online.

59. *Through Grown-up Eyes*, p. 41.

60. Her letter (additionally plugging the recent *London* book and Bobby's movie) appeared in the *Herald*'s 'Somerset Notes and Queries' column (12 November 1949, p. 2).

61. These were Dent's 1982 double volume *Green Leaves; and, London Under Fire 1940–45* and the Chivers large-print *Milou's Daughter* (1987).

62. Running to 186 pp. Demy 8vo (c. 56K words, in larger print than usual), priced at 12*s.* 6*d.*, it includes a black and white frontispiece showing Bobby on the studio set's grand staircase and twenty-two black and white double-sided photographic plates credited to Ted Reed, the unit's studio stills photographer, and to Leslie Baker. Originally intended to be placed together between pp. 74 and 75, the plates were finally tipped in at irregular intervals throughout the text and captioned by names or phrases (not by quotations from the text as in previous books). There are twenty-one chapters with fifty-three scene breaks corresponding to the narrative's diary structure. The verso of the Illustrations page contains a complete 'unit list' of '*The Lost Illusion*' crew. Two end papers similar to D. L. Ghilchik's illustrated maps in the earlier books were drawn as Mé directed by John Hawkesworth, one of the set decorators, who also designed the jacket. More online.

63. Updated passage, p. 28. *London* ran to 290 pp. Demy 8vo (c. 101K words) containing sixteen chapters, three of which are divided into subtitled sections,

with twenty-six scene breaks overall. The running heads and section titles are
set inconsistently, suggesting different press processes. There are also two uncredited end paper drawings in red showing 'The Future Piccadilly Circus And
Its Surroundings In 1656' (front) and 'Piccadilly Circus And Its Surroundings
In 1948' (back). More online.

64.   Letter to Elizabeth Snapp in Mona Searcy Carrico, 'The Madeleine
Henrey Collection at Texas Woman's University', Texas Woman's University
School of Library Science dissertation, 1975, pp. 32–33.

65.   *Philippa* ran to 316 pp. Sm. 8vo (c. 94K words), price 9*s*. 6*d*., with twenty-seven chapters and forty-three scene breaks. The unsigned jacket represents
the young lovers in a watercolour impression of the novel's village setting. According to the letter to Snapp (see previous note), this setting was inspired by
the vestiges of ancient Littleton Park on the site of Shepperton Studios in 1947.
More online.

66.   *Matilda*, p. 34.

67.   *Matilda, p. 255.*

68.   *Matilda*, pp. 17-21.

69.   *Matilda, pp.* 261–64.

70.   *Matilda, p. 207.*

71.   *Matilda, p. 290.*

72.   Running to 304 pp. Demy 8vo (c. 112K words) bound in Dent's standard
black cloth boards, it was illustrated with fifty line drawings by Diana Stanley,
who went specially to Villers for the job. (It was she who did the famous colour
illustrations for the Borrowers series by Mary Norton also published by Dent a
few years later.) Clad in a green jacket with Stanley's drawing of the farmhouse
in a kind of dream cloud seen through a five-barred gate, *Matilda* has nineteen
chapters and sixty blank-line scene breaks corresponding as usual to Mé's daily
writing stints rather than to actual story developments. More online.

73.   *Vienna*, p. 6.

74.   A travel diary running to 274 pp. Demy 8vo (c. 92K words), price 16*s*.,
Vienna has twenty-eight chapters and seventy-eight scene breaks, a colour
frontispiece and end papers, sixteen black and white single-sided uncredited
photographic plates, and four black and white uncredited maps in the text. The
coloured jacket in the same nursery wallpaper style as the frontispiece and end
papers is like them uncredited. More online.

75.   Joyce Reynolds, 'Dancing the New Year In', *Country Life*, December 22
1950, pp. 2174 and 2176.

76.   It ran to 350 pp. Demy 8vo (c. 156K words) bound in black cloth boards,
price 12*s*. 6*d*. with gilt spine titling and a plain grey jacket with maroon titling.
A watercolour frontispiece by I. Le Tournier. represents the Paris fortifications.
This long book has twenty-eight chapters with only twenty-seven scene breaks
(none at all before p. 88), suggesting structured composition rather than the
habitual free flow of memory. (Mé's habitual 'dressmaker' technique based on
successive writing stints never resorted to patterns. She usually wrote extem-
pore as she cut her dresses—freehand.) The text begins with a nice piece of

typographic symbolism: a ten-line-high drop cap 'I' bearing a cameo portrait of a little girl in long blonde ringlets. It may have been borrowed from a children's alphabet, but to someone versed in the Henrey universe it looks awfully like like a jewellery clip.

77.   *Little Madeleine*, p. 30.

78.   The school at this time is vividly described in Richard Gosnell's old boy memoir <https://www.oldnorthavianassociation.co.uk/newsletter_2004.html>.

79.   *Through Grown-up Eyes*, p. 74.

80.   *Paloma* ran to 264 pp. Demy 8vo (c. 87K words) bound in black cloth boards with gilt spine titling and a black and white photographic portrait frontispiece of Paloma in full finery. The book has twenty-seven chapters and as many scene breaks. All the chapters, save one with twenty-five pages, extend to fewer than fifteen pages and ten to fewer than six. The watercolour on the jacket represented three elegantly-dressed women with a little dog standing and conversing in the Green Park. It was the first of many jacket illustrations done for Dent's Mrs Robert Henrey books by Phyllis Ginger, who had illustrated *London* remarkably for the same publisher and author in 1948. More online.

81.   *Paloma*, pp. 132 and 175.

82.   *Madeleine Grown Up* ran to 313 pp. Demy 8vo (c. 128K words) price 15*s*. bound as usual in black cloth boards with gilt spine titling. There was a much publicised 'second large impression' the same month and a further one in 1953. A fourth impression would come out in 1975.

83.   'Madeleine Henrey' was her signature on letters.

84.   *Sunday Times*, 20 April 1952, p. 4.

85.   *A Farm in Normandy; incorporating, The Return to the Farm* ran to 398 pp. Demy 8vo (c. 132K words) with a black and white photographic frontispiece representing Mé walking hand in hand with Bobby in front of the farmhouse. There are no other illustrations, whereas the earlier editions had each contained over a dozen. The green jacket design was based on the end papers of the original editions. More online.

86.   Bob's log is a useful hand-list running from July 1946 to December 1978. Kept among his literary papers at Villers it is typed by year on embossed 'From Mrs. Robert Henrey' letterhead and must be partly or wholly retrospective, presumably compiled in the 1970s from old diaries which have not survived.

87.   *Journal*, pp. 240–41.

88.   *Journal*, p. 242.

89.   *An Exile in Soho* ran to 343 pp. Demy 8vo (c. 112K words) price 16*s*. bound in black cloth boards with gilt titling. The jacket design by Phyllis Ginger bore a watercolour depicting the book's first scene (a little man in a bowler hat trudging head bowed across St Giles's churchyard) in a 123 mm diameter medallion. The title was yellow, the author's name white, the rest uniformly black. More online.

90.   *Madeleine's Journal*, p. 241.

91.   Letter dated Villers-sur-Mer, 27 May 1974, published facsimile as

…magnificently mistress of her trade. A Letter From Madeleine Henrey on Feminine Writers. With an Introductory Note by Mary Evelyn Huey. Denver: Texas Woman's University Press, 1979.

92.   *Madeleine's Journal* ran to 295 pp. Demy 8vo price 16*s.* with eighty-seven scene breaks, a number of long conversations and a fistful of letters quoted verbatim. The jacket and title page contained an uncredited line and wash fashion sketch signed undecipherably ('S. Maita' ?). It seems to have pleased the authoress, as somewhat similar sketches of her in fashion poses would appear later on the covers of Dent's hardback and paperback editions of *Mistress of Myself* and *The Dream Makers*. More online.

93.   *Month*, pp. 84-85 and 95.

94.   *Month*, p. 171.

95.   *A Month in Paris* ran to 244 pp. Demy 8vo (c. 79K words), priced 16*s.*, with twenty-seven chapters and eighty-two scene breaks. More online.

96.   In a letter to Elizabeth Snapp at Texas Woman's University, 7 April 1975, Madeleine Henrey wrote (Carrico dissertation, p. 38): 'I dislike writing articles. I did a few for the London Star in 1951, I think, but mostly about the fashion houses in Paris and about my friend Schiaparelli but writing articles is a very different technique to writing books, and they bore me.' A passage in *Golden*, pp. 101–104, confirms that the trip to Gstaad in 1953 (*Journal*, pp. 248–68) was undertaken to prepare this book, initially for Bob's features pages in the *Star*. Their son's unpublished 'Conversations', chap. 11, mentions his parents' work on Schiap's memoirs.

97.   *Madeleine—Young Wife: The Autobiography of a French Girl* ran to 380 pp. Demy 8vo (c. 141K words) with a jacket showing a fanciful *vue cavalière* of the farmhouse in watercolours. The omnibus fell into four parts. Chapters one to fourteen contained the complete text of the 1952 rewrite of *A Farm in Normandy*. Chapters fifteen and sixteen headed 'London Interlude' contained a new selection of rewritten extracts from *A Village in Piccadilly* in which 'we' became 'I', 'ours' became 'my' etc. Chapters seventeen to twenty-four contained the complete 1952 rewrite of *The Return to the Farm*. The final chapters twenty-five to thirty headed 'The Days of Peace' contained an entirely new text beginning when 'I' returns to 'my farm' in 1945 and ending at Christmas 1951 spent by 'I' at 'my farm' with 'my son', 'my mother' and for once 'my husband'. More online.

98.   *Madeleine Young Wife*, pp. 331, 342, 366, 348, 366, 362 ('The Days of Peace' extracts), ,

99.   *La petite Madeleine* ran to 392 pp. 8vo (c. 156K words) price 690*fr.* paperback, with a colour gouache by François Salvat on the front cover representing an imaginary sad little girl on a Montmartre place. Mé dedicated the book to movie director and screenwriter Fernand Marzelle, no doubt hoping for a screen adaptation. It didn't materialize.

100.   *Milou's Daughter* ran to 239 pp. Demy 8vo (c. 77K words) price 16*s.* bound in black cloth boards with gilt spine titles. The shiny gilt jacket reproduced a watercolour of 'Nice from the Corniche Road' by Gordon Home. The

dedication page bore a thirteen-line invocation of 'Milou!' from p. 186 of *The Little Madeleine*. There were twenty-five chapters with sixty-six scene breaks reflecting the fragmentary nature of the narrative. More online.

101.   *She Who Pays*, p. 33.

102.   *Bloomsbury Fair* ran to 231 pp. Demy 8vo (c. 74K words) priced 16*s.* bound in black cloth boards with gilt spine titles. The white end papers represented scenes from the story sketched in black, with handwritten captions on blue line maps of Bloomsbury (front) and Mayfair (back) signed David Ghilchik, who had drawn similar end papers for the farm books in the 1940s. Part of the front end paper was reused for the jacket in black on a light blue background with red titling. More online.

103.   *Madeleine jeune fille* ran to 331 pp. prelims included (c. 123K words), paper bound price 690*fr.* with a colour cover presenting an artist's impression of Madeleine in a bustling London street against a backdrop of St Paul's cathedral, More online.

104.   *Dream, p. 5.*

105.   Bromley Abbott, 'This glossy world the girls do live in!', *Sunday Dispatch*, 29 November 1959, p. 2.

106.   *This Feminine World* ran to 217 pp. Demy 8vo (c. 67K words) bound in black cloth boards with gilt spine titling. More online.

107.   *A Daughter for a Fortnight* ran to 202 pp. Demy 8vo (c. 63K words) bound in black cloth boards with gilt spine titling. The jacket was daughter pink with blue lettering and a white mirror frame on the front, while the back and back flap boasted a list (with review quotes) of the twelve previous 'books by Mrs Henrey' on sale from Dent. According to this list *The Little Madeleine* was in its fourth impression, *An Exile in Soho* in its second, *Madeleine Grown Up* in its third, *London* in its fifth, *Paloma* in the second impression of the 'cheaper edition' at 7*s.* 6*d.*, while *A Journey to Vienna* was (rather surprisingly) available in a 'cheaper edition' too at 8*s.* 6*d.*, probably mistaken by the punters for a pocket guide now that the borders were open again and the tourist travel allowance had been increased to £100 per year. More online.

108.   *The Virgin of Aldermanbury* ran to 253 pp. Demy 8vo (c. 88K words) bound in black cloth boards with gilt spine titling, fourteen chapters with sixty-nine scene breaks. It came out with a watercolour frontispiece of the church and garden by Phyllis Ginger—reused on the jacket—as well as fourteen black and white drawings in the text by the same artist. A map with little figures and handwritten captions by David Ghilchik similar to his end papers in previous books was placed as a black and white spread on pp. 18 and 19. It was the first of the books in the corpus to have a modern copyright notice ('© Mrs Robert Henrey' and the year), the previous titles having carried just the year of first impression and 'All rights reserved' or 'This book is copyright'. More online.

109.   *Mistress of Myself* ran to 248 pp. Demy 8vo (c. 80K words) price 20*s.* bound in black cloth boards with gilt titling on the spine. There are fifteen chapters with 108 scene breaks. More online.

110.   Thompson, otherwise unknown (perhaps a *Woman's Own* artist), may

also have designed the anonymous jacket for *The Dream Makers* judging by the style of the drawings.

111. *Mistress*, p. 3.

112. *Mistress*, p. 47.

113. *The Dream Makers* ran to 248 pp. Demy 8vo (c. 100K words) price 21s., bound in black cloth boards with gilt spine titling, twenty chapters with 109 scene breaks, and came out with an uncredited blue jacket showing a Madeleine figure with bobbed hair saluting front covers of *Marie Claire, Woman's Own* and *Grazia*. More online.

114. *Spring in a Soho Street* ran to 234 pp. Demy 8vo (c. 76K words) price 21s., with eighteen chapters and seventy scene breaks bound in black cloth boards with blue top edging, red gilt titling and St Giles's clock tower on the spine. The watercolour jacket imitating Phyllis Ginger signed Prue Seward shows a slim red-headed elegant in a white dress and high heels leading a black poodle through Berwick Market. More online.

115. Carrico dissertation, p. 38.

116. *Her April Days* ran to 217 pp. Demy 8vo (c. 75K words) price 21s. bound in black cloth boards with gilt spine titling, ten chapters with fifty-eight scene breaks. The dedication page bears a kind of epitaph attributed to Shakespeare (from the third sonnet, in fact): 'Thou art thy mother's glass, and she in thee | Calls back the lovely April of her prime.' The last page is subscribed: 'Villers-sur-Mer, Calvados. January 1963.' The jacket front and spine were brown with fancy pink titles and the author name in white Garamond. The front flap carried the blurb, the back flap a list of previous titles. The jacket back adopted a new design incorporating a full-page puff that would be reused with variations for several years. 'Critics all over the world', it claimed, ranked the original Madeleine trilogy 'amongst the great books of the present century'. To date, Mrs Robert Henrey had sold 'over half a million books—quite apart from paperback sales'. They had been translated 'into six foreign languages'. She was 'one of the few authors of our time with a huge and happily loyal readership'. More online.

117. *April*, p. 159.

118. *April*, pp. 118–19.

119. *April*, p. 124). The 'lines of Victor Hugo' are from 'Les Pauvres gens', part of *La Légende des Siècles* (1859), recited by generations of French schoolchildren as 'La Cabane du pêcheur'.

120. Telephone conversation with the author, 1 April 2022.

121. *Wednesday at Four* ran to 251 pp. Demy 8vo (c. 104K words) price 25s. bound in black cloth boards with gilt spine titles. There are sixteen chapters with eighty-nine scene breaks. On the jacket front, the top two-thirds are white with the title in black italics under a half-tone portrait of the authoress speaking with raised hands holding a fountain pen, while the bottom third is red with white lower-case sub-title and upper-case author name in Garamond roman. The jacket back reproduces the 'Critics all over the world...' puff. More online.

122. *Wednesday*, pp. 110-15.

123.   *Wednesday*, pp. 101-102.

124.   Judith Burnley, *Unrepentant Women*. London: Heinemann, 1982. Reprint: Arrow, 1983 pp. 25–29 and 97–100. After *Woman's Own*, Judith edited the 12-volume *Penguin Modern Stories* series and wrote novels, poetry, plays, and the life story of her partner the *Sunday Times* drama critic John Peter.

125.   *Winter*, p. 4. The expression parodies the legal phrase 'His Majesty's Dominions' referring to the realms and territories of the British sovereign.

126.   The book launch party was for Stanley Jackson's *The Savoy: The Romance of a Great Hotel*. London: Muller, 1964. Mé thought she was in the book, but wasn't. Monsieur Adolphe was.

127.   *Winter*, p. 84

128.   *Winter Wild* ran to 204 pp. (c. 86K words) Demy 8vo price 35*s*. bound in black cloth boards with gilt spine titling. It had eight chapters and fifty-five scene breaks. The dark green jacket front, uncredited, suggested abstractly a frosty prospect superimposed by a blue title and pink author name. The white jacket back bore the standard 'Critics all over the world...' puff. More online.

129.   *Winter*, p. 92.

130.   *Winter*, p. 92

131.   *Winter*, p. 120.

132.   *Winter*, p. 92.

133.   *Winter*, pp. 141-42.

134.   *Winter*, pp. 165-68.

135.   *She Who Pays* ran to 199 pp. (c. 77K words) Demy 8vo price 30*s*. bound in black cloth boards with gilt spine titling, nine chapters with seventy-two scene breaks. The olive green jacket front had a green on black and white vignette of the farm's garden front by Raymond Piper placed between the title in ornate white italics and the author name in black Garamond caps. The white jacket back bore the standard 'Critics all over the world...' puff. More online.

136.   G.L. Apperson, *English Proverbs and Proverbial Phrases: A Historical Dictionary*. London and Toronto: Dent & Sons, 1929, 'Cloud and clouds', p. 108, col. 1, no. 5.

137.   *London Under Fire 1940–45* ran to 255 pp. Demy 8vo (c. 82K words), price 30*s*. (glossed also as new-style £1.50), bound in black cloth boards with gilt spine titling and identical red end-papers showing the three-dimensional street map of Piccadilly, Shepherd Market and 'Our Flat' that had been used for the front end paper of the wartime editions. The jacket front bore the 'Dawn after the Raid' photograph from *A Village in Piccadilly* (a tin-hatted fire-watcher clambering over a heap of rubble), partly overprinted with a fiery red rectangle punning on the title, which appeared at the top in white reserve with the author's name in black Garamond caps. The white jacket back carried the standard 'Critics all over the world...' puff. There were twenty-six half-tones (not twenty-four as announced on the front flap) selected from the total of fifty photographic plates in the original editions (eleven from *A Village in Piccadilly*, eight from *The Incredible City*, seven from *The Siege of London*). These illustrations were irregularly tipped in throughout the book in recto-verso pairs. The volume was

divided into five sections by year. The edited versions of the three originals
were spread over this section structure, each announced within the structure by
its title in centred caps at the top of a recto with a blank verso. Titles and years
were repeated in the running heads. More online.

138. *Incredible*, pp. 62-63.

139. *Julia* ran to 251 pp. Demy 8vo (c. 90K words) prelims included, price
£2.10, with seven chapters and forty-three scene breaks. The jacket front was a
full-page watercolour by Phyllis Ginger showing a summery Regent Street busy
with people, cars and buses, and two girls, a blonde and a brunette in pink and
black respectively, standing chatting at the entrance to number 130, the Galeries
Lafayette's Carrington Building (*sic*). The white jacket back carried the standard 'Critics all over the world...' puff in red and black. More online.

140. *A Girl at Twenty* ran to 224 pp. Demy 8vo (c. 88K words), price £3.25,
with nine chapters and fifty-two scene breaks. The background of the jacket
front and back is orange with black text. The usual 'Critics all over the world...'
puff occupies the back.The jacket front—similar to the overall cover design for
An Exile in Soho—bears a 123 mm diameter watercolour medallion by Phyllis
Ginger (drawn from a photograph) showing Mé standing in front of Piccadilly
Circus in 1926, in the actual dress she wore. It seems a lot of trouble was taken
to find a photograph of the Circus without the statue of Eros, which had been
removed during work on the new Tube station. Bob wrote to Bobby: 'It is a
wonderful likeness of her and I love it.' More online.

141. Letter of John Sundell, 27 June 1983, kept at Villers.

142. Running to 195 pp. Demy 8vo (c. 76K words) prelims included, price
£3.50 bound in black cloth boards with gilt spine titling, *Green Leaves* has
twelve chapters, twenty-four scene breaks and many quotations of letters and
poems. The verse is set off in blocks, the prose is mostly quoted in the text,
sometimes over several pages. The jacket is, unsurprisingly considering the
title, shades of green. The front carries a rectangular black and white profile
drawing of Mé pen in hand by Thurston, otherwise unknown. The blurb on the
front flap is slightly off-key, making out that she somehow 'followed in the footsteps' of the brilliant women in her husband's ancestry. The back flap has the
usual raised-hands authoress photograph and legend, and the jacket back bears
the ritual 'Critics all over the world...' puff. More online.

143. *The Golden Visit* ran to 232 pp., prelims included, Demy 8vo (c. 85K
words), bound in black cloth boards with large top to bottom gilt spine titling.
It had twelve chapters and eighty-two scene breaks. The jacket was uniformly
gold-hued with russet lettering and a 123 mm diameter medallion containing a
watercolour by Phyllis Ginger showing Mé and her grand-daughter smiling at
one another seated side by side against a wall of the farm. The jacket back bore
the final version of the 'Critics all over the world...' puff. *The Golden Visit* was
printed by Biddles at Guildford and bound on the remaining machines at Dent's
Aldine Press at Letchworth, soon to be dismantled like the rest. More online.

144. *Golden*, p. 109.

145. *Golden*, p. 110.

146.   *Golden*, p. 108.

147.   Biddles reprinted the original Demy 8vo pages from photographic reproductions, using cheap stiff white offset paper. Unfortunately, someone cocked up the layout, producing an editorial mess that Bob would never have tolerated. Instead of being placed after the title page of *Green Leaves*, the Foreword mistakenly appeared at the head of the combined volume on unnumbered pages, followed by the original text of *Green Leaves*. On what should have been page 197 a new title page appeared, imprint and all—unnumbered, of course—followed by the contents list and epigraph from the 1969 omnibus *London Under Fire 1940–45*. To add to the mess, the new Introduction on unnumbered pages was followed by the text of the first edition unaltered except for the page numbers starting at nine. This meant that there was a discrepancy of four between the page numbers of the two editions, and that the final page of the combined volume, which should have been page 448, was numbered 251. The re-paginated signatures were bound in green cloth boards with gilt spine titling at Biddles's newly acquired bindery at Kings Lynn, Dent's splendid old machines at Letchworth having finally been disposed of. More online.

148.   Letter of Guy Newton, Weidenfeld's financial controller, 27 May 1988.

149.   John Whale, 'French writer who endeared herself to Britain', *Guardian*, 30 April 2004.

150.   Robert Henrey, *Through Grown-up Eyes*, pp. 161-62.

About the Books

From 1937 to 1949, the titles were first published by Heinemann, Peter Davies or (predominantly) Dent as by Robert Henrey, thereafter as by Mrs Robert Henrey.

Dent's prelims listed them under headings which evolved over time ('The Farm Books', 'The London Trilogy' and so on). Non-Madeleine or straight Robert Henrey titles were—depending on authorship issues—either excluded from the prelims altogether or listed under Mrs Robert Henrey's 'other books'.

From 1955 the Madeleine series was grouped separately by title with glosses such as '*(her girlhood)*' or '*(her love story and marriage)*'. It was listed from 1975 as '*Mrs Robert Henrey's autobiographical sequence in chronological order*' meaning Madeleine's biographical order.

The official Mrs Robert Henrey canon omitting several titles appeared from 1980 in *Who's Who* based on an incomplete recension drawn up by Robert Henrey in his literary testament dated 23 May 1980.

The key 'More online' in the Notes refers to the companion website:

https://qr.net/eV6DqB

Henrey, Thomas Selby. *Attic Salt*. London: James Nisbet & Co, 1913.

Henrey, Robert [Selby]. *A Century Between*. London, Toronto: William Heinemann, 1937.

———. *A Farm in Normandy*. London: J.M. Dent & Sons, 1941.

———. *Letters from Paris 1870-1875*. London: J.M. Dent & Sons, 1942.

———. *A Village in Piccadilly*. London: J.M. Dent & Sons, 1942.

———. *A Journey to Gibraltar*. London: J.M. Dent & Sons, 1943.

———. *The Incredible City*. London: J.M. Dent & Sons, 1944.

———. *The Foolish Decade*. London: J.M. Dent & Sons, 1945.

———. *A Journey to Gibraltar*. London: The Travel Club, 1945.

———. *The Siege of London*. London: J.M. Dent & Sons, 1946.

———. *The King of Brentford*. London: Peter Davies, 1946.

———. *The Siege of London*. London: The Right Club, 1946.

———. *The Return to the Farm*. London: Peter Davies, 1947.

———. *Delphine and Other Stories*. London: Peter Davies, 1947.

———. *A Film Star in Belgrave Square*. London: Peter Davies, 1948.

———. *An Attic in Jermyn Street*. London: J.M. Dent & Sons, 1948.

———. *London*. London: J.M. Dent & Sons, 1948.

———. *London*. New York: E. P. Dutton, 1949.

Henrey, Robert [John Edward]. *Through Grown-up Eyes: Living with Childhood Fame*. Clifton-upon-Teme: Polperro Heritage Press, 2013.

Henrey, Mrs Robert. *Philippa*. London: J.M. Dent & Sons, 1949.

———. *A Journey to Vienna*. London: J.M. Dent & Sons, 1950.

———. *Matilda and the Chickens*. London: J.M. Dent & Sons, 1950.

———. *The Little Madeleine*. London: J.M. Dent & Sons, 1951.

———. *Paloma*. London: J.M. Dent & Sons, 1951.

———. *Madeleine Grown Up*. London: J.M. Dent & Sons, 1952.

———. *An Exile in Soho*. London: J.M.Dent & Sons, 1952.

———. *A Farm in Normandy; and, The Return to the Farm*. London: J.M. Dent & Sons, 1952.

———. *A Village in Piccadilly*. London: J.M.Dent & Sons, 1952.

———. *Madeleine's Journal*. London: J.M. Dent & Sons, 1953.

———. *Madeleine Grown Up*. New York: E. P. Dutton, 1953.

———. *The Little Madeleine: The Autobiography of a Young Girl in Montmartre*. New York: E. P. Dutton, 1953.

———. *A Month in Paris*. London: J.M. Dent & Sons, 1954.

———. *Madeleine's Journal*. London: Non-Fiction Book Club/Dent, 1954.

———. *Madeleine Grown Up*. London: Reader's Union, 1954.

———. *Madeleine Young Wife: The Autobiography of a French Girl*.

New York: E. P. Dutton, 1954.

[————.] *Shocking Life by Elsa Schiaparelli.* London: J.M. Dent & Sons, 1954.

————. *La petite Madeleine.* Paris: La Table ronde. 1954.

————. *Milou's Daughter.* London: J.M. Dent & Sons, 1955.

————. *Bloomsbury Fair.* London: J.M. Dent & Sons, 1955.

————. *Paloma.* New York: E. P. Dutton, 1955.

————. *Madeleine jeune fille.* Paris: La Table ronde, 1955.

————. *Bloomsbury Fair.* London: The Quality Club, 1955.

————. *This Feminine World.* London: J.M. Dent & Sons, 1956.

————. *Milou's Daughter Madeleine: A Sentimental Journey to the South of France.* New York: E. P. Dutton, 1956.

————. *A Daughter for a Fortnight.* London: J.M. Dent & Sons, 1957.

————. *The Virgin of Aldermanbury: Rebirth of the City of London.* London: J.M. Dent & Sons, 1958.

————. *Mistress of Myself.* London: J.M. Dent & Sons, 1959.

————. *Madeleine Young Wife.* London: J.M. Dent & Sons, 1960.

————. *The Dream Makers.* London: J.M. Dent & Sons, 1961.

————. *Spring in a Soho Street.* London: J.M. Dent & Sons, 1962.

————. *Her April Days.* London: J.M. Dent & Sons, 1963.

————. *Wednesday at Four.* London: J.M. Dent & Sons, 1964.

————. *Winter Wild.* London: J.M. Dent & Sons, 1966.

————. *She Who Pays.* London: J.M. Dent & Sons, 1969.

————. *London Under Fire 1940-45.* London: J.M. Dent & Sons, 1969.

————. *Julia: Reminiscences of a Year in Madeleine's Life as a London Shop-Girl.* London: J.M. Dent & Sons, 1971.

————. *A Girl at Twenty: Six Months in the Life of the Young Madeleine.* London: J.M. Dent & Sons, 1974.

————. *Green Leaves.* London: J.M. Dent & Sons, 1976.

————. *Green Leaves.* Bath: Firecrest, 1976.

————. *The Golden Visit.* London: J.M. Dent & Sons, 1979.

Henrey, Madeleine. *Green Leaves; and, London Under Fire 1940-45.* London: J.M. Dent & Sons, 1982.

————. *Milou's Daughter.* Bath: Chivers, 1987.

Henrey, Robert. *Through Grown-up Eyes: Living with Childhood Fame.* Clifton-upon-Teme: Polperro Heritage Press, 2013.

Acknowledgements

Robert Henrey showed me his father's literary papers and allowed me to paraphrase and quote from them, as well as from his parents' and his own published and unpublished works. The London Library and AbeBooks provided many kilos of reading matter. The British Library's Newspaper Archive was an invaluable source of book reviews and background material, as was Gale's Artemis. The special collection of Madeleine Henrey papers at Texas Woman's University was shared with me by Kimberly Johnson and her librarians. In a memorable telephone conversation Judith Burnley described 'RH' as she knew him. Yohann Deguin helped with Proust. To all, many thanks.

Not forgetting the indefatigable diarist (see next page):

Lundi 11 mars 85 - Il fait froid - mais il y a
du soleil - J'ai travaillé un peu sur l'herbage
mais avec douleur, tant j'ai mal au dos -
Mardi 12 mars 85. Toujours très mal au dos -
Rien au courrier - Le soir au lit, j'ai commencé
les Pensées de Marc Aurèle - Grande péroraison de
Matthew Arnold, et ce n'est qu'à la fin de
ce long essai que je découvre Matthew Arnold -
Évidemment c'est le fils du Head master de
Rugby - mais n'ayant jamais rien lu de lui
j'en suis enchantée -
Mercredi 13 mars - Il neige il fait très froid -
Mon jeune ouvrier est venu vider le bac pour
le cimenter - J'ai horriblement peur qu'il
prenne froid quand je le vois descendre dans
ce gouffre, il en remonte tout souriant -
Ah, me dit-il votre petit chien est très taquin
avec vos poules, il en tirait une par l'aile,
j'ai dû les séparer -
Jeudi 14 mars - Sainte Mathilde - C'est le
nom de ma mère et le mien - Je nous souhaite
bonne fête, mais je ne suis pas gaie - Cependant
il y a les premiers daffodils dans le jardin -
et je suis allée déjeuner ez Hélène Vincent -

A page from her unpublished holograph 'Number Six'

INDEX